Translation Practices Explained

Translation Practices Explained is a series of coursebooks designed to help self-learners and teachers of translation. Each volume focuses on a specific aspect of professional translation practice, in many cases corresponding to actual courses available in translator-training institutions. Special volumes are devoted to well consolidated professional areas, such as legal translation or European Union texts; to areas where labour-market demands are currently undergoing considerable growth, such as screen translation in its different forms; and to specific aspects of professional practices on which little teaching and learning material is available, the case of editing and revising, or electronic tools. The authors are practising translators or translator trainers in the fields concerned. Although specialists, they explain their professional insights in a manner accessible to the wider learning public.

These books start from the recognition that professional translation practices require something more than elaborate abstraction or fixed methodologies. They are located close to work on authentic texts, and encourage learners to proceed inductively, solving problems as they arise from examples and case studies.

Each volume includes activities and exercises designed to help self-learners consolidate their knowledge; teachers may also find these useful for direct application in class, or alternatively as the basis for the design and preparation of their own material. Updated reading lists and website addresses will also help individual learners gain further insight into the realities of professional practice.

Sara Laviosa
Sharon O'Brien
Kelly Washbourne
Series Editors

Scientific and Technical Translation Explained

A Nuts and Bolts Guide for Beginners

Jody Byrne

Routledge
Taylor & Francis Group

LONDON AND NEW YORK

First published 2012 by St. Jerome Publishing

Published 2014 by Routledge
2 Park Square, Milton Park, Abingdon, Oxon OX14 4RN
711 Third Avenue, New York, NY 10017, USA

Routledge is an imprint of the Taylor & Francis Group, an informa business

ISBN 13: 978-1-905763-36-8 (pbk)
ISSN 1470-966X (*Translation Practices Explained*)

Typeset by
Delta Typesetters, Cairo, Egypt

British Library Cataloguing in Publication Data
A catalogue record of this book is available from the British Library

Library of Congress Cataloging-in-Publication Data
Byrne, Jody.
  Scientific and technical translation explained : a nuts and bolts guide for beginners /
Jody Byrne.
     p. cm. -- (Translation practices explained)
  Includes bibliographical references and index.
  ISBN 978-1-905763-36-8 (pbk. : alk. paper)
1. Technology--Translating. 2. Communication of technical information. I. Title.
  T11.5.B968 2012
  418'.035--dc23
                              2011052578

For my beautiful daughter, Áine

Contents

List of Figures

Acknowledgements

This book is based on my experience over many years as a technical translator, technical writer, trainer and researcher and it draws on various aspects of my work with numerous translation agencies, localization vendors, translators and academics to provide what is, hopefully, a useful and accessible resource on scientific and technical translation. In particular, the many students I have taught at Dublin City University and the University of Sheffield as well as the people who asked insightful questions at conferences and guest lectures have played a vital role in determining which information is included in this book and how it should be presented.

I am particularly grateful to the series editors who provided helpful comments on the various drafts of this book. My sincerest thanks go to John Kearns and to Kerry and Rick Gilchrist who, despite their heavy workloads, read sections of this book and provided invaluable comments, suggestions and feedback. I would also like to acknowledge and thank the SCIgen group, Oxford University Press, Henkel Ltd., Avocent and Elaine McAndrew at Merrill Brink International for their kind support for reproducing some of the texts used in Chapter 4.

My undying gratitude goes to my wife, Janice, for her eternal patience, support and love during this project. Thank you (again)!

About this book

The purpose of this book is to introduce you to the issues involved in translating scientific and technical texts and to provide you with the skills and knowledge to deal with them. Despite varying estimates as to the true monetary value of scientific and technical translation, few people could deny that it is one of the most important areas of translation, both from a professional and, increasingly, from a training point of view. In this book, you will gain an overview of scientific and technical translation, explore its origins and its professional context and develop the knowledge and skills necessary to deal with a wide range of texts.

One of the main difficulties for anyone interested in scientific and technical translation has always been the chronic lack of resources on the subject. This has been an issue since I was an undergraduate translation student and unfortunately, if comments from students and trainers are anything to go by, the situation has improved very little since then. This book is aimed, therefore, at students who are interested in scientific and technical translation, both as a career choice and as a research area, but who have found it difficult to find sufficient information to help them get started. This book is also aimed at anyone who simply wants to learn more about the area.

In writing this book, I had three main aims. The first was to provide as broad and holistic an introduction to scientific and technical translation as possible so as to give a better understanding of this complex interdisciplinary area. By positioning scientific and technical translation within the field of technical communication, it will be apparent that communicating technical information between languages requires more than just a good dictionary and an ability to write clearly. This approach will also highlight areas of common interest between translation and other aspects of communication, and hopefully stimulate ideas for further research.

My second aim was to provide practical advice to help those starting out or intending to work as technical translators. While it is not possible to prepare translators for every eventuality, it is possible to highlight some of the more common scenarios and provide suggestions on how to deal with them. This means novice translators will not find themselves completely unprepared for the reality of professional scientific and technical translation.

Finally, I wanted to provide a range of practical activities to help students practise their skills and to familiarize them with the processes in scientific and technical translation. These activities can be found at various points in each chapter.

By presenting typical translation strategies drawn from professional practice and from various other sources, this book will help you to explore scientific and technical translation in more detail and develop your own translation strategies. The learning activities in particular are intended to inspire and encourage trainers and students to develop their own learning and teaching methods.

Using this book

This book is designed to provide knowledge and skills that can be applied in practical translation scenarios. It is not intended solely as a theoretical exercise, although it does draw, where necessary, on theory to provide a context for the practical strategies proposed. It also explains that scientific and technical translation is highly interdisciplinary, both as an activity and as a field of study.

This book can be used in a number of ways. It can be used in conjunction with classroom-based practical translation courses with individual sections and chapters being referred to as necessary. Chapters 1 to 3 can also be used as initial reading at the start of a semester. Individual students will also find that the various activities are useful as self-study strategies as part of their independent learning.

Chapter 1 begins by identifying scientific and technical translation and by describing what it is and, more importantly, what it is not. We will then examine the professional, organizational and theoretical context within which scientific and technical translation operates.

Chapter 2 introduces the idea that scientific and technical translation should not be regarded just as a type of translation but as part of the broader field of technical communication. This is necessary not simply because technical communication is the traditional source of the texts which we will translate, but because of the shared interests and, in many respects, the overlap in activities and skills. This chapter introduces you to technical communication and emphasizes the role of scientific and technical translation as a communicative process that is aimed at specific audiences. Given the overwhelming importance of the audience in the translation process, it is important to understand their needs, their expectations and even their idiosyncrasies so that we can tailor our translations accordingly. The chapter concludes with some suggestions on how to go about gaining a better understanding of audiences.

Chapter 3 examines the typical features of scientific and technical language before examining several main categories of texts. This is important if we are to understand the ways in which audiences' needs are met by particular types of text. For each main category, a discussion of the main features and content is provided with observations as to how some of these factors may affect the translation process. The chapter concludes by looking at how Translation Studies can help us to categorize and make sense of the various text types we will encounter.

After the preparatory background information provided in the previous chapters, **Chapter 4** looks at some of the main types of text you may be asked to translate. The first two examples are accompanied by document profiles, which highlight the main features of the text as well as a list of problems you are likely to face and how to deal with them. To help develop your text analysis skills, you will need to produce profiles for the remaining text types yourself, although Appendix 4 contains sample profiles, which you can consult if you need to.

Chapter 5 looks at some of the general translation approaches, which may come in useful when translating scientific and technical texts. Starting with generic translation strategies with which most translators are familiar, the book looks at how strategies such as modulation, recategorization (which was once known as transposition) and borrowing are used in the context of scientific and technical translation.

We will also look at other more radical strategies such as restructuring, recycling information, expansion and contraction, again illustrating how they are applied to the translation of technical documentation. Next, we look at the different types of translation you may be expected to produce. Understanding what each type of translation involves will help you decide which translation macrostrategy is the most appropriate for a given project. This chapter also draws on the idea of the translation brief proposed by Skopos theory as a way of identifying what it is your translation is supposed to achieve. Again, this will help you decide how you need to tackle a particular translation.

Chapter 6 is perhaps the most practice-orientated chapter and in it we look at specific aspects of scientific and technical texts and the challenges they can pose for translators. These aspects cover a range of areas such as culture-specific features, errors in the source text, authoritative translations, and formatting issues that will require either a cautious approach, direct action or even no action at all. Finally, a glossary of key terms and other useful resources are also provided as appendices at the end of the book.

I hope that the topics covered in this book, together with the practical strategies and learning activities will do justice to what is an interesting, rewarding and demanding field of translation.

Jody Byrne

Dublin, May 2011
www.jodybyrne.com

Find out more on Facebook
facebook.com/ScitechExplained

1. Scientific and Technical Translation

In this chapter

This chapter introduces you to scientific and technical translation and explains its origins and its importance both from a historical perspective and in terms of its current position within the language and other industries. This chapter will also show that while scientific translation and technical translation are closely related fields, they are not identical and the terms scientific and technical cannot be used interchangeably. We will discuss the significance of this type of translation before examining how theories of translation can help the translator. You will also learn about who is involved in scientific and technical translation and gain an overview of the typical tools you will need to use as a translator. This chapter will discuss your responsibility as a scientific and technical translator from a legal and ethical point of view before presenting some practical activities to help you practise what you have learned.

1.1   Introduction

> Scientific and technical translation is part of the process of disseminating information on an international scale, which is indispensable for the functioning of our modern society.
>
> (Pinchuck 1977:13)

Translation is an important driving force of modern society. It facilitates the flow of ideas, expertise, values and other information between different cultures. It is also essential for scientific and technological advancement. In today's information age, the role of scientific and technical translation is more important than ever. It has facilitated some of the most significant scientific and technological advances of recent decades. These advances have transformed our daily lives to the extent that the world around us is virtually unrecognizable from fifty, or even twenty, years ago. Virtually every aspect of our lives from education and work to entertainment, shopping and travel has been swept along by a seemingly unstoppable wave of new inventions and technological advances. What many people do not realize is that these inventions and advances are accompanied at almost every step of the way by translation in its capacity as a vehicle for disseminating scientific and technical knowledge.

Although in terms of translation studies, scientific and technical translation is just one of a number of fascinating areas of study, it is, however, an area of translation which has had a profound impact on society. Furthermore, as a field of translation activity, it is one which will have most impact on the vast majority of translation students, as it is here that many translators find a sizeable amount of their income.

1.1.1 Some distinctions
Despite their similarities, technical and scientific translation are not interchangeable terms.

The aim of this book is to introduce the fundamental features of scientific and technical translation and the skills needed to engage in this type of activity. It is important to realize, however, that the terms *scientific* and *technical* are not identical and that the expression *scientific and technical* is not a tautological reference to the same type of translation. Part of the decision to group these areas together has to do with the way in which these subjects are traditionally taught, rather than any similarity between the two. The majority of translator training institutions offer modules with titles such as "Scientific & Technical Translation" or "Advanced Translation – Scientific & Technical" and presumably, this is a convenient way of organizing teaching provision.

Another reason is that the lines separating scientific and **technical texts** are becoming increasingly blurred. As we will discuss later, it is not uncommon for texts to combine elements of both scientific and technical texts and all of the issues that this entails. So, while the two areas are separate in many ways, the ways in which they appear in the real world mean that they need to be considered together.

Pinchuck (1977:13) identifies three key categories of information, which provide the materials for scientific and technical translation:

1. The results of pure science;
2. The results of applied scientific research carried out in order to solve a particular problem; and
3. The work of technologists, which is intended to result in an industrial product or process, which can be sold.

Pinchuck quite rightly points out, though, that there is always a significant amount of overlap between these categories and that the work of today's scientists, i.e. theoretical scientific information, is likely to become tomorrow's technology and as such give us various tangible products, devices, services and so on. From this perspective, it is worth remembering this relationship as we examine scientific and technical translation in this book; while the texts may differ and the information may take different forms, their foundations are ultimately built upon largely the same information. However, the way in which this information is presented and used varies quite significantly between scientific and technical translation. So, while a **technical text** is designed to *convey* information as clearly and effectively as possible, a **scientific text** will *discuss, analyze* and *synthesize* information with a view to *explaining* ideas, *proposing* new theories or *evaluating* methods. Due to these differing aims, the language used in each type of text, and consequently the strategies needed to translate them, may vary significantly.

It could even be said that scientific translation has just as much to do with literary translation as it does with technical translation. While the common view of scientific writing is that it is dry, highly objective and impartial, with all traces of style and linguistic creativity chased from the discourse like a fox from a chicken coop, the reality is quite different. Locke (1992) comprehensively dismantles the idea that there is no place for individualism, style, metaphor and creativity in scientific discourse. Indeed, he argues that the very nature of science means that individual style and creativity are intrinsic parts of the scientific process. He cites, for example, the use of metaphors as a foundation of scientific language with terms such as the *Big Bang* and the *Greenhouse Effect* owing their existence to the creativity of scientists and writers. The implication of this for translators, then, is that they must be able to recognize and negotiate culture-bound metaphors in much the same way as literary translators must.

1.1.2   Historical significance
Technical translation's long and colourful history helps us understand its importance today.

Translation is practically as old as writing itself and for almost as long as humans have been writing they have been translating. Indeed, evidence of this can be found in ancient clay tablets containing bilingual Sumerian-Eblaite glossaries (Deslisle & Cloutier 1995:7). Some have gone so far as to say, rather humorously, that translation is the "second oldest profession" known to humanity (Baer & Koby 2003:vii). To many, translating sacred texts such as the Bible or Koran immediately springs to mind when we speak of translation in historical terms. However, the translation of scientific and technical texts has a history, which is as long as that of religious translation, if not longer. That translation has accompanied virtually every significant scientific and technological discovery throughout the ages is well documented and it is difficult, if not impossible, to find a single example of an invention or discovery which was not exported to another language and culture by means of translation.

While translation has always facilitated the dissemination of knowledge, it was not until the 15th century that it really came into its own. In 1447, Johannes Gutenberg developed what is widely credited as being the first moveable type printing system which revolutionized printing and made it much easier to produce and, indeed, own books. That this invention had such an impact on translation and the dissemination of scientific and technical knowledge is due to the ensuing explosion in the number of books produced in Europe. Tebeaux (1997:14-30) describes how, during the English Renaissance, countless books were written on topics such as medicine, farming methods, animal husbandry, fishing, gardening, household management, horse riding, falconry, fencing, military science, navigation, road building, carpentry, stained glass making and so on. Gutenberg's press permitted unprecedented levels of distribution for these books thanks to the relative ease and cost-effectiveness with which they could be produced. Not only did this make it easier to distribute original language texts, it also made it easier to disseminate information in translation.

And so, translation, newly empowered by widespread printing, continued to play a central role in the dissemination of scientific and technical information for centuries. However, it was only during the last 100 or so years that translation really made its mark on science and technology. This was a time when scientists were making countless new discoveries and writing about their findings in their own native languages. With other researchers eager to acquire new knowledge and learn new techniques, the demand for translations of these scientific texts was unprecedented. This translation activity in turn fuelled new research, which resulted in even more new discoveries. Imagine how under-developed science would be, were it not for translation; each language area would be intellectually isolated and each language community would have to discover the entire body of scientific and technical knowledge for itself. This would not simply be a case of reinventing the wheel, but of reinventing the wheel dozens, if not hundreds, of times.

The following are just a few examples of significant scientific pioneers and the languages in which they published their work:

- **Physics**: Max Planck and Albert Einstein (German), Nils Bohr (Danish), Robert Boyle (English), Hideki Yukawa (Japanese);
- **Biology and genetics**: Camillo Golgi (Italian), Tang Dizhou (Chinese);
- **Radiology and medical diagnostics**: Pierre and Marie Curie (French), Wilhelm Conrad Röntgen (German);
- **Bacteriology**: Alexander Fleming (English), Louis Pasteur (French);
- **Psychiatry**: Sigmund Freud (German).

The advent of printing also marked the start of a new era in translation itself, which, it could be argued, saw the way in which translation was viewed and carried out change quite significantly. In the centuries before printing, there existed a manuscript culture with texts being handwritten, fragile and almost ephemeral objects. Texts, usually of a scientific or technical nature, were copied by scribes and were often modified, whether intentionally or unintentionally, through the addition, omission or modification of information. This resulted in variability and uncertainty with regard to texts and the problem became even more pronounced when translation was added to the mix. At the time, translating lacked the standards of accuracy and quality that we expect today with the result that mistranslations or even omissions of difficult passages were common (Montgomery 2002:178).

Indeed, such was the extent of the problem it was not uncommon for copies of the same work held, for example, in libraries in Paris and Oxford to differ quite significantly in terms of content (Grant 1992:367). As Grant points out: "knowledge was as likely to disappear as to be acquired" as a result of the translation process. This was made all the more problematic when we consider that there might only have been one copy of the source text and this would have been written on fragile vellum or papyrus. This trend can be traced back to ancient Rome and Greece where the concept of intellectual property as we currently know it simply did not exist. In Greece, for example, the demand for knowledge, particularly of a scientific and technical nature, gave rise to what we now call compilers. These compilers, whose name comes from the Latin "to plunder", effectively "misappropriated" whole chunks of texts, usually through translation and presented them as their own work (Stahl 1962:55). Translators at the time used source texts as the basis for new books and combined the ideas of the original with their own ideas, opinions and suggestions.

Consequently, many of the great works by some of the most important scholars such as Posidonius or Ptolomy have effectively been lost; despite numerous publications purporting to contain the writings of these scholars, there is no trace of their actual writings left as a result of countless publications which combined, modified, assimilated or falsified their work. Roman translators were no less cavalier in their approach to scavenging knowledge and passing it off as their own. Indeed, the Romans described these practices as **inventio** (invention), which involved the rewriting or rewording of the original during translation, and **contaminare** (contamination), which involved combining translations together from different sources to form an entirely new work.

This changed quite significantly, however, with the advent of relatively high volume printing as facilitated by Gutenberg's invention. Texts became fixed – objects to be respected rather than ragged scraps of vellum, which could be written and copied by anyone. The process of printing texts on paper and binding them gave the knowledge they contained a legitimacy and permanency which had rarely existed previously. In the case of translation, the existence of a fixed and standardized source text made translators more accountable for omissions and mistranslations because it was easier to consult the original source text. We could argue that printing raised standards within scientific and technical translation and that, ultimately, it was instrumental in the emergence of various translation theories and concepts such as equivalence, faithfulness or **loyalty** and later concepts such as adequacy.

> **Practical Exercise 1: The language of science**
> Think of three major scientific discoveries and find out who are the main scientists associated with them. What is the nationality and working language of each scientist? Now identify three products or inventions that make use of one or more of these discoveries and find out in which country they were made.

1.1.3   *Modern scientific and technical translation*
Various factors over the centuries have changed the way we look at technical translation today.

In today's globalized economy, scientific and technical translation in many respects represents the backbone of international trade and the scientific endeavour which fuels it. Virtually every product sold or specialized service provided – whether MP3 players, telephone conferencing systems, luxury cars, flame retardant cladding for use in the construction industry, online shopping websites, mobile phone services or designing a steel mill – will require the involvement of scientific and technical translators at some point in its lifecycle. This involvement may come as early on as the design and consulting phase, during development and manufacture, as part of sales and marketing activities or to provide support to customers and users.

It has been estimated that scientific and technical translation now accounts for some 90% of global translation output (Kingscott 2002:247). Of course, this figure is unlikely to be completely accurate for a number of reasons – one of which relates to how we define scientific and technical translation (see Byrne 2006:3). However, even assuming that the figure is exaggerated due to various confounding variables, this figure is unlikely to be too far off the mark. This is all the more likely when we consider that the localization industry, which tradition- ally makes extensive use of scientific and technical translators, is estimated to be worth around US$12 billion (DePalma & Beninatto 2006:4).

Indeed, scientific and technical translation forms such a crucial part of mod- ern industry and society that it is the subject of numerous laws, regulations and directives and many international scholarly scientific journals, even those which publish papers in various languages, require translations of abstracts at the very least.

Practical Exercise 2: Exporting languages
Make a list of the electrical appliances you have in your home and note the countries in which they were designed and/or built. With your national language at the centre, draw a diagram illustrating the languages from which documents relating to your appliances have been translated.

Try to find some of the documentation that came with these appli- ances. Are there any features, for example style, subject, language or formatting which you think would pose problems for a translator? If you had to translate one document yourself, how would you ap- proach these features?

1.1.4   Some legal dimensions
Understanding how various legal factors affect how and why we do our work.

One of the most compelling reasons for studying scientific and technical transla- tion is that in many cases the translation of documents in these domains is an activity which is required by law. In Europe, EU Council Resolution C411 specifi- cally states that in order to be able to legally sell or distribute technical products and appliances, all **technical documentation** relating to the product must be translated into the language(s) of the country where the product is to be sold (Council of the European Union 1998). A result of the Directive is that products are only regarded as being complete when they are accompanied by full operating instructions in the users' own language; if there are problems or inaccuracies in the instructions, the whole product can be regarded as defective. To put this into perspective, any product that involves some form of technology, be it electronic, electrical, mechanical, chemical etc., must be accompanied by documentation in a variety of languages. Assuming that few companies have the resources to employ **technical writers** to produce documentation in each of the languages concerned, it is fair to say that there is a huge demand for translators (usually **freelancers**) who can translate this documentation into different languages.

The translation of **technical documentation** is also subject to a range of other laws, regulations and directives. Another provision of Resolution C411 is that instructions must be clear, comprehensible and must provide clear warnings to prevent misuse of products and to advise users of possible risks and hazards. Since in practice these translations are not regarded as translations *per se*, but rather as original **target language** documents, the regulations regarding technical writing and documentation will apply.

Other pieces of legislation which affect scientific and technical translation include Directive 2001/95/EC, which deals with general product safety, and Directive 88/378/EEC, which deals with the safety of toys. Both state that clear warnings about possible risks must be given in the users' own language. Similarly, Directive 90/385/EEC, which deals with medical devices, and Directive 76/768/EEC, which relates to cosmetics, state that documentation must be translated and it must anticipate potential risks (Byrne 2007:16). But even after translations have been produced, the law still plays an important role because translators can be held liable for mistakes in their texts as a result of contractual obligations or as a result of other liabilities arising from tort law (*ibid.*).

Practical Exercise 3: Translation and liability
Consider the following scenario: When translating an installation manual for a gas heater, a translator notices that the source text contains a serious factual error. It says that the gas supply ***must not*** *be turned off* before starting work. It should have said that the gas supply ***must be turned off***. However, the translator retains this incorrect information in the target text. An engineer installing a gas heater follows the instructions and as a result, the heater explodes, killing the engineer and three other people who were working nearby.

What are the key issues to be considered in this case? Who do you think is responsible for the deaths? Should the translator be found negligent and fined/imprisoned? Why? Are there any mitigating factors?

Practical Exercise 4: Finding legal resources
An important aspect of law is that in many jurisdictions it is constantly evolving as a result of new court rulings, laws and legislation. Websites such as EUR-Lex [http://eur-lex.europa.eu] provide a wealth of information on legislation in the EU.

Using the Internet, your local library or whatever information sources are available to you, find three sources of national case law and legislation for your own country and three sources of international legislation. Try to identify any cases or laws which relate to translation or the provision of specialized technical information.

1.2   A place for translation theory?
What can translation theory tell us about translating technical documentation?

Translation theory has always been a problematic area of study. Part of the problem is that it seeks to understand and explain translation, which is itself a complex and notoriously difficult concept to pin down. In the rush to explain the various facets of translation - and possibly to justify translation as a discrete field of study - a plethora of theories, models and approaches have emerged, some of which are extremely insightful and useful, but amidst the noise created by so much work it is sometimes difficult to make sense of it all.

An introductory book intended to explain the practice of scientific and technical translation is not the place for a lengthy discussion of translation theory, although it is necessary to mention briefly some of the more relevant theoretical approaches which relate to this area. The following paragraphs will provide a very brief outline of how translation theory can be applied to scientific and technical translation.

One of the most difficult aspects of translation theory is that scientific and technical translation have traditionally been neglected by scholars and none of the mainstream theories really addresses scientific and technical translation specifically. Some models have been developed as general theories of translation while others have emerged from particular types of translation, such as literary translation or bible translation. As a result, applying any of the available theories to scientific and technical translation is fraught with difficulty.

Difficulties also arise because, as Chesterman (2000:49) points out, many theories of translation adopt a binary approach to translation consisting of diametrically opposed extremes. Some examples of this include *formal* vs. *dynamic* equivalence (Nida & Taber 1964), *semantic* vs. *communicative* (Newmark 1977) and **covert** vs. **overt** (House 1977). While this approach certainly serves to make the theories neater and easier to describe, it represents a rather oversimplified vision of the translation process. Translation inevitably involves shades of grey – new scenarios, unusual combinations of factors and so on – which means that trying to shoe-horn a translation into one category or the other is often uncomfortable, if not impossible. Conversely, having too many categories or options can make classifying a particular translation scenario equally challenging.

While a lot of valuable work has been done in the field of **LSP** (Language for Special Purposes) and text typologies, which help us to understand why and how texts are produced in specific communicative contexts, there is still a lot to be done before we can comfortably apply a theoretical model to scientific and technical translation. Typologies are discussed in Chapter 3 but for more information see, for example, Göpferich (1995) and Trosborg (1997).

1.2.1   Recreating the source text

Traditionally, the source text has been regarded as the most important element in translation, particularly as it is the starting point for the whole process and the basis upon which **target texts** are produced. The prevailing view has been that, for a translation process to exist there has to be a source text, otherwise we would not be translators, we would be writers. In recent years, however, the focus of translation theory has, particularly in non-literary spheres, shifted away from frameworks based on the source text towards a more communicative approach. This means that translation is increasingly being regarded as a communicative process and, as such, the guiding factors are the message and recipient, i.e. the content and the target audience. This change of focus has made the study of translation clearer in that we can relate it to actual real-world events with real participants.

The emphasis on the source text is perhaps most apparent in the numerous definitions and types of **equivalence**, which all rely on one thing: a link or bond of some sort between the source text and the target text. It is this relationship that, according to Kenny (1998:77), allows the **target text** to be considered a translation of the **source text**. As Catford (1965:49) explains, "the TL text must be relatable to at least some of the situational features to which the SL text is relatable".

The focus in equivalence theory on the need to have a strong link between the source and target texts is unfortunately taken to extremes, however, with the result that the source text can erroneously be regarded as the most important component in the translation process, with translators striving to create as close a replica of the source text as possible. Indeed, some would argue that it should be the sole guiding principle for translators. Taking this approach to its natural conclusion, we would have a situation where we could never separate the source text and target text; the target text could not function as a translation without the ever-present source text.

While this is clearly problematic in many ways, to deny that there must be at least some link would also be misguided. Quite simply, without the source text there can be no translation. While this relationship can, to a certain extent, be abused through, for example, an insistence on excessively literal translations motivated out of an unquestioning and sometimes misguided loyalty to the author, often to the detriment of the target language (**TL**) reader, the fact remains that the source text forms the basis for the translation.

Perhaps the most well known types of equivalence are *formal* and *dynamic equivalence* proposed by Nida in 1964. Formal equivalence is concerned with the message in terms of its form and content. With this type of equivalence the message in the TL should match the different elements in the source language as closely as possible, be they lexical, syntactic, stylistic, phonological or orthographic. According to Catford, a formal correspondent (or equivalent) is "any TL category (unit, class, structure, element of structure, etc.) which can be said to occupy, as nearly as possible, the 'same' place in the 'economy' of the TL as the given SL [source language] category occupies in the SL" (Catford 1965:27).

Dynamic equivalence, on the other hand, is based on the notion that the **TT** should have the same effect on its audience as the **ST** had on its own audience. With dynamic equivalence, the emphasis is not so much on finding a TL match for an SL message but rather on creating the same relationship between the target audience and the message as that which existed between the SL audience and the message (Nida 1964:159). The aim here is to produce a target text which is natural and idiomatic and which focuses on the TL culture. According to dynamic equivalence, a successful translation needs to capture the sense of the ST and not just the words. As such, it can only be regarded as a successful piece of communication if the message is successfully transmitted to the target audience.

Nida & Taber make the point, however, that eliciting the same response from two different groups of people can be difficult, particularly when we consider that no two people from the same language group will understand words in exactly the same way (1969:4). This sentiment is also expressed by Steiner (1975:28). What we are left with, therefore, is an approach which is theoretically quite desirable but difficult to implement and imprecise in practice. Applying the idea of formal and dynamic equivalence to any type of translation, not just to scientific and technical translation, rarely produces anything tangible or specific for a translator to make use of because they are such vague and subjective concepts.

There are a number of systems, which have been put forward to examine the levels of equivalence (see, for example, Komissarov 1977, Koller 1979, Baker 1992). One of the most enduring of these is the scheme proposed by Koller (1979:188-189), according to which equivalence can occur on the following levels:

- *Denotational meaning*, namely the object or concept being referred to;
- *Connotational meaning*, which is, according to Koller divided into language level, sociolect, dialect, medium, style, frequency, domain, value and emotional tone;
- **Textual norms**, which are typical language features of texts such as legal documents, business letters etc.;
- *Pragmatic meaning*, which includes reader expectations;
- *Linguistic form*, namely devices such as metaphors, rhyme and so on.

Each of these levels then gives rise to a particular type of equivalence, which can be used to describe the relationship between the ST and TT. In scientific and technical texts, achieving equivalence on any of these levels might require the translator to focus more on the information being communicated (denotational meaning) in the case of an instruction manual, on the *way* in which information is expressed (linguistic form) in a popular science article or on set phrases and document conventions (textual norms) in the case of a certificate of conformity (see Chapter 4). In order to emphasize equivalence on one of these levels, translators may find themselves having to settle for lower levels of equivalence on one or more of the remaining levels.

It has become rather fashionable to dismiss equivalence when discussing professional translation (Pym 1995 & 2010). The insistence of equivalence-based approaches on maintaining what some would regard as excessively close links between the target text and the source text and its original audience seems incongruous when the point of translation is to communicate to a new audience. Equivalence can also be criticized for its general difficulty in incorporating real-world, extratextual issues such as time constraints, preferred terminology and style, reader expectations, etc. However, to dismiss equivalence out of hand because it appears old-fashioned, excessively concerned with the source text and isolated from the world in which translation takes place is like saying that walking is not as useful as running and should be banned. In reality, both running and walking have their advantages and their disadvantages, it all depends on what it is you are trying to achieve.

These levels of equivalence give us, in theory at least, the ability to compare source and target texts, once a translation has been produced. However, we need to be wary of trying to use the various types of equivalence to *dictate* how a translation should be produced and how the ST and TT should relate to one another. They are simply not designed to do this; equivalence cannot tell us which of its various levels should be used, primarily because it has difficulty taking account of the fact that, as Toury (1995:26) says, a translation is a fact of the target language that hosts it. This means that scientific and technical translations will be governed and judged in the context of the norms, expectations and rules of the target text. In other words, they will be treated as if they were originally produced in the target language and not as translations. Moreover, equivalence does not take into account those real-world issues which play as much a role in shaping the translation process as the source and target languages, the text and its content etc. All that we can realistically expect to achieve using the various levels of equivalence is describe how the source and target texts relate to one another after the translation has been completed. A more helpful way of using equivalence is to employ its levels and types during the translation process as a set of tools or policies which can be selected in order to achieve some translation goal. In practice, this might mean that when translating an instruction manual, for instance, we would decide that denotational equivalence is more important than equivalence of linguistic form or connotational equivalence and that we would concentrate on conveying the information rather than on recreating the particular stylistic features of the source text.

The difficulty in adopting this type of approach, as hinted at above, is that we do not know which of the various levels of equivalence and, by extension, which aspects of the source text, are the most appropriate for a particular context. Simply knowing the different ways in which a source text and target text *can* be equivalent does not mean that a translator will choose the most appropriate one for a particular project. As a result, translators are usually left to their own devices in choosing the most appropriate translation strategy and may or may not choose the right one.

1.2.2   *Focusing on the target text*

Skopos theory was developed by Hans Vermeer in 1978 and was the first theory to fully recognize the professional reality of translation and that, unlike equivalence, the target text, or more precisely the **purpose** of the target text, is the most important in determining the way we should translate texts (Vermeer 1982; 1987a). This theory is based on the principle that translation is a communicative activity, which is performed for a specific reason; a text is written for a specific purpose and it is translated for a specific purpose. It is this purpose, which is known as the **Skopos**, which governs the translation process, unlike equivalence, where the ST and its effects on the SL audience determine the translation process, or for that matter **functionalism**, where the ST function defines the TT function and the translation process.

Skopos theory maintains that the translation process is determined by the Skopos of the TT as specified by the commissioner and the translator. A text, according to Skopos theory, is an *offer of information*, i.e. the raw materials from which any number of possible translations can be produced (Vermeer 1987b). The way in which a translator selects the "correct" translation depends on the intended purpose of the translation being known. While this may seem rather vague, it does in fact reflect the reality of translation. For example, the way in which we translate a document will depend on who is going to read it, how they are going to use it, the way in which the text will be distributed and so on. These factors do not necessarily remain constant between source and target text and they are particularly important in scientific and technical translation.

Take, for example, a situation where we are asked to translate the user guide for a toaster. In both languages, such texts are expected to have an informative function so the primary function will not change. In the original source language culture, it is normal for such documents to adopt a tone which emulates an expert "speaking down" to a layperson who is instructed to follow certain procedures. However, target language readers would react quite badly to what they would perceive as a patronizing and demeaning, almost insulting, tone. If this document were being translated for distribution in the target country, the appropriate course of action would be to translate the text in such a way that this expert-layperson register is replaced by a peer-to-peer register where the reader is *advised* to follow certain procedures. A translator would be entirely justified in making such changes, as the translation would fail in its purpose otherwise.

However, if the user guide is simply being translated for use by a service engineer, the emphasis will be on the information and the reader is unlikely to be "offended" by harsh orders and will not need to have the translator explain every concept in simple terms. Ultimately, we would have two quite different translations originating from the same source text. But if, according to Vermeer, an ST is an offer of information and can give rise to any number of potential translations (Nord 1991:23), how is the translator to know which one is the most appropriate one? If it were left to chance, there is the risk that the translator may pick the wrong one, i.e. translate the text in a way that does not meet the client's requirements.

Rather than leave such an important strategic decision to chance, Skopos theory introduces the notion of the **translation brief**, which is defined as a form of project specification which sets out the requirements for the translation (Byrne 2006:39). This brief is intended to form the basis for identifying the Skopos of the translation and is supposed to, among other things, clearly define what the translation is to be used for and who will use it. In his definition of translation, Sager (1993:116) acknowledges the need for some form of brief or instructions "from a third party" on the basis of which the translation is carried out. Unfortunately however, producing a translation brief is quite a hit and miss affair with clients rarely able to provide anything more relevant or specific than "I have a 7,500 word document that I need translated. It's got something to do with electronics and I need it by the end of the week."[1] In such cases, the translator generally needs to ask certain probing questions such as "is the text for publication?" etc. and on this basis construct some form of translation brief. This unfortunately weakens the effectiveness of Skopos theory somewhat.

This problem is compounded by the fact that nobody seems to know exactly what should go into a translation brief although the general consensus seems to be that it should provide some form of information about the target audience, intended purpose of the text and any stylistic or terminological requirements. Sunwoo (2007), in her paper "Operationalizing the translation purpose (Skopos)", seeks to address this problem and presents a detailed "model for constituting the translation purpose from the translation commission" and a way of situating the text. The result is a very detailed analysis although it is probably much too complex for practical use.

Skopos theory can be tricky to use in practice because of the vagueness of the notion of the translation brief and also because it does not actually say how we are to fulfil a particular Skopos. But it does help us to concentrate on the most important aspects of the translation process.

From this very brief description, we can see certain limitations which are also indicative of other theoretical approaches to translation. For example, while equivalence gives us theoretical criteria with which to compare translations against their originals and which can be used as strategies if needed, it cannot account for the numerous factors which exist outside texts but which nonetheless play a crucial role in translation. Nor for that matter does equivalence tell us which of the various levels and types of equivalence is the most appropriate for a given translation scenario. Equivalence frequently places too much emphasis on the role of the source text to the detriment of all other factors.

While the introduction of **functionalism** (see House 1977, for example) was a groundbreaking step in that it lessened the emphasis of translation on purely textual factors, it still, unfortunately, maintained the excessive importance attached to the source text. Skopos theory, on the other hand, is valuable in that it explicitly addresses the professional context of translation and takes a more holistic approach.

Unfortunately, it can be problematic from the point of view that the Skopos of a translation is based on the undefined notion of the translation brief, which is open to interpretation and may, in some cases, be very difficult to formulate

---

[1] I once received an email asking whether I would be available to translate a medical text. Before agreeing to take the job I asked to see the text first, whereupon it emerged that the text was actually about guns, not medicine. The company for whom the text was to be translated normally made medical devices but had diversified into manufacturing accessories for guns.

because translators are rarely given meaningful translation briefs or commissions. Moreover, because Skopos is intended as a general theory of translation, it is not really in a position to offer explicit instructions or guidance on how to achieve specific Skopoi.

One method of reconciling the problems outlined above might be to combine the best features of Skopos theory, equivalence theory and work carried out on text typologies. This would involve using Skopos theory to determine what it is we need to achieve with our translation. This gives us our general overview of what type of translation is required.

When combined with a knowledge of text typologies we can then produce a clearer picture of what precisely our translation will look like in terms of features such as language, terminology and content, based on what we know about comparable texts in the target language. Then, with this knowledge, we can use the various levels of equivalence not as criteria for comparing texts, but as guidelines, informed by our understanding of the purpose of the target text which will aid us when translating.

However, there is much more to translation theory than the examples given above. There are numerous other models and approaches available such as relevance theory (Gutt 1991), translation norms (see Schäffner 1999), descriptive translation studies (Toury 1995) and functionalism (Reiß 1971), some of which may have something to offer scientific and technical translation. It is essential to realize however, that while none of the existing theories of translation on their own can provide an infallible model of the translation process, particularly for scientific and technical translation, they do provide adequate raw materials with which we can develop an informed and acceptable working theoretical model to guide our practical work. The challenge here is to examine the various theoretical approaches and models and then cherry pick those aspects which appear to be most relevant. It is quite conceivable that all of the components for a robust and reliable theory of translation, not just scientific and technical translation, are available to us already. All that remains is to assemble the various pieces into a basic usable theoretical framework.

> **Practical Exercise 5: Skopos versus equivalence**
> Draw up a list of the advantages and disadvantages of using (1) just equivalence and (2) just Skopos theory to explain scientific and technical translation. Compare the results of both lists. If you had to choose just one theory, which would it be and why? How would *you* combine the two theories?

1.3   Tools of the trade

As well as linguistic skills, we also need to use a variety of software and tools as part of our work.

When we consider the long association between translation and various innovative technologies over the centuries it comes as no surprise to find that technology plays a crucial role in scientific and, perhaps more so, technical translation. While for the most part translation has traditionally facilitated the dissemination of new scientific and technical knowledge, science and technology have also had a tremendous impact on translation.

Commercial translation (as distinct from interpreting), the point of which is to provide a written alternative to some foreign language, has always required the use of certain tools whether a clay tablet and stylus, quill and parchment or typewriter, telex and fax. Such tools, while requiring some acclimatization, more so in the case of typewriters and telexes, were unlikely to have any radical impact on the work of the translator; they were simply improvements on existing methods. The benefits to translators were modest and came in the form of slight improvements in the presentation of translations or faster delivery of texts. Translation only underwent a genuine metamorphosis as a result of technology with the advent of computers and the Internet.

Despite the fact that computers and the Internet have existed in one form or another for decades, their everyday use was virtually unheard of only thirty years ago. Computers at that time were bulky, room-sized contraptions which required teams of scientists to tend to their idiosyncratic and temperamental needs. The modern PC, as we know it, was at that time but a distant glimmer on the horizon. The Internet, too, was at an embryonic stage, consisting of a dozen or so computers located at military bases, research laboratories and universities in the USA. It is only since around the mid-1990s that the Internet has truly made its mark on translation. In 1971, Sykes referred to typewriters as a staple part of any translator's office. Some 25 years later, O'Hagan's (1996:5) reference to the fax as the most popular form of communication shows that the Internet had yet to establish itself as a core component of the translation landscape.

Computers and the Internet have changed business models throughout the world, in all industries and business sectors and have gone hand in glove with globalization. In the translation industry, it has created new demands for translations and placed new demands on translators, requiring them to adopt new technologies and practices as part of their day-to-day work. Indeed, technology has almost created its own demand by facilitating global business; it creates a demand for new processes which inevitably involve the use of technology. This process which has seen translation become a computer-based activity (Austermühl 2001:1) has transformed both the type of work we do and the way in which we perform this work. Nowhere has this impact been more pronounced than in the fields of scientific and technical translation.

Perhaps it is because scientific and technical translation coexist so closely with technology that they have experienced such a drastic technological transformation, or perhaps it is because working with companies and organizations where technology plays such a crucial role in their activities has required translators to become part of the technical landscape. Whatever the reason, the nature of scientific and technical translation means that the basic word-processing skills, which would once have been sufficient and are still sufficient for most translators, are simply not enough any more, particularly for those working in scientific and technical domains.

Today's scientific and technical translator has to contend not only with word-processing and sending files by email or electronic file transfer, but receiving documents in a bewildering array of file types which often have to be handled using specialized software. This software is often so far removed from mainstream computer use that someone outside our profession would never even know about them, let alone be expected to use them. The translator, who translates documents produced in industries where such software is commonplace, needs firstly to be able to recognize such files and technologies, and secondly to know what to do with them.

Virtually all translators - irrespective of the types of texts they translate – have to contend with the increasing levels of technology necessary to do the job. Where once the translator's role was quite distinct from that of a graphic designer, desktop publishing (DTP) specialist or even programmer, the expectation now is that translators need to be able to deal with various technologies, file formats and tools.

To help us make sense of the vast array of technologies and tools with which the technical translator must contend it helps if we group them into three broad categories:

- General tools
- Text processing tools
- Translation tools

1.3.1   General tools

This category of tools is used by virtually everyone, not just translators. This category forms the basic level of IT competence which is needed to be able to function in any career and it consists of general PC skills such as basic maintenance, installation and deinstallation of software, data archival and backups, file compression, CD creation and PC security. Perhaps more importantly, this category also includes the increasingly important communicative functions of the Internet such as online research using search engines and databases and communications using email, Internet telephony, instant messaging and video conferencing as well as sending data using **FTP** servers etc. Nearly all translators have to deal with this level of technology as part of their day-to-day work.

1.3.2   Text processing tools

Text processing tools are the staple of any translator's toolkit; they are the very means by which we do our work. Again, all translators need to be proficient in the use of basic word-processing packages, regardless of the translator's specialism. For many translators, a solid understanding of Microsoft Word or possibly OpenOffice is more than enough to be able to work effectively as a translator. However, for certain groups of translators, most notably those of a scientific and technical persuasion, the situation can become much more complex indeed.

Most documents are produced using word processors such as Microsoft Word. But despite the rather impressive range of features offered by this type of software, word processors are actually at the lower end of the text processing spectrum in terms of complexity and the powerfulness of their features. Certain types of documents, such as those produced for highly technical products including software, machinery or vehicles are so large and complex as a result of formatting, cross-referencing and graphics that they cannot be produced using typical word processing software. Instead, they are produced using **DTP** software such as Adobe FrameMaker, InDesign or PageMaker.

These are complex professional applications which allow authors to combine text and graphics to produce documents with complex layouts for distribution either in traditional print format or in a number of electronic formats for distribution via the Internet or on disk. Indeed, a large proportion of documents, particularly in IT-related domains are never actually printed – they are intended to be distributed electronically and read on-screen. Consequently, technical translators may receive documents in **PDF** format or in a mark-up language such as **HTML** or **XML**. However, such electronic documents are not solely produced by DTP applications.

The emergence of what is commonly referred to as "Web 2.0" (O'Reilly 2005) has caused an explosion in the volume of information published online. In comparison to the static information traditionally produced by the people who operated websites, the "new" web has become a platform for dynamically and often, collaboratively, produced data which is shared by everyone in a more fluid and democratic way than previously possible thanks to online content management systems, social networking sites and blogs. The ubiquity of what can best be described as "Internet-related documents", means that technical translators need to be comfortable with, although not necessarily expert at, using technologies such as HTML, XML, scripting and programming languages. This is so that they can identify the text to be translated in a file and translate it without damaging the technical parts of the file which make it work. Often, texts which are not even of a technical nature but which are in HTML format, for example, are sent to technical translators simply because, as a rule, they have more experience translating this type of file.

1.3.3   Translation tools

There are, of course, tools which are designed specifically for translators and which are therefore unique to translation. These tools are specifically aimed at assisting translators in performing their daily tasks. In many cases, a translator's familiarity with such tools is a key deciding factor in whether the translator is actually awarded a project. Frequently referred to as **Computer-Assisted Translation** or CAT tools, they include **translation memory** systems, terminology management systems, electronic corpora and sometimes machine translation (see Austermühl 2001 and Bowker 2002). When **CAT** tools initially emerged, it was widely believed (and indeed feared) that they would radically transform the face of translation and change the role of the translator immeasurably.

To a certain extent, this is true but the impact of such technologies did not transform all areas of translation, primarily because CAT tools are only suited to particular types of texts in particular subject areas. As such, they do not feature as prominently in the work of all translators. Taking translation memory tools as an example, it is clear that, because they can only reuse existing translations, they are only of use when translating texts which contain a lot of repetition or which will be updated frequently. It is unlikely that such tools would be very useful when translating literary, marketing or **commercial texts**. In fact, they are most commonly used in technical translation where the nature of documents means that there is frequently a high proportion of repetition and where new product releases require existing documents to be updated.

Similarly, terminology management systems are at their most useful in situations where there is a large amount of terminology which must be used consistently. Admittedly, technical translators do not have the monopoly on such tools but they do represent perhaps the largest group of users.

For the technical translator, CAT tools require significant investment in the form of purchasing software, upgrading infrastructure and obtaining training. Initially, the expense and effort may seem counter-productive as the translator spends time learning how to use software which would otherwise be spent earning money. Translators also need to grapple with alternative payment schemes introduced as a result of translation memory systems (see Austermühl 2001 for example). However, proficiency in translation tools opens up a much larger pool of potential work for translators for which they would otherwise not be considered.

Another benefit of translation memory tools, particularly for the technical translator is that they can lessen the need to have experience of using the various DTP applications. Many translation memory tools provide filters which make it possible to extract the translatable text from files produced in different applications so that they can be translated in a single translation environment. So rather than having to learn how to use five or six different DTP applications, a translator simply needs to learn how to use one translation memory tool.

1.4   Who's who in scientific and technical translation?
Translation involves more than just a translator, a text and a mysterious target audience.

As both Sykes (1971:1) and Byrne (2006:11) point out, scientific and technical translation is a service, a communicative service carried out for people, by people. Scientific and technical texts are produced in response to a demand for information of a scientific or technical nature; such texts are translated because someone in a different language community wants to access or use the information these texts contain.

But who are the people involved in this process? An extremely basic response would be to say that scientific and technical translation involves the author, the translator and the reader, but this is much too simplistic, particularly in view of the vast global industry that has developed around the process of translating texts from one language into another (Byrne *ibid.*). The clear oversimplification notwithstanding, this basic categorization does provide a neat starting point for our examination of the people involved in scientific and technical translation.

Sager (1993:93-94) provides a relatively detailed breakdown of the participants in the translation process which is indicative of what happens in real life. He identifies the following participants:

- **Producers**: defined as the author of the source text whether a professional or subject-specialist who writes occasionally;
- **Mediators**: translators, editors, revisers; essentially anyone who modifies the text;
- **Communication agents**: the commissioner of a text or translation;
- **Recipients**: the intended end user or some person other than the addressee who may have different expectations.

A similar categorization of participants consists of the following (Byrne 2006:12-15):

- **Document initiator**: The person or entity responsible for setting in motion the production of a document. This is the person who wants to communicate something and "orders" the creation of a text. This may be a company that manufactures a product.
- **Writer**: The person or persons actually responsible for writing the document. In some cases, this might be a staff writer or a freelance writer.
- **Translation initiator**: This is the person responsible for initiating the translation process. It may be the same person as the document initiator or it may be a third party who "encounters" the document and wants to understand it.
- **Translator**: This is the person who actually produces the translation although strictly speaking it falls under Sager's category of mediators.
- **User**: The intended recipient of the translation, this person is concerned with accessing the information contained in the text as effectively as possible. Users of scientific and technical translations expect translations to function as authentic target language texts.

As complex as this may seem, it gives only part of the story because there are numerous other people involved in the process of translating scientific and technical texts: agencies, localization vendors, vendor managers, translation technology specialists, experts, editors/proofreaders, project managers, in-country reviewers, DTP and graphic artists, software, website and computer game engineers etc.

Given the fundamental role played by the client, who initiates the translation process and the translator, who is responsible for carrying out the work, we should examine their roles in more detail.

1.4.1   *The translator*

At the very heart of the translation industry is the translator, performing a role that is both essential and extremely complex. In any discussion of translation, we often see references being made to translators as some faceless, anonymous, almost mythical creature. For the most part, however, the actual nature of the translator's work and the conditions under which this work is carried out receive little attention.

Just as there are different types of text and subject, so too are there different types of translators and the types of work they do can vary significantly. Bear in mind that in referring to types of translators we do not mean broad distinctions such as legal translator, financial translator or technical translator, but rather more practical organizational distinctions.

Some translators, known as *staff translators*, are employed by large companies and translate documents produced by the company. In many cases, staff translators work for engineering or IT companies although some legal firms, financial institutions, government bodies and international organizations (see Wagner *et al.* 2002, for example) employ their own translators directly. The motivation for employing staff translators is generally a matter of finances: companies with a large and sustained demand for translations will generally find it more cost effective to employ their own translators who are constantly available and who receive a salary instead of being paid per translation.

Other motivations include the need to develop a skilled and experienced in-house team to ensure consistency, accuracy and quality. Staff translators generally deal with specific subject areas and quite often, specific range of text types. For example, a staffer working for a chemicals producer may typically translate packaging and labels, chemical data sheets, lab reports, chemical assay reports, instructions for use, health and safety documentation and as well as regulatory documents such as declarations of conformity.

Similarly, a staff translator working for a manufacturer of agricultural machinery may translate **user guides**, repair and maintenance manuals, spare parts lists, conformity documentation and test reports from product authorization bodies as well as the odd press release or article for trade journals. What this type of translation job may lack in variety - depending on the company, the texts and subjects rarely change – it makes up for in the sheer detail and level of specialized knowledge translators gain. As they are working on the same subject virtually all of the time and dealing with new developments and innovations, staff translators gain highly specialized knowledge of the subject area and of the documents produced in that area. Such expertise is often difficult to rival.

In-house translators, like staff translators, are employed by companies on a full-time basis but, unlike their staff translator colleagues, they work for translation companies or localization vendors. Working for a translation company can, depending on the individual company, provide scientific and technical translators with a greater variety of texts and subject areas and as such might appeal more to those who like the challenge of not knowing what project is around the corner. Of course, to justify the expense of hiring in-house translators, agencies may require their translators to deal with more than just scientific and technical texts during quiet periods or where there is an urgent non-technical job. This often requires translators to work outside their comfort zones and while some translators may shy away from this, others may find this an appealing prospect. In certain large translation companies, teams of translators may be assigned to certain key clients, often forming a "virtual translation department" for that client. Such teams will deal exclusively with projects for a specific client and, in this respect, the job of the in-house translator closely resembles that of a staff translator.

However, the most significant group of translators are not employed by large multinationals or by translation companies. Instead, they work for themselves as freelancers. *Freelance translators* are self-employed and are responsible for finding their own work, whether directly from clients, through agencies or other translators or any combination of these sources. Some freelancers may also join an online **translator community** such as ProZ, Aquarius or Translators Café to find work but such practices are widely criticized by professional translators who blame sites like this for reducing rates of pay for translators and promoting the use of unqualified translators (Ricketts 2010).

Practical Exercise 6: Translation forums
Visit the Aquarius.net, ProZ.com and TranslatorsCafe.com websites and compare the features available to translators. What costs are involved? What types of projects are typically posted on these sites? Do projects offer a fixed price or do they ask translators to suggest a price?

Freelance translators pick their own subjects and decide which projects they want to take on. This gives them the potential to have as much or as little variety as they want. In reality, however, the need to achieve a reasonable level of income means that many freelancers will often need to take on work in several areas, sometimes outside their main specialisms. This is not necessarily a bad thing as it helps freelancers to expand their expertise and as such remain competitive. In some cases, freelancers may join forces with other freelancers in order to take on translation projects which are too large for one translator to handle within the time available. They may even group together to share rented office space in order to keep costs down while at the same time having access to a professional workspace which is separate from the translator's own home.

Freelance translators represent the largest group of translators in the world. This may sound surprising, but the vast majority of all translation work is carried out by freelancers. Whereas thirty years ago most translators were staffers, nowadays around 80% of all translators work on a freelance basis in what is a highly fragmented industry (Boucau 2005:28). In the current economic climate, not just in individual countries but across the globe, this means that there are relatively few jobs available for full-time in-house or staff translators. Many companies cannot afford the expense of employing full-time translators and so choose to outsource their work to agencies or directly to freelancers. This reality is something which deters many students from pursuing translation as a career altogether (Byrne 2003). Often students do not feel sufficiently ready for freelancing when they leave university. Others are deterred by the uncertainty of not having a regular, fixed income and the need to be completely self-sufficient.

While in many respects, the ideal career path would involve at least some in-house experience before setting up as a freelancer, sometimes there is no other option but to take the plunge and go straight into freelancing. As a career option, freelancing is demanding in that it requires motivation, determination and courage but the rewards make the effort worth it: choosing your own working hours, flexibility, variety and, quite often, higher levels of income than in-house or staff translators.

Regardless of the different types of job scientific and technical translators may find themselves doing, the actual work they do remains fairly constant. As a scientific and technical translator, your duties go beyond merely translating texts. Depending on your level of experience, you may well be called upon to edit or proof another translator's work or to revise the work of less experienced translators. Often, translation projects are so large and have such short turnaround times that it is simply not possible for one person to produce a translation. In such cases, several translators may work in a team, with each person translating a section of the text. Of course, there needs to be another translator who works as an editor to combine the various sections and ensure consistency in terms of style and terminology.

A client may not know whether or not to commit to the expense of having a document translated; this is especially true of larger documents. Rather than adopt a "wait and see" attitude, translators may be asked to provide a "gist" or indicative translation, which is a very rough form of translation giving the basic meaning of a text but without any stylistic "polishing" or finesse. The idea of such translations is simply to give the client an idea of what the text is about so that they can access key information, for example to see if a foreign patent constitutes an infringement of another patent, or decide to have a full translation produced.

Senior translators are often called upon to set and evaluate test translations which are given to job applicants. This is not quite the straightforward task it may seem. Test translations are typically quite short, i.e. in the region of 500 words, which means that it is vital to select a text which is suitably challenging, but fair at the same time, in order to select the right candidates. Evaluating test translations is made all the more challenging because, depending on the level of the position being applied for, the applicant may be permitted to make a certain amount of mistakes and still be considered for the job.

As cultural experts, translators may also be asked to provide reports on the cultural appropriateness of various types of communications. Examples might include assessing television or newspaper advertisements to determine whether they contain anything which is likely to cause offence in their own culture or indeed, whether the advertisement is likely to be effective. This cultural insight also comes into play when translating or localizing websites: translators can and should advise customers if a website contains images, colours, language or content which is likely to prove problematic in the target culture. A variation of this type of cultural consulting involves assessing corporate brands, including company names, to ensure they are appropriate for the target market.

1.4.2   The clients

As mentioned previously, scientific and technical translation is a service provided to people who need either to communicate or access scientific or technical information. Such a broad definition inevitably means a vast range of potential clients for translators. Assuming that every organization involved in scientific research or the development and production of some form of product will need translated documents at some point, it is fair to say that clients are to be found in virtually every sector of industry and business.

Such general statements do little, however, to explain where a scientific and technical translator's work comes from. Although many translators deal almost exclusively with translation agencies, not least because agencies relieve translators of the effort of finding clients, translators are ultimately providing translations for individual clients. Agencies aside, obvious clients for scientific and technical translators include:

- **Engineering**: Usually manufacturing products or providing services related to some form of engineering, whether it is mechanical, electrical, electronic, chemical or medical. The texts involved generally relate to different fields and applications of chemistry, physics or biology.
- **Transport**: Companies involved in the aerospace or automotive industries, railway engineering, public transport, logistics, agricultural and works vehicles.
- **Information technology**: In its broadest sense this includes software and hardware companies, companies involved in some way with the Internet, either providing services, software or systems, and providers of telecommunications solutions including hardware, infrastructure, software, design and management.
- **Research organizations**: Government think tanks, standards institutions, safety organizations (e.g. product approval bodies or road safety agencies), public service bodies such as meteorology centres, universities, laboratories, regional development authorities and trade associations.

Other, less obvious, clients might include:

- **Commercial entities**: Insurance companies (e.g. technical reports on accidents or structural reports for buildings), banks and venture capitalists who may require detailed technical information in order to invest in new innovations or purchase new technologies, lawyers, business

consultants who advise various businesses on improving processes and
systems, auditors, etc.

- **Service providers**: Training centres, technical consultants, architects,
  town planners (e.g. public transport, environmental engineering, etc.),
  car dealerships, consumer associations, estate agents, etc.
- **Individuals**: Anyone who, for whatever reason, needs to access scientific
  and technical information whether for personal reasons (e.g. translating an obscure maintenance document for a classic car) or for research
  reasons (e.g. academic research or deciding which electronic components to buy for a project).

In the next chapter, we will examine the context within which technical documentation, the raw materials for scientific and technical translators is produced.
Building on the descriptions of the key stakeholders involved in the translation
process, Chapter 2 will also examine the recipients of our translations in more
detail.

Suggested Reading

Baer, Brian J. & Geoffrey S. Koby (2003) *Beyond the Ivory Tower: Rethinking Translation Pedagogy*, Amsterdam/Philadelphia: John Benjamins.

Byrne, Jody (2006) *Technical Translation: Usability Strategies for Translating Technical
Documentation*, Dordrecht: Springer.

------ (2007) Caveat Translator: Understanding the Legal Consequences of Errors in
Professional Translation. *Journal of Specialised Translation*, 2007 (7): 2-24.

Delisle, Jean & Judith Woodsworth [eds] (1995) *Translators Through History*, Amsterdam: John Benjamins.

Esselink, Bert (2000) *A Practical Guide to Localization*, Amsterdam/Philadelphia:
John Benjamins, 2nd edition.

Finlay, I.F. (1971) The Staff Translator. J.B. Sykes (ed.) *Technical Translator's Manual*,
London: Aslib.

Heyn, Matthias (1996) Translation Memories: Insights and Prospects, In L. Bowker
et al. (eds) *Unity in Diversity? Current Trends in Translation Studies*, Manchester:
St Jerome, 123-136.

Sykes, J.B. [ed.] (1971) *Technical Translator's Manual*, London: Aslib.

Tebeaux, Elizabeth (1997) *The Emergence of a Tradition: Technical Writing in the
English Renaissance 1475-1640*, New York: Baywood Publishing Company.

2. Translation and Technical Communication

In this chapter

This chapter discusses translation from the point of view of technical communication and it will show that we need to consider scientific and technical translation as part of a much larger communicative environment which is based on the development and dissemination of scientific and technical information. This chapter will describe what technical communication is and you will discover what type of information is communicated and how it is presented in different texts. By the end of the chapter, you will have learned about the key features of typical technical texts and how they affect translation. You will also learn how the target audience is the most important variable when communicating technical information and you will learn useful strategies for understanding their needs.

2.1   Introduction

It is easy to think of translation in isolation, as if it were an island completely cut off from the shore and everything around it. We can forget that translation, for all of the theorizing, debating and, sometimes, arguing, is essentially a type of communication. Even then, it's not the *only* type of communication. Many of the issues involved in translation are not unique to translation; they are shared by other forms of communication too.

In practice, there are almost always several ways of looking at a problem, and simply by holding something upside-down or sideways we can examine it from a completely different angle and gain a completely new insight into how it works.

By remembering that translation is just one of many types of communication, we allow ourselves not only to better understand what it is we are doing but also to access different bodies of knowledge, knowledge which is developed and added to by communicators from other areas who are working on similar problems, albeit from different perspectives. This gives us an insight which is both highly relevant and useful for our work as translators of **technical documentation**. When we talk about scientific and technical translation, our closest and most helpful neighbour is **technical communication**.

2.2   What is technical communication?

> Producing technical communication involves creating, designing, and transmitting technical information so that people can understand it easily and use it safely, effectively, and efficiently.
>
> (Markel 2001:4)

Any time you read a text that contains technical information which either explains how something works, how to do something or which helps you to understand technological concepts, the chances are that you are reading a product of technical communication. Whether you are reading a science textbook, a user guide for your car, an environmental impact statement, a journal article or even a health and safety leaflet, you are reading a technical document.

Technical communication, as the above definition suggests, seeks to help an audience understand a subject or to carry out a procedure, it helps people perform things quickly and safely, and may even help readers avoid dangerous situations or making mistakes when using something. Technical communication does this by combining text and graphics with an understanding of how to present information in such a way that what should be complex information is readily available and easily accessible for a particular audience in a particular context.

Technical documents are generally produced by two types of people: *technical professionals* and *technical communicators*. Technical professionals are typically the subject experts who develop the data or knowledge being communicated in the texts in the first place. In many cases, these engineers, technicians or scientists write their own texts in addition to performing their traditional engineer tasks. Some estimates put the proportion of time scientists and engineers spend on writing at about 40% (Markel 2001:4). This is a lot when you consider that their primary training is in science and technology and not necessarily in communication. In fact, there is evidence to suggest that many do not even want to spend this amount of time writing and that they may be doing so because they have to, not because they want to.

The other producer of technical documentation is the technical communicator. This person is the full-time communication professional whose job it is to produce and communicate technical information. Unlike the technical professional, the technical communicator may not always have the same in-depth technical knowledge but they will have a much more detailed understanding of how best to communicate information and are generally doing the job because they like to write.

To leave this description of who produces technical documentation as it is would be to omit another equally important producer. Translators are, without doubt, an essential part of the technical communication environment but they rarely, if ever, merit a mention in books on technical communication. For various reasons, most technical documentation will land at some point on a translator's desk and it is up to the translator to deal with this material, to present it to a new language audience who will treat it as if it were an original text.

Now the traditional definition of technical communication limits itself almost exclusively to *technical writing* and it means that translators are rarely mentioned in large sections of the literature. More modern definitions proposed by professional associations such as the *Institute for Scientific and Technical Communicators* in the UK and the *Society for Technical Communicators* in the USA and by translation researchers such as Schubert (2009), Göpferich (2009) and Byrne (2006) regard *technical communication* as a generic umbrella term which includes translating, editing and illustrating. In this sense, translators are included in the term "technical communicator" along with various other communication professionals. If we think back to the definition of technical communication given earlier, it is clear that translation has a rightful and important place in the process.

In practice, this means that technical communication consists of technical writing which provides the raw materials which translators will translate. To do this to the best of our ability, we therefore need to know what it is technical writers do and how they do it. As Schubert (2009:26) points out, the solutions technical writers opt for when designing and producing texts ultimately become controlling influences which affect translators' work. Herman (1993:12) nicely sums this up when he says that the "principal stylistic goals of technical writing, are simultaneously those of technical translation" and that in order to be a good technical translator, you need to be a good technical writer. While the demands and expectations for quality placed on technical writers equally apply to translators (see Byrne 2007), it is important not to overstate the similarities between technical writing and technical translation.

As well as the obvious task of writing texts, technical writing involves various factors such as information design, fonts and typography, graphics, page layout, and various decisions regarding the type and format of the document. Most, if not all, of these things are beyond the normal remit of a translator and cannot be changed during translation. Nevertheless, as translators we can benefit from understanding the documents writers produce and how they produce them, as well as from adopting the writing strategies and audience analysis methods they use.

2.2.1   Generic features of technical communication
Understanding the main features that shape technical communication

There are numerous different types of documents which fall under the category of technical communication and defining them all would be next to impossible. In just the same way as the subject material is vast and varied, so too are the texts used to convey this information. That said, there are certain key features which are common to most if not all types of technical document and they can help us appreciate the complexity of the task being performed.

Technical communication addresses specific readers
All technical documents are produced for a specific purpose, whether it is to help users perform a task, to demonstrate a particular concept, or to provide sufficient information to allow a decision to be made. In other words, technical documents can be thought of as **task-orientated** tools aimed at a particular group or groups of people. Sometimes the identity of this audience is made quite clear, for example through specific requests from a client or as a result of an identified need, and this means a document can be carefully tailored to that audience's needs. Some documents will be read by multiple audiences, some of whom may not even be the intended audience, and this may even require writers to prioritize these audiences and cater for their needs accordingly. Regardless of how many potential audiences there are, a technical document is conceived, designed and produced with the needs of a specific group in mind.

Technical communication is a tool

Whether it is performing a task, understanding a concept or making a decision based on clear facts, the aim of a technical document is to help readers to do something. Most people will read a technical text not because they enjoy it, but because they need to in order to do something else. Texts, therefore, are tools, a means to an end which is outside the text itself. Consequently, the text should not be the focus of attention. It is not there to entertain nor is it supposed to be a vehicle for the writer's literary talents and aspirations – the aim is to convey the right information to the right people in the right format so that they can get on with their jobs.

There is, of course, an exception to this general rule and that is the sub-category of scientific writing. In this category of text, we are communicating a different type of information, information that is less pragmatic and more theoretical. Here, writers may need to invent terms for new concepts, use various rhetorical devices in order to convince readers of the merits of the information being presented and, particularly in the case of popular science texts, to entertain them.

In these cases, creativity and literary prowess are often essential in order to achieve a communicative goal. Imagine trying to describe the concept of a *Red Giant* (a type of star) or the *Big Bang* (a way of explaining the origins of the universe) without using literary creativity. This dichotomy of function, however, involves very specific and easily identifiable instances and it does not detract from the basic premise.

Technical translation is creative too!
Even though technical texts – as opposed to scientific texts – do not use ornate, prosaic and fancy language, it does not mean that they are not creative. The fact that technical language is supposed to be clear, straightforward and functional places significant constraints on writers and translators as they try to communicate technical information when the number of ways in which they can say something is severely limited. By effectively excluding vast sections of a language which could be used to nicely explain various complicated ideas, these constraints mean that only some of the linguistic tools can be used. While the language is restricted, the information, events and situations it is supposed to convey are not. Like subtitlers who need to convey large amounts of information in a very small box measuring just 40 or so characters across, technical writers and translators who are working with such limited resources need to come up with some pretty creative solutions in order to get the message across. For a good example of creativity in technical translation, see *Scenarios and examples* on page 170.

Technical communication is often produced collaboratively

Unlike letters or essays, which are usually the work of one single person, technical documents are frequently the product of several people working together. In certain companies, documents may be produced by teams of technical writers or other contributors, each writing specific sections of the text. But even where only one writer is involved, documents invariably pass through several cycles of review by various people such as technical experts, marketing people, lawyers and users with changes being made to each iteration or version of the document. With several people working on a documentation project, it is very easy for stylistic inconsistencies to make their way into the text simply because different people have different ways of writing and they may not adhere to style guides consistently.

For translators, this means that sometimes the same concept is referred to using different terms throughout a document or the text suddenly stops making sense when we reach a particular chapter. In extreme cases, a text may suddenly become incredibly difficult to translate because the style and clarity of the text suddenly deteriorates in comparison to the rest of the document. Similarly, technical documents are often translated by teams of translators, particularly in the case of large documents with short delivery times. Again, the problem of inconsistencies in style has to be dealt with, usually by an editor or a senior translator, but also by a lone freelancer.

Technical communication uses design to improve usability

Simply presenting information in clear and carefully crafted prose is not a guarantee that the audience will understand it or that they will be able to do so easily or efficiently. Often, seemingly simple factors such as the font and its size, the colours and amount of white space in a document can make the world of difference to how effectively readers absorb information (see Byrne 2006:68ff). Beyond these cosmetic factors, technical documents frequently use graphics to reinforce and support textual information or to convey large amounts of information quickly and clearly.

As a translator, it is not particularly likely that you would need to concern yourself with issues such as fonts, page layout and graphics (unless they have particular cultural connotations and need to be changed), but, as we will discover later on, you will have to work with and around them and you can also play a significant role in ensuring the **usability** of information in documents.

Technical communication uses a variety of technologies

As we discovered in Chapter 1, technical translators can expect to be exposed to a range of technologies which are used to produce technical documents. This is because the writers themselves use a range of tools to create and disseminate their documents. Often, the nature and complexity of a document will necessitate the use of one tool or another. For example, a simple one-page instruction leaflet can be comfortably produced using a basic word processor, whereas a complex document comprising several hundred pages containing graphs, design blueprints, equations, conditional text, variables and hyperlinks will need to be created using sophisticated tools such as FrameMaker or using mark-up technologies such as DITA. Whatever the scenario, the variety of media used to produce and distribute technical information is a key characteristic of this area.

Structured writing
An important theme in contemporary technical communication is the idea of *structured writing*. DITA, which stands for *Darwin Information Typing Architecture*, is a prime example of a structured writing tool. Based on the **XML** mark-up language, it is used to identify information by type and not by content. For example, definitions are marked as definitions, concepts and tasks are clearly identified as such. Individual document types are used to present information relevant to a particular task and they can contain predetermined types of information and sometimes in a specific order. The aim is to improve the consistency, accuracy and comprehensibility of information, and because it separates information content from its presentation, specific information can be reused in a variety of contexts without the need for rewriting or extensive editing. An example would be technical information written for a user guide being re-used easily on a website or in a help system. This is known as Single-Source, Multi-channel Publishing and makes it possible for information producers to gain as much use from their information as possible. A wealth of information on DITA is available on the DITA World website (www.ditaworld.com).

2.3   Who reads technical documentation?

If technical communication is an activity which is aimed at providing people with information, then it makes sense to find out a little more about these people and what it is they want. By looking at what an audience needs, how they expect information to be presented and the way in which they are going to use that information, we can better understand the challenges facing us as translators and formulate strategies for translating texts.

This is particularly true if we think back to the discussion of Skopos theory in Chapter 1, where we learned that it is essential to understand the purpose for which a translation is produced in order to translate it properly. In those all-too-frequent cases where the translator is not provided with a specific translation brief, we have to resort to knowledge of what the typical text **function** is and an understanding of what the typical audience for a particular text is.

2.3.1   Understanding audiences
As obvious as it might seem to say that translations are produced with a specific audience in mind, it is worth taking a little more time to understand our audiences in more detail.

Once upon a time, it was fairly safe to assume that the only people who would read a technical text were technical people: engineers, technicians, scientists, all people whose jobs revolved around science and technology. This meant that you could be pretty sure that whomever you were writing for would have good, if not excellent, knowledge of the subject matter. This basic assumption led some translation scholars (for example, Hervey *et al.* 1995) to imply that there is no such thing as an absolute novice or lay reader.

We now know that this is untrue, particularly when we consider the sheer volume of products and services being documented these days. Is it really fair to expect and assume that your grandmother has a background in electronics and communications technology before she reads the instructions for the mobile phone you bought her for her birthday? Probably not. Granny will read the instructions and they will have to present information in such a way that she can understand them, even without a degree in telecommunications.

The same applies to pretty much every other act of technical communication. Nowadays, it would appear that background knowledge has been replaced by interest, or most likely necessity, as a key assumption about our audiences. People read technical documents either because they are interested in the topic or, in the majority of cases, because they have to, whether this is due to their jobs or because they cannot get something to work.

But back in the days when people assumed that only "technical" people would read technical texts, writers and translators only had to worry about making sure that texts were accurate and relatively comprehensible. As such, you could take a lot for granted in terms of background information. This meant that additional explanation, examples and clarification would rarely be necessary because the chances were that the reader was an expert in that area or a very close area and would not want every little abbreviation, acronym and technical term to be explained, nor would they need to be told every single step in a basic procedure.

The traditional technical writing approach to the issue of audiences has been to categorize readers into hypothetical categories based on the typical jobs or roles they hold (see for example Price 1984: 32). This gives us an insight into what people will use a text for, how they will use it and how they expect the text to look. There are various examples of how readers can be categorized. Van Laan & Julian (2001:89ff) focus on readers' job titles, functions and duties, to propose *novice users, power users, programmers* and *system administrators,* although these will typically only apply to texts in a software context, not to a broader technological area. Similarly, Markel (2001:99-100) describes *experts, technicians, managers* and *general users.*

A more widely applicable set of categories comes from Horton (1994:28-29) who describes *novices* as having little background knowledge but who are curious to learn more yet cautious about making mistakes and *occasional users* who may once have mastered a concept but through infrequent use may forget certain information. *Transfer users,* according to Horton, are knowledgeable of a similar subject area and try to apply this existing knowledge in a new context (we can think of these people as "super educated laypersons").

The final categories defined by Horton include the self-explanatory *expert user* and the *rote user*. Rote users use information or a product without knowing or understanding much about the hows or whys of what they are doing. They follow explicit instructions, often in repetitive, unchanging scenarios and run into problems when new or unknown situations arise. Figure 1 combines the categories provided by Horton and Markel and gives a brief overview of how a user's role affects their needs and their interactions with technical documentation.

It is also worth noting that different types of reader may use documents in different ways depending on their needs, attitudes and expectations. Expert users, for instance might be expected to skim through a document or dip in and out at certain points as they look for specific information. Certain types of novice user may read entire chapters carefully and in sequence while rote users will skip straight to the section containing step-by-step instructions. This will affect various aspects of a text but from a translator's point of view may require headings, for example, to be written consistently to allow readers to identify quickly sections or to use short, simple sentences to ensure instructions are easy to follow.

Reader	Reasons for reading	Considerations
Expert User	A quick overview to get started, then detailed information.	Different types of user: system administrators, programmers, etc. Usually in a hurry and will quickly skip to relevant sections of text.
Technician	Identify and perform procedures, locate components etc.	Often reads in a work area – information must be easily accessible and digestible, physical document needs to be large print and fold open on a desk or the floor.
Transfer User	Problem-solving, to fill in gaps in existing knowledge	Tries to solve problems alone but needs clear help when previous knowledge proves inadequate. May need comparisons and trouble-shooting information.
Rote User	Interested in clear step-by-step instructions needed to perform a very specific task.	Instructions must be clear, unambiguous and short. There should be no unnecessary information and may contain lots of diagrams.
Novice	Needs a general overview and introduction to subject; to solve problems and in time, more detailed information.	Usually has very little background knowledge and requires slower pace of information with frequent explanations and definitions to build up background knowledge. Requires carefully paced step-by-step information.
General Reader	General interest, curiosity, boredom	Does not need to understand everything. Could be a potential customer or employee so documents need to be grammatical, professional and well presented to create good impression of company.

Figure 1: Sample reader roles and their needs

While this approach is useful in that it helps technical communicators to think actively about their audiences, it oversimplifies the situation somewhat and it does not take into account a range of other factors which previous research[1] has shown to be essential when communicating technical information (see Schriver 1996 and Hoft 1995, for example). The problem is also that the nature of technology has changed quite substantially, even in the last ten to fifteen years and this has necessitated a new approach to technical communication. As audiences grew and became more diverse, so too did the documents and the variations of document types. With this came new methods – linguistic, graphical and pedagogical – for achieving the goals of technical communication and – from the point of view of translation – for understanding how to make technical information available to new audiences.

As we mentioned above, you will often know who the audience for a particular text is, either through explicit references or implicit clues in the text, from a **translation brief** or some other means, but equally there are just as many cases where you will not immediately know who your audience is.

Normally when we write certain types of text we do not need to give as much thought as we would for other types of text, generally because we usually instinctively know, either from the context or from the type of document, what is expected of us and of our writing. But when it comes to technical translation, it is very important that we have as detailed an understanding of our target audience as possible. In fact, the audience is probably the most important factor in technical writing and technical translation. Getting a translation right depends in so many ways on understanding your audience that virtually every translation decision you make will depend on how well you understand your audience and the environment in which they are working. Such decisions might include whether to use one term over another, whether a particular phrase needs to be reworded, either to make it clearer or to make it less patronizing, or whether to change the order of sentences because your audience expects logical and chronologically accurate instructions.

From a purely writing perspective, understanding the target audience affects not just the type of information we want to convey but also the language we use to convey it in a particular context. In translation, things are more complicated and our understanding of the text's audience will shape our translation strategies and will ultimately play a big part in whether or not we are successful in our translation efforts. This is because not only are we trying to produce the same type of document in another language but, because different languages and cultures are involved, the number of factors is essentially doubled since what may be appropriate information to one audience may be unacceptable for

---

[1] Schriver (1996), for example, says that the design, layout, sequencing and even content of texts can affect their communicative effectiveness. Hoft (1995) describes a range of "international variables" such as political, social, educational, linguistic and technological factors which play an important role in communicating technical information. Hoft's international variables are discussed in "What is the native culture?" on page 38.

another and what may be an appropriate and effective means of expressing it in one language may be wholly inadequate in another.

Understanding people & culture

An important factor in understanding audiences is their culture. It can help you learn a lot about people and why they do some of the things they do, and it can help explain those instances when people do not behave in ways which you would expect. With an understanding of the source and target cultures, you will be better able to work around their idiosyncrasies. There are various definitions of culture but they usually share a common theme in the idea of a shared set of attitudes, values, goals, beliefs and practices that characterize a particular group of people and which evolves over time. Bates & Plog (1990:7) define it as "the system of shared beliefs, customs, behaviours, and artefacts that members of a society use to cope with the world and with one another, and that are transmitted from generation to generation through learning". This is quite a lot of information to try to learn. The "Iceberg Model" was developed in 1975 by Selfridge and Sokolik as a way of illustrating the complexity of culture and categorizing it. It divides cultural knowledge into surface, unspoken and unconscious rules.

- Surface rules are the most visible and obvious traits of a culture and they include such things as political, economic, social, religious, educational, linguistic and technical factors, and practical manifestations such as currency, numbers, date and time formats etc.
- Unspoken rules are less obvious and include things like etiquette, appropriate forms of address, tipping etc.
- Unconscious rules are more deep-seated elements of a culture's collective psyche which people do or observe without realizing it, for example, dependence on context, notions of time and distance, rate and intensity of speaking etc.

As translators, we need to know who the audience is for the source text, who the audience is for the target text, and then decide whether the two are compatible. If they are not, we need to find a way of smoothing over the bumps in communication to ensure the target text does what it is supposed to do. If you understand the audience, it follows that you understand their language, culture, expectations, knowledge etc. Virtually all of the decisions you make as a technical translator will be directly related to these issues and they will be easier to make, the more you know your reader(s).

There are various ways in which you can get a better understanding of the audiences who are most likely to read the text and then tailor the text towards their needs and expectations.

Practical Exercise 7: Analysing cultures
Using the Iceberg Model, create a short snapshot of your own culture and produce a crash course in local customs and traditions for a particular group of foreign visitors to your city. This document should contain a list of tips or key pointers which are presented under the categories of *surface, unspoken* and *unconscious* rules.

Practical Exercise 8: Planning for different audiences
Imagine you are asked to write two training guides explaining how to use the latest version of a word processor. One of the guides is for a group of transfer users who have used a rival word processor. The other guide is for a group of novices with no previous knowledge or experience of word processors. Write a sample table of contents to indicate the topics you might need to cover in each document.

2.3.2 Finding out who the audience is
Knowing who is going to read your translation means you can write specifically for them and give them the type of text they need.

The notion of audience is one with which most of us are very familiar. Look in any book on translation and you will see numerous references to the target audience, reader, intended audience, and various other synonyms. But despite the ubiquity of the audience, it is still a surprisingly abstract and fuzzy concept, which is difficult to define in any concrete way.

This is not unique to translation. Technical writers, too, struggle with figuring out who their audience will be. In many cases, it is simply not possible to create a detailed profile of our audience so we have to resort to other methods in order to gain some understanding of what they need, want and expect. Rosenberg (2005:9) acknowledges both the need to identify your audience as well as the difficulty in doing this. He proposes two simple questions which, when properly followed through and analyzed, can provide a wealth of information to help us:

- What does my audience already know about this technology?
- What is the native language of my audience?

While both questions are aimed primarily at technical writers, they are highly applicable to translation scenarios. By understanding what the audience knows about a particular technology we can decide whether or not we need to provide additional explanations and foreground particular facts or whether we can omit certain facts; this also tells us whether we need to avoid specialized terms and acronyms or whether we can use them comfortably.

The second question is motivated by the fact that, in English at least, a sizeable proportion of the audience of a technical text do not speak English as their first language and texts need to cater for their particular circumstances and abilities. From a translation point of view, it seems quite unnecessary to ask this question because translators know into which languages they translate. It seems about as useful as reminding yourself of your own name. But if we take this question and examine it in a more profound way, it can pay dividends. The idea of language does not just refer to the words people use to refer to things and the rules they use to string them together.

Instead, language combines various factors such as culture, customs, norms, conventions and countless other factors that make up a language community. If we make the question even more specific and say which specific variety of language the audience speaks, this question might make more sense, i.e. US English, Swiss German or Canadian French. Incidentally, this is quite similar to what people in the localization industry call a "**locale**".

Language or locale?
Simply referring to Arabic or Spanish or Russian is fine for people who are not concerned with communicating across cultures. But for those of us who are, we need to be much more specific because the same language can be used in different countries by people with different cultures, and to group them together would not only be politically and culturally insensitive, but also inaccurate. For this reason, it is helpful to think in terms of *locales* rather than simply in terms of target languages.

The best way of understanding a locale is in the context of multilingual computing where it represents a combination of language **and** the country **and** the culture where it is used. A locale can be defined as a set of attributes which are specific to a particular language and geographical region. These attributes include such settings as the display language, number formats, date/time formats, time zone, daylight saving time, currency formats and keyboard layout. Examples of locales include English (U.S.) or Arabic (Morocco).

Instead of users having to manually change these settings themselves, locales are used to store all of the relevant information so that the computer can implement the changes automatically and the software will work properly. It ensures, for example, that a word processor uses the correct dictionaries for spellcheckers, that the correct currencies are displayed in an accounting program and that the paper sizes are correct when you print something.

In the context of translation, a locale equates to the various linguistic, cultural, social, political and historical factors that make the target audience what it is.

As useful as these questions are, they are still rather vague and prone to arbitrary results depending on who asks them. It would be better if we were able to have a more detailed way of understanding audiences.

2.3.2.1 ASKING THE RIGHT QUESTIONS

While we may never know exactly who will be reading our texts, we may be able to deduce who our audience is from the context or from the text type. Sometimes the best you can hope for is to come up with a prototypical, generic outline of who the audience is. While not ideal, it is better than nothing and it will still help you to translate effectively. In his discussion of audiences, Rosenberg (2005:9-20) proposes a number of categories which we can usefully turn into questions to help us gain a clearer picture of our audience.

What is the general education level?
This will help us understand the general levels of literacy among the audience. For less literate audiences, a text which is written in overly complex language will be less effective and possibly even counterproductive. Conversely, pitching the language level too low may, in some circumstances, frustrate more literate audiences.

What experience and expertise does the audience have?
What is the background of the audience in terms of their work experience, level of expertise and job seniority? How familiar are readers with the subject matter and the work area in which the information is needed? This information will determine how much detail we can present in the text and how we present it.

How wide and diverse is the audience?
Is there one audience or multiple audiences? Although it is a bad idea to try to cater for too many audiences within a single document, certain types of texts are produced for multiple readerships. These readerships will need to be categorized into primary and secondary audiences so that the appropriate level of attention can be paid to the needs, expectations and experiences of specific groups. This may require us to clearly label sections or structure information so that they are separated for the different audiences.

What is the native language?
Even if all of our readers speak English, for example, there may be significant variation in their ability to speak it. This may be because it is not their first language, or even their second or third language. Readers may have only a very limited knowledge of a language as used in a specific subject area. In such cases, it may be necessary to limit the range of vocabulary used in texts and define new or specialized terms and abbreviations when they are first used in the text. Other strategies which can be of benefit to non-native speakers of a language (although generally useful to everyone) include using the active voice and avoiding long sentences because it makes sentences clearer, more direct and less complicated.

Similarly, there are numerous regional varieties of languages such as English, Arabic (see Wilmsen & Youssef 2009), Spanish and Portuguese, which means not all terminology will be standardized and not all cultural references will be commonly intelligible. There may even be preferences with regard to grammatical structures or forms of address.

In the case of product names (see "Translating brand names" on page 64) and medicines it may be necessary to swap them for generic names or replace them with country-specific equivalents. Some examples might include *paracetamol* which is sometimes referred to as acetaminophen while the drug *clopidogrel* (used to prevent blood clots) is marketed in different countries under its generic name *clopidogrel* and also under the trade names *Plavix*, *Ceruvin* and *Clopilet*. An asthmatic who uses *albuterol* inhalers may have difficulty in knowing what *Proventil* is if they are more familiar with *Ventolin* inhalers. Even fast-acting cyanoacrylate glue is referred to as either *Super Glue*, *Krazy Glue* or *The Original Super Glue* depending on the market in which it is sold. Clearly, knowing the variety of a particular language and the intended country can have significant implications for the text and the people who will read it.

> **Practical Exercise 9: Different country, different name**
> Identify three products from around your home. They can be anything from foods to cleaning products, drinks, medicines or whatever you can find. Find out if they are sold in any other countries. If so, what are they called? If not, what are the nearest comparable products available in that market?

What is the native culture?

As we saw earlier, culture is something which can transcend nationality and physical geography and may consist purely of a group of people with a shared interest in some particular area, for example, computer games, electronics, steam engines or even crime. The nature of the cultural norms, expectations and dynamics within the target audience culture affects texts in a variety of ways, such as the use of slang and jargon, forms of address and cultural references based on the assumption of shared knowledge. The native culture of the readers will also determine practical issues such as date and time conventions, currencies and even references to laws, institutions and government departments.

But this category opens up a much richer avenue of analysis to help translators understand the text and its audience and to identify appropriate translation strategies. In her book, *International Technical Communication*, Nancy Hoft presents a series of approaches for identifying "international variables" (1995:62ff), which she says will help us to identify firstly, what the essential components of technical documentation are and secondly, to decide which aspects of a text need to be changed in order for the text to be effective in another culture.

But before we look at these factors which are drawn from the work of Hall (1976), Hofstede (1991), Victor (1992) and Trompenaars (1993), a word or two of warning is in order at this point. When discussing cultures it is important to remember that we cannot equate one culture with one language or vice versa. There may be numerous parallel cultures located within a particular language group and they may be quite different from each other. It is for this reason that in the following paragraphs we will not refer to nationalities or languages the way Hoft does, only to groups who *tend to* exhibit particular characteristics or preferences.

Similarly, the approaches proposed by Hoft are very useful but they are generalizations, rules of thumb to help broadly categorize audiences. It is important to remember this and not to resort to indiscriminate stereotyping of cultures, nationalities and audiences, because there are no hard and fast rules and there will always be exceptions and anomalies. However, when used with the right level of caution and flexibility the following points can provide us with a better insight into how our audiences *tend* to work.

In addition to identifying any differences and similarities between the source and target audience in terms of educational systems, literacy levels, learning style, political, religious and social climate, we can also compare our source and target audiences in terms of their approaches to context, authority and uncertainty.

Understanding Context

The role of context in intercultural communication was highlighted by Hall in 1976. In his book *Beyond Culture*, he proposed a model which allows cultures to be classified as either **high context** or **low context**. The difference between a high and a low context culture depends on the level of explicit verbal information which members of a culture tend to use in their communicative interactions.

The basic idea is that meaning is a combination of explicitly stated information and implicit non-verbal information derived from the context. The model says that the more a culture relies on context in communication, the less likely it will be to communicate information explicitly. Such an audience is then regarded as high context. Conversely, low context audiences depend less on the context, preferring instead to explicitly communicate information.

Although the idea of contexting is popular when discussing cultures and communication, the validity of the model and its propositions has been questioned by Cardon (2008), who says that it has not been fully verified experimentally. For this reason, care is needed when classifying entire cultures or nationalities as being high or low context so that we do not stereotype or overstate what is simply a tendency. An example of this can be seen in work by Victor (1992), who ranks ten countries in terms of their context-dependency, with Japan regarded as a high context culture and Swiss-Germans as a low context culture. Again, while this may be useful, we need to remember that cultures and nationalities consist of discrete sub-cultures which may not exhibit the same tendencies.

The notion of context provides us with a way of assessing how much detail there should be in a technical document in order for it to be understood by the intended audience. Context is the amount of explicit information we need to include in a given communicative act so that the recipient can understand us. There are, according to Hall (1976), two broad categories of culture, high context and low context, although in reality both Hall (*ibid.*) and Victor (1992) acknowledge that there is a continuum linking the two extremes along which individual cultures may be placed.

One example of how such a continuum might look is provided in Figure 2, which is based on an illustration produced by David Katan (1999:183):

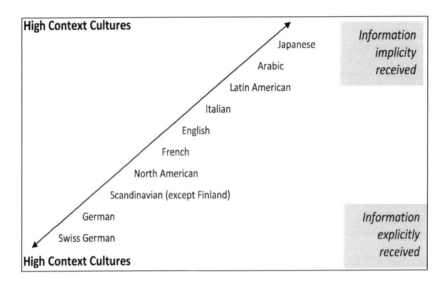

Figure 2: High and Low Context Cultures (Katan 1999:183)

For translators, this means that texts aimed at certain groups will need to be very explicit and detailed whereas other texts may be more vague and lacking in detail because the audience will be able to use the context of the communication to determine the meaning. For a high context culture, a text written for a low context culture may be perceived as overly prescriptive, patronizing and possibly insulting, whereas a text written for a high context culture may be regarded as defective, sketchy or confusing by a low context culture. We can also relate this to our efforts as translators to correctly gauge the prior knowledge and expertise of the target audience for a text.

Authority and, in particular, a culture's attitudes to authority can affect how information is presented in technical documentation. Hofstede's (1991) notion of *power distance* seeks to explain how members of a group (in his study, subordinates) react to authority figures (in Hofstede's study, managers). The relative power distance, i.e. low or high, is likely to determine the relationship between those in a position of authority and those who are not. In the case of technical communication, it can help us to determine what is and is not an appropriate way of addressing readers or issuing instructions. It can even affect the emphasis on or extent to which certain types of information need to be foregrounded in a text.

The final factor presented by Hoft relates to another concept developed by Hofstede, namely *uncertainty avoidance*. This seeks to establish whether an audience will react favourably or unfavourably to uncertainty or unclear situations and information. From the point of view of scientific and technical translation, such situations might affect the nature and amount of explanation provided in an instruction manual or the way in which users can navigate around a website.

In a culture with low levels of uncertainty avoidance, readers tend to work things out for themselves and are unlikely to be adversely affected if information is missing, inaccurate or not explicit enough. Cultures with high levels of uncertainty avoidance regard unknown situations as "threatening" (Hoft 1995:87) and readers will require explicit details if they are to successfully assimilate the information.

Admittedly, this is potentially a huge amount of information to gather and process. Remembering and applying it will be just as much of a challenge unless we can come up with some way of managing it. For this reason it makes sense to use some form of standardized, repeatable and, more importantly, easy-to-use tool to ease the information burden. Hoft, for example, proposes a checklist for analyzing and comparing source and target audiences. Although her checklist was designed for technical writers who are producing information for readers in other countries, it is also useful for translators. While it is by no means perfect, comprehensive or applicable in every translation scenario, it is still a useful starting point and can be customized according to the requirements of a particular translation project.

	Political	Economic	Social	Religious	Educational	Linguistic	Technological
Similarities							
Differences							

Figure 3: Worksheet for profiling a target audience (Hoft 1995:61)

Practical Exercise 10: Comparing cultures
Using the worksheet shown in Figure 3, create a profile for your source language culture and your target language culture. What, if any, are the main differences between the two? Are there more similarities than differences? Try to think of a number of hypothetical scenarios when these similarities/differences would affect communication.

> **Practical Exercise 11: Creating cultural profiles**
> Use the various questions and criteria mentioned in this chapter to create a cultural profile for your source language and for your target language. Look for areas that they have in common and areas where they differ. What impact would these differences have on the type of information contained in (a) an advertisement for a car; (b) a report on home entertainment systems in a specialist magazine; (c) an instruction manual for a lawnmower?

2.4   Knowing what you're talking about
You cannot be an expert in every technical area but there are strategies for dealing with new topics.

Once we have identified our audience and their needs, we still face the challenge of communicating complex information to them in an appropriate manner. This poses problems for translators at every stage of their careers. If you are just starting out, you are asked all the time to state your specialisms but, unless you happen to have a background in a technical subject already, you are essentially starting your career with a blank canvas. If you are an experienced translator, the challenge is how to stay abreast of ever-changing subjects where knowledge and expertise, which has taken years to accumulate, can be rendered obsolete as a result of a single journal paper or patent application, or in the case of software with the release of a new software version.

At the start of your career, it is very hard to have a definite specialism and you may need to take on pretty much any job you can, within reason of course, to push yourself and to help you to firstly gain as much experience as possible and eventually to develop a specialism. You should also take advantage of the various transferable skills which you develop as a translator. These skills include the ability to carry out research, solve problems, analyze information and use computers, and they make the process of acquiring new specialisms easier.

Naturally, a bit of common sense is essential when taking on jobs – agreeing to translate a text on a subject where you have absolutely no understanding or familiarity of even the most basic aspects of the text is hardly a wise or advisable course of action. That said, taking on a text which will require you to spend some time doing research is a good thing; this is how you learn and add to your repertoire.

Some specialisms are, thankfully, quite easy to acquire either because you have a natural talent for them, because you know something about a related area, or because there are lots of resources available. Once you have acquired a specialism, it is surprising how others develop out of it.

Sometimes a text will require you to have an understanding of more than one specialism. What is supposedly a text dealing with software and computer networks may suddenly turn into a complicated discussion of meteorology and financial accounting because the software is really a platform for syndicating and distributing meteorological data to airports via the Internet. Not a problem if you understand this new subject matter and if you have had a chance to research it, but if it comes as a surprise midway through a project, you may find yourself in trouble. For this reason, no matter how experienced you are or how well you think you know a subject area, never accept a translation project without first seeing the text and having a chance to read through it quickly. While pushing yourself (and even scaring yourself in the process) with new subjects is part of what makes translation interesting, overstretching yourself means you risk either not being able to finish the translation or producing a substandard piece of work.

One of the most frequently asked questions among aspiring translators, particularly those who want to specialize, is how to gain a specialism. As a graduate of a translation programme your expertise will, naturally, be in translation. But unless you have qualifications in other fields or have taken classes in specialized translation, you will not yet have a clear area of specialization. Developing the subject-specific knowledge to allow you to deal with different texts and, ultimately, to develop a specialism is an ongoing challenge for translators and one which needs to be taken every bit as seriously as maintaining your language skills. Unfortunately, there is no easy way of solving this problem but there are some useful tips, which can help:

1. **Read everything and anything!** No matter what it is, whether the label on a bottle of ketchup to the instructions that come with a power drill or a car magazine you find while waiting for your dental appointment, read it. Regardless of whether you are interested in the topic or even whether you understand what you are reading, you will gain a familiarity with different writing styles, terminology and even small snippets of subject knowledge. As a translator, no knowledge is wasted and you will be surprised how the sticker you read on the side of a washing machine five years ago will suddenly come to mind in the middle of a translation when you are looking for a word or phrase.

2. **Do your research.** If you are interested in a particular area or if you seem to be getting a lot of work on a particular subject, turn it into a hobby and set yourself the challenge of finding out as much about it as you can. Reading popular science magazines, school books, basic college texts or even "*...For Dummies*" books can help you develop your understanding of various areas. If you are not sure what areas you should look at, start with the basics of physics, chemistry and biology. Once you have a good knowledge of these areas you can look for more and more detailed sources of information in specific areas.

   Above all, the most valuable asset a translator can develop is the ability to research a topic quickly to find the most important information and then assimilate it. Some people are born researchers, while the rest of us have to develop this talent over time, but do persevere and keep a note of the best places to find information whether online or in the real world. Remember to practise and refine your use of keywords and phrases when searching online.

Fine-tuning your search strategies

While modern search engines provide access to vast amounts of information, sorting through it to identify the most relevant and reliable information can be time-consuming and difficult. With Google, for example, you can narrow your searches using some quite simple techniques:

- **-** Add a minus sign to the start of a word you want to exclude from your search.
- **~** Add a tilde to the start of a word to search for synonyms.
- **""** Use quotation marks to search for a specific phrase.
- **site:** Use the site parameter to search for information on a particular site (e.g. site:jodybyrne.com) or type of site (e.g. site:.org).
- **filetype:** Use the filetype parameter to search for specific types of files such as *pdf*, *doc* or *html*.

Certain databases, such as library catalogues, allow you to use Boolean operators to make your searches more specific:

- **AND**: Type AND between two words to find resources that contain both words.
- **OR**: Type OR between two words to find resources that contain either word.
- **NOT**: Type NOT in front of a word to exclude resources that contain this word.

3. **Take a night course.** Most local community colleges and adult education centres run a range of part-time night classes on a huge range of areas from cake decoration to car maintenance, woodwork, electrical systems and computer programming. Not only are you learning useful skills, which will help you in day-to-day life, but you will also expand your knowledge in a specialized area. This is also a great opportunity to get out of the house and meet people – quite useful if you have spent all day sitting in front of a computer screen. Courses like this can also count towards the Continuing Professional Development (CPD) requirements of some professional translators' associations.

4. **Talk to experts.** If you know someone who is an engineer or a nurse or a botanist (or know someone who knows one), make use of their expertise. These people have amassed many years of expertise and are a goldmine of useful information. They can often answer questions more quickly than you can type a keyword into a search engine. You do need to brush up on your interview skills to get the right information because subject matter experts do not necessarily know anything about translation, so you will need to ask the right questions and make sure that you are as clear and concise as possible.

Some people suggest cold-calling experts, i.e. looking in the phone book for an expert and calling them at random. This may or may not work but remember that just like you, these people need to earn a living and every minute spent talking to you or answering emails is lost money to them. If you happen to know where the local engineers hang out in their free time you could try befriending them!

Practical Exercise 12: Researching technical subjects
Pick a random topic that interests you from the latest issue of the *New Scientist* or any other popular science magazine. Try to find as much information on this topic as you can from a variety of sources including a library (university and public), the Internet, encyclopaedias etc. Write a brief report explaining what the area is about for a complete novice. Create a glossary explaining key terms, concepts and phrases. You can also create an online forum or group blog to share your reports with colleagues or fellow learners. You might also find it useful and interesting to produce a multilingual dictionary of terms based on these reports.

To make things even more interesting, try to locate a subject matter expert. This can be a professor in your university or someone you find in the phonebook, a friend or even a friend of a friend. Contact them and ask to interview them about their research in the area. This is a chance for you to practise your interview skills and a chance to practise communicating about a subject with an expert audience. When you have conducted the interview, write a short summary of what you learned from the expert.

Practical Exercise 13: Create your own knowledge network
This task involves surveying your friends and family about the scientific and technical specializations of their immediate and extended circle of friends and acquaintances. Who knows an engineer? Do any of your friends know a microbiologist or a computer programmer? Once you have compiled a list, create a chart to represent graphically the different fields of knowledge you have access to.

In the following chapter, we will build on this overview of technical communication by examining technical documentation in more detail. This examination will involve a discussion of the main types of document, their key characteristics and their implications for translators.

Suggested Reading

Hoft, Nancy (1995) *International Technical Communication*, New York: Wiley.
Herman, Mark (1993) Technical Translation Style: Clarity, Concision, Correctness, In S.E. Wright & L.D Wright (eds) (1993) *Scientific and Technical Translation*. Amsterdam: Benjamins, 11-20.
Schubert, Klaus (2009) Positioning translation in Technical Communication Studies. *Journal of Specialised Translation*, 11: 17-30.

Horton, William (1994) *Designing and Writing Online Documentation*. New York: John Wiley & Sons.

Markel, Mike (2001) *Technical Communication*, Boston: Bedford/St. Martins, 6th edition.

Online Resources

- **How Stuff Works** is a useful site which explains various scientific and technical concepts and associated technologies in clear, easy-to-understand language. This site is great for getting some background information on anything from communications and cookery to science, technology and nature: www.howstuffworks.com

- **The New Scientist** provides free access to a range of useful articles on different aspects of science and technology. The articles are very accessible and extremely well-written and will help you develop your subject knowledge and become familiar with clear scientific language: www.newscientist.com

3. Understanding Technical Documentation

In this chapter

This chapter looks in greater detail at the different types of texts which are translated by technical translators. By the end of the chapter, you will have learned about the key features of typical scientific and technical texts and how these features affect translation. These factors will include issues relating to language, structure, content and non-verbal features. You'll learn some strategies for identifying various text types and the challenges they pose.

3.1   Introduction
In order to translate a text properly, you need to be able to tell what kind of text you are dealing with.

Technical information is ubiquitous and appears in many different places and formats. As a result, it is often difficult to tell exactly what is – and what is not – a technical text. If a technical text is supposed to contain technical information, does that mean that a text that contains other types of information is no longer technical? How do we distinguish between a scientific and a technical text? These are not easy questions to answer with anything other than an "It depends" or "You learn to get a feel for what type of text it is". This is not much use when you are learning how to become a technical translator. While the question of whether a text can be classified as purely technical, purely scientific, or something else really does depend on a number of factors, it is possible to identify certain basic characteristics, which give a good indication of what we are dealing with when presented with a text.

Generally speaking, technical documentation has a number of key characteristics which, although not always exclusive to technical documents, do help us to understand why they are the way they are and how we can translate them. Armed with this information we are in a better position to be able to recognize them in the first place.

3.1.1   *Specific features of technical documentation*
Identifying the main linguistic, terminological, structural and content-related features of texts

In Chapter 2, we examined a variety of generic features which can be used to define technical communication and its associated texts. Nevertheless, different types of technical information will be communicated to different people for different purposes. This variety of information shapes the entire nature of individual documents and gives rise to a range of different text types, each of which addresses the particular needs of a particular audience in a particular context. This combination of audience and purpose, which determines the texts we encounter, is referred to by Markel (2001:92) as the "writing situation".

In this section, we will look in more detail at specific characteristics of scientific and technical texts, which go beyond the more environmental factors previously outlined. While the following features could conceivably apply to both scientific and technical texts, they are presented here as general rules of thumb; each category contains features, which are usually typical of scientific or technical texts, or which vary in their implementation depending on whether it is a technical or a scientific text.

3.1.1.1 LANGUAGE

Keeping it simple is the key to technical texts and making sure that the language they contain is both clear and to the point is one of the core values of technical communication. This is not just an altruistic and caring principle aimed at making life easier for readers; it actually makes sense for a variety of reasons. If you bear in mind that in reading technical texts, readers are usually trying to do something else and need the text do help them do it, then we do not want to distract them from this task by making them decipher overly complex language or fantastically creative and ornate, but ultimately unintelligible, language.

So, by keeping things simple, we reduce the amount of work readers have to do and we reduce the risk that something will be misunderstood or otherwise impede the smooth flow of information. This is particularly important where readers are in a hurry, are stressed or where they are not native speakers of the language. Some of the key ways in which the clarity and simplicity of technical texts is improved is to use simple declarative information instead of complex sentences and to provide clear and simple instructions which are in chronological order or which present a logical cause and effect structure.

- SAUBER HK 10F is not classified as a dangerous substance in accordance with the relevant laws governing chemicals.
- The detector automatically checks the condition of the batteries.
- The HA-100B is a wireless glass-break detector that provides easy and reliable protection against robbery.

Example 1: Simple declarative sentences

- From the main menu, select "Installation" and then "New Installation".
- If the cycling device triggers an alarm, mount the unit in a different location.

Example 2: Clear and Logical Instructions

Scientific texts also make use of simple language to a certain extent, but owing to the different aims and intentions, they need to use a broader range of linguistic devices to do this. So while a technical text seeks to get information across as clearly and effectively as possible, scientific texts are not always concerned solely with conveying information as much as they are with creating some sort of effect or eliciting some response from the reader. As a result it is not unusual to see passages of text composed of quite long, complex sentences involving the type of language more commonly associated with more conventionally creative types of text. This can be seen in the following example taken from a scientific textbook:

- In cystic fibrosis, the combination of thickened secretions and repeated viral, *S. aureus* and *H. influenzae* infections in early life lead to severe bronchiectasis; chronic infection with *Pseudomonas aeruginosa*, and sometimes *Burkholderia cepacia*, results in fatal destruction of the lung in spite of frequent courses of potent i.v. and nebulized antibiotics. (Murray *et al.* 2005:36)

Example 3: Complex sentence structure in a scientific text

Romani ite domum!
Example 3 also illustrates a rather interesting feature, which typically sets scientific texts apart from technical texts: Latinisms. Whether as an acknowledgement of the scientific tradition or as an essential part of scientific discourse, the use of terms and phrases in Latin is an extremely common feature of scientific language, particularly the binomial nomenclature used in biological and life sciences. Naturally, this has its roots in the status of Latin over many centuries as being the language of knowledge and of the educated. A word of caution is needed, however. While Latin was used as a *lingua franca* (now I'm doing it!) for the global scientific community, it would be unwise to assume that all languages use Latin as part of their scientific discourse. What is commonplace in certain language families might be unheard of for language families which have never come into contact with Latin or which cannot trace their ancestry back to Latin. We will discuss the issues relating to the use of Latinisms in Chapter 6.

The following example – taken from a popular science book entitled *Oxygen: The Molecule that Made the World* – displays complex language and a concerted effort by the author to help readers understand the implications and associations of the information being conveyed. The result is, admittedly, a rather challenging sentence.

- We emerge blinking, then, from the great Varanger ice age – the last snowball earth – which ended some 590 million years ago, into a world in which the surface oceans and the air are well oxygenated – well enough for us to breathe – but the deep oceans are still stagnant, like the Black Sea today, saturated in hydrogen sulphide. (Lane 2002:69)

Example 4: Complex and figurative language

In addition to longer sentences, in certain types of scientific texts, particularly but not exclusively popular science where the function is to entertain as well as educate, authors may resort to prosaic imagery in order to make certain concepts easier to comprehend, to establish a proximity with the reader, and to make the subject more interesting. As a result, we see quite vivid language such as the following, which is taken from a scientific monograph on radio-telescopy.

- In the splendour of a moonless night, far from the pollution of the sky by artificial lighting, the first revelation is that of the stars. (Schatzman & Praderie 1993:1)
  Example 5: Vivid imagery in scientific language

Popular science publications provide an even richer supply of vivid, literary language and imagery:

- An awful fate befell many of the young women hired to paint radium onto the dials of watches, so that they would glow in the dark. [...] Within a year their teeth began to fall out and their jaws disintegrated. (Lane 2002:109-110)
- We are each so atomically numerous and so vigorously recycled at death that a significant number of our atoms - up to a billion for each of us, it has been suggested – probably once belonged to Shakespeare. A billion more each came from Buddha and Genghis Khan and Beethoven, and any other historical figure you care to name. (Bryson 2003: 176)
  Example 6: Vivid imagery, literary style and varied rhetorical devices

Metaphors
Often thought to be the sole preserve of literary language, metaphors are an incredibly useful tool for writers of both scientific and, to a slightly lesser extent, technical texts. Metaphors are particularly valuable in scientific texts where they help authors to put a concrete name to an abstract concept. Metaphors such as *Black Hole*, *Greenhouse Effect* and *Double Helix* are some of the better known scientific metaphors and it is quite clear that they are beneficial in providing not just a neat and tidy term for the various concepts, but also a way of explaining what they mean in a way to which readers can easily relate.

Metaphors (and similes) are also used to explain complex processes and systems by taking advantage of readers' existing knowledge and understanding of the world around them. Looking at another example taken from Nick Lane's book on oxygen, we can see how the biological necessity for genetic variation and mutation is explained through the metaphor of a bank robber.

- [...] a genetically static population is a sitting target for pathogens and predators. In the same way it is much easier to rob a bank if you have memorized the unchanging patrols of security guards. (Lane 2002:235)
  Example 7: Metaphors in scientific texts

But it is not just scientific writers who can craft a clever metaphor to convey their ideas. Technical texts are also littered with metaphorical language and it too serves an important purpose. Whether we are using terms like *worm screws* in mechanical engineering texts or referring to concepts such as *communities* or *groups* in technical white papers for website software, it is difficult to avoid language which is metaphorical on some level. From the examples given above, worm screws are so named because the shape of the screw is reminiscent of a worm. In the field of computer science, the notion of communities and groups such as those seen on social networking sites are user-friendly ways of expressing what is essentially a relationship between different types of data in a database. Other familiar technical metaphors relate to computer *viruses* such as *Trojan Horses*, *worms* and *zombie* computers while *handshake* protocols refer to the various steps in the process of connecting a computer to a server.

Terminology

One of the most immediately noticeable features of both technical texts and scientific texts is the terminology they contain. Perhaps more noticeable in a technical text because of the relative simplicity of the surrounding language, the strange, complex-looking and often scary words such as *hydrogen sulphide*, *angioplasty* or *polymerization* can often have people scrambling for their dictionaries.

In reality, however, specialized terminology accounts for just a small proportion of the total words in a technical text. Peter Newmark (1988:151) once estimated that 5-10% of a text is made up of specialized terminology, although this will naturally vary depending on the specific text we are dealing with; in the case of patent extracts, for example, specialized terminology might account for anything up to half of the total word count. Alongside highly specialized terminology, a technical text is likely to present us with abbreviations and acronyms, which are just as specialized, and which may have a number of different meanings depending on the subject, the context or even the company or organization which produces the text. In the following example from the instruction manual for a satellite receiver, we can see both specialized terminology and acronyms:

- You will need a multi-feed antenna with a *6° differential*, two *universal LNBs* and a *DiSEqC* or *sound burst switch*.
Example 8: Specialized terminology and acronyms

In the following examples, we can see acronyms and abbreviations relating to units of measure.

- Operating Frequencies: 315 MHz or other *UHF* channels where permitted by local regulations.
- The unit is rated for use at the following voltages: 120 *VAC*, 60 Hz / 9 VAC, 700 mA;
Example 9: Specialized acronyms and units of measure

Once we have overcome the initial shock of specialized terminology, we then need to contend with specialized terms which pose as general terms. These ordinary-looking general terms, which look as if they could appear in an ordinary non-specialized text, have quite specific meanings depending again on the context and subject area. For example, the word *jumper* means a small metal clip, which is used to create an electrical connection between two terminals in an electrical device but in general language it can be used to describe a woollen garment or even a person who is jumping!

- The INS/DEL *jumper* should be closed if you want the system to react immediately.
  Example 10: Sentence containing a term with both general and specialized meanings

Similarly, the words *salt* and *suspension* are frequently used in ordinary everyday language but when they appear in the technical datasheet for an industrial chemical, they adopt much more specific meanings.

- The product contains the sodium salt of a special, low molecule polycarbon acid which is a highly effective component for stabilizing minerals which are in suspension in water-based solutions.
  Example 11: Sentence containing terms with both general and specialized meanings

Other fairly standard terms such as *sandwich*, *neighbourhood* or *cycling* can be taken to mean quite different things if they are in the technical specifications for building materials, an online help system for a website or an installation guide for an alarm system.

- The protective film must be removed from the *sandwich* panels no later than 2 months after manufacture (or after a maximum of 2 week's exposure to the elements).
- When a user creates an account on the community website, a list of available *neighbourhoods* is displayed on the welcome page.
- If the *cycling* device triggers an alarm, mount the unit in a different location.
  Example 12: General terms with specialized meanings

3.1.1.2 FACTS AND SPECIFICATIONS

Setting aside issues of language for a moment, the whole point of technical documentation is to communicate something. There is, however, a limit to what can be expressed in smooth, clear prose. Sometimes the only way to convey information effectively is to present bare facts and figures, whether it is incorporated into a sentence, presented as a bullet point in a list or in a table without any textual "padding".

- The recommended dose is between 50 and 80 mg per litre of water.
- Pack Height: max. 710 mm
  Pack Width: 1010 mm for construction widths of 200-300 mm
  Pack Length: max. 14.0 m
  Pack Weight: 4.0 t

Example 13: Extract from list of technical specifications

In a scientific text, we also find hard facts, although the structural and linguistic style of such texts means they are likely to be presented in sentences rather than as bulleted lists.

- The estimated average probability of experiencing a major cardiac adverse event after treatment for in-stent restenosis with a follow-up period of 9±4 months was 30.0% (25.0–34.9%, 95% confidence interval) with strong evidence for heterogeneity between study specific results (P = 0.0001). (Radkea *et al.* 2003:266)

Example 14: Extract from a research paper on cardiac surgery

- The density of these clusters varied between 0.29–0.46 mm^2 (an average of 0.34 mm^2) on the basis of measurements of over 800 mm^2 of sample area in both microstructures. (Chandran 2005:304)

Example 15: Extract from an article on material testing

- In 1997, 46% of U.S. commercial aircraft were over 17 years of age and 28% were over 20 years. In 2001, 31% of the U.S. commercial fleet were over 15 years of age, and those aircraft accounted for 66% of the total cost of maintenance per block hour. (MacLean *et al.* 2005:1)

Example 16: Extract from a scientific report on aircraft safety

3.1.1.3 REFERENCES

Often in a text, whether technical or scientific, an author will refer the reader to information which is contained elsewhere in the document or in other documents. This can take the form of references to laws, directives and standards in the case of technical texts or to books and journal papers in a scientific text. In some cases, particularly in software-related documents, references may also be made to diagrams, interface items, menus or accompanying documents. This is often done so as not to impede the flow of information or to overload the reader with too much information at once. The decision to split a document into multiple smaller documents can be a way of keeping the size of individual documents to a minimum, and sometimes it is simply due to the medium chosen to disseminate the document, for example, online help, websites, leaflets or brochures.

- This product has been tested with regard to:
  EMC Emissions: EN 50081-1 1992
  RFI: EN 55022 1998
  EMC Immunity: EN 50082-1 1997

Telephony: TBR21 1998
Safety: EN 60950+ Am1(93), Am2(93)

- The device complies with the provisions of European Directive 1999/5/EC
Example 17: References to standards and laws

Scientific texts use more traditional academic referencing methods in order to
draw the reader's attention to additional information. This also serves to reinforce the arguments being made and to convince the reader of the validity of
the information and the trustworthiness of the author. It could be argued that
it is similar to the referencing of laws and standards which takes place in technical documents where, in addition to identifying additional information, the
references may show that, by conforming to a particular standard, a product is
reliable and safe. Footnotes are also used in scientific texts either as a way of
providing readers with additional, incidental information or as a way to provide
references to other works.

3.1.1.4 GRAPHICS

A key feature of technical texts, particularly those aimed at consumers and those
which have an instructional **function**, is the use of graphics and illustrations. Such
graphics may include diagrams, graphs, schematics, photographs, screenshots
or any other visual representation or information. This is particularly true of
documentation for software products where providing a picture of what users
are supposed to see on a screen is infinitely more effective than any amount of
verbal descriptions.

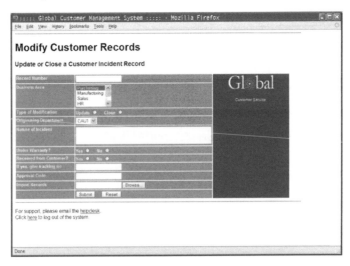

Figure 4: Example of a screenshot for a software application

Using screenshots to illustrate a software interface does mean, however, that
a document which contains these references is inexorably linked with an entity

which is outside the document. In order for such a text to be coherent, i.e. to make sense within its situation (Baker 1992:239), it must accurately reproduce the text contained in the software interface. As a result, any changes to the software will necessitate changes to the document. It also means any textual references to the software which are contained within the text must be phrased consistently and accurately. From this point of view, the text effectively becomes something of a multimedia, and possibly even a multimodal, text.

Other graphical references, which can be found in all types of technical documentation, relate to diagrams in which various components or items are labelled. Again, the aim is to convey information to readers clearly, quickly and effectively.

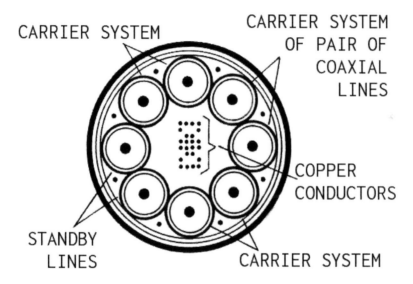

Figure 5: Technical diagram with labels

Practical Exercise 14: Creating screenshots
There are numerous ways of creating screenshots. Some involve specialized software tools for creating screen captures which offer all sorts of sophisticated functions and options. On a Windows PC, you can use the PrintScrn button to create screenshots without the need for any special software.

To take a picture of one window, press Alt+PrintScrn. If you want to take a picture of everything that is displayed on your monitor, just press PrintScrn. Now, open up your word processor or graphics package and press Ctrl+V to paste your screenshot into a new file. Try creating screenshots of software and websites and paste them into new Word documents or into your graphics editor.

3.1.1.5 Formulae, equations and scientific notation

Second only to specialized terminology in its ability to make scientific and techni-cal texts look incredibly intimidating and complex to an unsuspecting translator is the use of formulae, equations and scientific notation. These are fundamental components of how scientists and technicians communicate and they perform a number of essential functions in texts, the most important of which is that they allow abstract concepts and ideas to be expressed clearly and concisely.

One of the most basic methods for expressing complex scientific and techni-cal information is *scientific notation*, which is also known as *standard form* or as *exponential notation*. This makes it easier to present figures which are too large or small to be conveniently written in standard decimal notation. The examples shown in Table 1 show how scientific notation works:

Ordinary decimal notation	Scientific notation
900	9×10^2
8,000	8×10^3
4,370,000,000	4.37×10^9
−0.0000000031	-3.1×10^{-9}

Table 1: Expressing decimal numbers in scientific notation

Unless we are dealing with purely mathematical texts, numbers, whether in ordin-ary decimal or scientific notation, will rarely appear in isolation. In the majority of cases, numbers are used to quantify something and unless we know what it is we are quantifying, the numbers are quite useless. For this reason, texts will feature a variety of units of measure. Units of measure are definite amounts of some physical quantity, such as length or weight. They are agreed upon, adopted and used by convention, and are represented by a unique symbol. In most cases, units of measure are governed by the *International System of Units*, known as *SI* for short. The SI sets out seven base units of measure:

- length - **metre** (Symbol: *m*)
- mass - **kilogram** (Symbol: *kg*)
- time - **Second** (Symbol: *s*)
- electric current - **Ampere** (Symbol: *A*)
- thermodynamic temperature - **Kelvin** (Symbol: *K*)
- amount of substance - **Mole** (Symbol: *mol*)
- luminous intensity - **Candela** (Symbol: *cd*)

Each of these units can be modified by means of prefixes such as *micro-*, *milli-*, *nano-*, *pico-* etc. Interestingly, the SI prefixes can also be used independently of

SI units of measure, for example with Imperial measures, with the result that you can conceivably see things like *kilofoot* (*kft*) or *microinch* (*μin*). In addition to the base units, there are various other units which are typically named after scientists who discovered them, such as *farad* (*F*) which is a unit of capacitance and is named after Michael Faraday, *volt* (*v*) the unit of electric potential difference which is named after Alessandro Volta or *watt* (*W*), the unit of power which is named after James Watt. All of these standardized units of measure are governed by the SI and are a staple of scientific and technical communication. Appendix 1 contains a list of other eponymous units of measure.

While metric measurements are rapidly becoming the norm internationally, you should not be surprised to see Imperial units of measurement sometimes being used in certain languages, particularly English. This is especially true in certain types of technical text such as workshop manuals, specifications or parts catalogues where inches, feet, pounds and ounces are still sometimes used.

A *formula* is a concise way of expressing information such as chemical reactions or mathematical operations in a symbolic manner. They can also be used to express general relationships between quantities or variables. The advantage of using formulae is that they are invariably more compact than any alternative verbal descriptions; they are accurate because there is no room for interpretation of words. Equally important is the fact that formulae are widely regarded as virtually universally intelligible. Indeed, mathematics was once described by Kasner and Newman as "a universal language, valid, useful, intelligible everywhere in place and time" (1940:358).

While scholars such as Montgomery might argue against this view of mathematics on the grounds that "even the most densely mathematical research takes place in a linguistic context" (2002:254) it is hard to imagine that this *context* would prevent a mathematician working in one language from comprehending equations written by a mathematician from halfway around the world. The reason for this is that equations are invariably accompanied by a list or brief paragraph which identifies and defines each symbol in the equation and assigns a value to it. A phrase which commonly appears after an equation to introduce these definitions is "*Where X equals Y*". As a result, providing the symbols have been clearly identified and explained, a mathematician should have no problem understanding any equation.

Chemistry	$CaCl_2(aq) + 2AgNO_3(aq) \rightarrow Ca(NO_3)_2(aq) + 2AgCl(s)$
Physics	$f = \left(\dfrac{v + v_r}{v + v_s}\right) f_0$

Figure 6: Examples of equations

Similarly, an *equation* is a mathematical statement, written in symbols, that two things are exactly the same (or equivalent); as a result, equations are written with an equal sign.

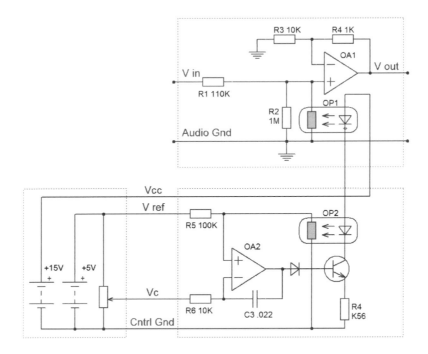

Figure 7: Schematic diagram with labels and measurements

Practical Exercise 15: Practise your maths skills
Calculate how many…

- grams there are in 27 kg
- seconds there are in 3 hours 2 minutes
- centimetres there are in 4.2 km
- meters there are in 4×10^4 km

3.2   Typical text types

While there are numerous types and variations of texts, the same general types appear regularly.

There are numerous different types of texts used to communicate scientific and technical information, and most of them are in a constant state of change. Each text has its own characteristics and content and is generally produced for a specific purpose. Some types of texts may merge to create new text types while others simply disappear. Given this state of flux, it would be very difficult if not impossible to identify, catalogue and describe each type of text here. This variety and variability notwithstanding, it is possible to group the majority of scientific and technical texts under the following headings:

- Manuals
- Applications and proposals
- Reports and scientific papers
- Presentations
- Regulatory documents
- Popular science

Rosenberg (2005:161ff) mentions websites as a category of texts but it is hard to say with any certainty that a website actually constitutes a text type of its own. The reason for this is that the web is a communication medium; it is a way of distributing documents. While certain document types may, over time, have evolved and changed to better suit the new medium, it can be argued that they are still essentially the same document type. It is, however, worth remembering that modern documents do not necessarily have to be published in printed format. Increasingly, documents which would previously only have been printed, such as manuals, brochures etc., are now often distributed only in electronic format. Similarly, there are texts which are designed purely for electronic dissemination, such as online help. Returning to the categories listed above, the following sections will provide a brief overview of their key features and the challenges they can present for translators.

3.2.1   Manuals

Manuals are educational documents. They are tools which help readers acquire new information to help them to learn how to do something or understand something. The aim of this type of document is to provide the reader with easy access to precisely the information they need at a particular moment and to ensure that it is clear and comprehensible. To achieve this, a number of types of manual have emerged in order to meet the requirements of readers and the circumstances in which they use the documents.

Cookbooks typically consist of a set of recipe-style units consisting of a bullet list of "ingredients" or prerequisites and a numbered list of steps to be carried out. This type of manual is best suited to describing information which is procedural and which can be broken down into discrete chunks or stages. Since this type of text is designed to give clear, step-by-step instructions of the type which might appeal to rote users (see Chapter 2) or to expert users in a hurry, it is essential that the flow of information be controlled so as not to overload the reader. For this reason, it is considered bad practice to combine multiple tasks into a single sentence no matter how elegant or compact the sentence is.

From a translator's point of view, you may need to intervene and split such a sentence into two separate steps to avoid confusion on the part of the reader as to what should be carried out and when. In the following example, the writer has managed to cram three separate tasks into a single sentence and it takes several attempts before a reader can figure out the order in which the tasks are to be performed.

> You can now insert the installation CD into the drive and run the set up program by typing "C:/setup.exe" in the *Run* dialog box providing you have logged in as an administrator.

By splitting the sentence into logical steps, we ensure that the reader immediately knows what to do and in what order:

> 1. Log on to the system as an administrator.
> 2. Insert the installation CD.
> 3. In the *Run* dialog box, type "C:/setup.exe" to run setup.

Tutorials are designed to provide readers with a basic introduction to a topic or product. This is usually achieved through a series of interrelated, **task-orientated** units which teach readers how to do specific tasks or activities. Often the tutorial, whether printed or online, is the very first contact a reader will have with a product or a concept so it needs to guide them relatively gently and in stages towards a certain level of competence. This can potentially be a stressful time for some readers, some of whom may be fearful of making mistakes, or concerned that they may not have enough experience to learn.

It is important, then, that a tutorial not make matters worse by giving information which the reader cannot understand, whether it is because the information is confusing, too advanced or just plain wrong. Karen Schriver (1996:216 and 224-227) discusses some interesting studies which show that most people (approximately 63% according to one study) tend to blame themselves for problems they encounter when following instructions in texts, even if it is clear that the texts are substandard.

Tutorials, therefore, are expected to be encouraging and supportive and to provide reassurance where appropriate and above all, they should not make the reader feel stupid. For this reason, it is not at all uncommon for tutorials to address readers directly or to acknowledge the difficulty of a particular task. It is important to remember, however, that not all tutorials are aimed at complete novices with little or no background information. As we mentioned previously, *transfer users* are users who have experience and knowledge of allied technologies or processes and who will have a reasonable understanding of concepts and processes similar to the one being explained. With these users you can take advantage of their experience and it will not be necessary to explain every single concept. The challenge, however, is not overly simplifying the text for them so that they feel patronized.

One of the key features of tutorials is the relatively slow pace at which information is presented. In comparison to other types of documents, the density of information is quite low, i.e. more words are used to convey less information, particularly at the beginning. As well as showing readers *how* to do something, tutorials will also try to help readers avoid making mistakes. This is also a legal requirement in Europe as a result of various Directives for product documentation to alert users to potential hazards caused by the incorrect use of a product.

Guides are designed to follow on from tutorials and to teach more advanced material to readers who already have a basic understanding of the subject. A typical guide will contain plenty of examples (which translators may need to adapt to the target language culture) accompanied by detailed descriptions, figures, tables and diagrams. Since readers already have a basic understanding of the subject, they will be less fearful of it and may even want or need additional background information to help deepen their understanding of the subject. This type of manual is usually used for products and technologies where steps are either not very obvious or where the product could be used in several ways depending on the user.

Tutorials and guides can also be incorporated into the same document. In such cases, it is important for you as the translator to remember that the function of such a document will most likely change after a couple of chapters, i.e. from instructional to explanatory as the reader gains a better understanding of the product. As a result, the language used to achieve these functions will change and you will need to modify the translation strategies you use accordingly.

Reference manuals represent a much more comprehensive body of information than tutorials or guides, and they are intended for readers who already have quite a high level of knowledge but who may need to refresh their memory as to certain details or to find information on less commonly used functions, for example. In a reference manual, the material is typically organized into focused topics and generally ordered either alphabetically or into logical sections of related topics. Each of the topics is a discrete unit of information which is independent of the others, i.e. each topic is designed to be read on its own without one necessarily having to read other entries. With this in mind, it is unlikely that a reference manual will ever be read from cover to cover, but rather will be dipped into as and when necessary. From a writing and translation point of view, this means that certain information may need to be repeated in a number of topics to prevent readers having to skip back and forth through the document.

Where cross-references are necessary - usually because there is too much information to repeat - the names of the topics or the sections being referred to must be accurate and consistent. This is particularly important for translators as they may be translating a reference to a section or even document which they may not have translated. If they have translated the section and they are using a translation memory tool, the tool should automatically suggest the correct translation. However, if the other section has been, or will be, translated by someone else, the translator needs to liaise with the other translator to ensure both will ultimately use the same wording.

An interesting development in the production of this type of document is the idea of an automatically generated reference manual. Certain types of software contain tools which scan through the various components and files which make up the application for programmers' notes and comments (small pieces of text explaining what a feature or module does – see Section 6.8 "Sample text and computer code" on page 162) and then compile them into a single document. While this is undoubtedly useful for companies in that it reduces the time and expense needed to produce documents, it does introduce a potential problem for readers and translators because programmers are not trained writers. As a result, the information in these documents may not always be of the same standard and may contain examples of poor or unclear writing.

Online help is a type of technical manual which is included with and accessed from within a piece of software. It is designed to provide information and assistance to users *in situ*. There are two main types of help system available to users: general help systems which users can search through, and context help which provides assistance depending on what the user is doing at any given time. Typical help systems consist of numerous topics, often task-based, which are linked together by means of hyperlinks, much like on websites. Each topic is typically assigned to one specific task and, as with a reference guide, is designed to function as a discrete, independent unit of information. This is because, like websites, tasks are discrete and can be accessed through a table of contents, list of keywords or search function; there is no way of predicting a user's point of entry into the system.

As a rule, help topics are designed in such a way that they can be read quickly and, ideally, displayed on a single help screen without the need to scroll down. As such, they are highly focused and feature short and simple sentences and possibly screenshots.

3.2.2   Applications and proposals

Like reports, which we will discuss shortly, applications and proposals are among the few types of documents that can be justifiably described as being both sci-entific and technical. A proposal is essentially a request to do or get something; a very complex and detailed sales pitch. In order to fulfil this function, the text is composed of several components or subtexts, each of which has its own func-tion, content and style of language:

- *Abstract*: A summary of all key points in the proposal.
- *Biographies*: More prevalent in scientific and academic proposals and used to emphasize the expertise of the proposers, and, in theory, the merit of the proposal.
- *Cover letter*: A standard letter from the proposers informing the recip-ient of their intention to submit a proposal.
- *Project description*: Perhaps the most important part of a proposal, it contains a significance statement, objectives and hypotheses, and methodological information.

- *Schedule*: Describes the proposed timeframe of the proposed project, including dates, contingencies and possibly risks to timely completion. This section may also contain financial information such as bonuses or lateness penalties.
- *Budget*: Provides key financial information.

The variety of information contained in a proposal – ranging from commercial to technical and financial – and the different ways in which this information is used pose an important challenge for translators who need to switch their strategies and style according to each section. Rather than having one single strategy for translating the document, it is necessary to have one macrostrategy for the whole document supported by local microstrategies for individual sections.

3.2.3 Reports and scientific papers

Perhaps even more so than proposals, scientific papers are a hybrid of science and technology, as they usually combine theoretical information with practical, applied information. Scientific papers and reports can take a number of structural forms but the main ones are:

- Introduction – Materials and methods – Results – Discussion (sometimes referred to as *IMRAD*).
- Abstract – Introduction – Materials – Procedure – Results – Conclusions – References.

Abstracts are one of the most important aspects of a text as they can determine whether or not the main text will be read. An abstract is a condensed summary of the main text and, together with the title, needs to function as a text in its own right in order to allow potential readers to accurately determine whether the paper contains the information they are looking for. If something is awkward or unclear in an abstract, as a translator you cannot simply shrug it off and assume that it will become clear when the reader reads the rest of the text because they may not read the text as a result of this ambiguity.

The **Introduction** seeks to provide background information to readers to show the context within which the current work was carried out. This will often involve the use of references and quotes from related literature which require particular attention from the translator when it comes to reproducing, translating or transcribing the information.

The **Materials** section contains a detailed summary of all of the materials in the study. This can often be quite technical and may contain various technical terms, including proprietary or trademarked names so correct spelling and orthography is essential.

Translating brand names
Texts may refer to materials by **brand name** only. If that particular brand is unknown or non-existent in the target language culture, we may have a problem. The instinctive solution might be to replace the SL brand name with a comparable TL brand name, if one exists, but this may be even more problematic than leaving the SL brand name in the translation. This is because the two products, although similar and possibly identical in most aspects, may have different characteristics, properties or chemical compositions, which in the case of a chemistry paper could have significant implications for the repeatability or even safety of the study. One of the safest ways of dealing with brand names which do not exist in the TL is to reproduce the brand name and accompany it with a brief phrase [in square brackets] which describes its function. Of course, this means you may have to do some research to find out what the product does in the first place. But this is part of a translator's job, isn't it?

The *Procedure* section contains relatively straightforward step-by-step procedural descriptions of the activities carried out. The key problems presented by this section include abbreviations, acronyms, units of measure and ellipsis. Other considerations include the need for consistency and absolute clarity; there can be no room whatsoever for inaccurate or unclear information, as it may affect the repeatability of an experiment, for example, and most significantly, render the study unreliable.

The *Results* section is an objective statement of the facts uncovered by the study. There is no discussion but rather a presentation of statistics, events, findings or other data. Such a section may include numbers, statistics (and standard statistical phrases regarding probabilities etc.), physical descriptions or reported speech from interviews (where you should translate exactly what is written, as it is written, even if it does not make perfect grammatical sense).

The *Discussion* section is where this information is analyzed, interpreted and explained. This section will more than likely recap on the hypothesis presented earlier in the document and will compare, contrast and interpret the data. It will contain set phrases which scientists use to express opinions, beliefs, probabilities and doubts. As such, the language will be much more complex. Good researchers will also use the discussion section to highlight and discuss any weaknesses or limitations with the methodology used.

Not all papers will contain a *Conclusions* section but where one does exist, it will provide a summary of the hypothesis, the results and the key conclusions derived from the discussion. It may also present ideas for future research.

References are not typically something we think about from a translation perspective, but from a practical translation perspective they are worthy of mention. While most journals will stipulate the preferred bibliographic style to be used, such as Harvard, MLA or APA, and it is not the translator's job to change these, the **content** of the bibliography is something where our expertise is required.

When translating between European languages, we can generally leave the references alone, but when translating from Chinese into English or from Russian into Arabic we are faced with a situation where the target audience is going to be presented with information in a script that they cannot decipher.

We may, therefore, need to decide ourselves or ask the client whether we need to transliterate the author names and book titles so that the target audience can read them. An ISBN number, if present, can be a very useful tool in finding out whether there is an official "gloss" or descriptive TL explanation[1] or method for transcribing this information. A small point, but one worth checking nevertheless.

An interesting variation on the report is the *case study*. This is a text which is used primarily for marketing purposes, but combines much of the content found in a technical report or paper with marketing and journalistic language. A case study is aimed at showing the benefits of a technology and/or the expertise of a company in a specific context. Such documents have a fairly standardized format which typically consists of identifying the client, explaining its needs (this can be regarded as the "problem"), and describing the solution and how it was put into effect.

This set structure is then typically followed by a testimonial section where the client expresses satisfaction with the company's solution and states how it has improved their operation or fulfilled their requirements. These sections will frequently be interspersed with journalistic-style quotes from key personnel involved in the project. The final part of a case study will often consist of paragraphs describing the companies involved, along with contact details. Such paragraphs generally have a more formal, less journalistic style, which is at times legalistic, and will be standard text for which there is usually an existing translation.

What makes case studies so interesting from a translation point of view is that they use a broad range of different writing styles to convey different information, such as highly complex technical data together with subjective personal opinions, reported speech and persuasive devices. Helpfully, they are incredibly easy to find on the Internet, and companies such as IBM, Avocent, Siemens and Hewlett-Packard have extensive repositories of case studies on their websites. Chapter 4 provides an example of a technical case study.

3.2.4 Presentations

Although not frequently acknowledged, the PowerPoint presentation has been identified as a specific text type by both technical writing and translation scholars (Myers 2000; Rosenberg 2005). For professional translators, presentations crop up with surprising frequency and apart from the technical challenges of translating these files, they can present problems which are more significant than their friendly, multi-coloured, animated and graphics-filled appearance would suggest.

---

[1] One way of presenting a gloss or transliteration would be "**SL title [TL title]**".

PowerPoint files, when properly constructed, will consist of text, graphics, figures and animations, which all work together to convey a message, or to support the speaker in conveying a message verbally. The constraints of space, time and legibility mean that most good presentations will be highly summarized and consist largely of bullet points – only bad presentations are crammed with paragraphs of text like a printed document. While this is good for the audience and the presenter, it is potentially bad news for the translator because there may be a lot of potentially ambiguous sentences in a presentation.

If you have ever seen handouts from a presentation you will know that most of the time, the slides only make complete sense if you have heard the presentation; on their own, they are not completely clear. In an ideal situation, you would be able to ask the client for clarification or, even better, for speaker's notes or the full version of the paper, but this is not always possible.

When translating these files, translators need to keep an eye on how long their translations are. Since presentations consist of text boxes which do not automatically resize, a translation which is longer than the original ST text will automatically be displayed in a smaller font. This is quite helpful, but if you add a lot of text, the font may become too small to be seen clearly when projected onto a screen. In the worst-case scenario, your ever-expanding translation may spill over the edge of the page, and this can clutter the presentation, harm the readability of the presentation and make the speaker look unprofessional. In case you were thinking that you can simply add a new slide...don't! At least not without checking with the client first because there may be limits on the number of slides they can use, or there may be timing or simply design issues.

Finding texts on the Internet
Using a combination of searches on the different language versions of websites, you can find parallel texts on the same topic in your target language. *Parallel texts* are similar texts on the same topic in your target language which can help you find target language equivalents for terms in the source text or give you a better insight into the style used in typical documents. For this reason, it is usually best when they are not translations. In the majority of cases they are much more useful than consulting a dictionary because they show how terms are used in context and they are often more up-to-date. To find parallel texts you firstly need to think carefully about your search keywords. Then think about things like which format the text is likely to be published in as it can help narrow your search. Documents like presentations are often published in PowerPoint (.ppt) or HTML format while case studies, reports and user guides are typically published on the web in **PDF** format. You can use Google to search only for those files which are in specific formats. To do this, type "filetype:" alongside your search terms. This has the added advantage of helping to narrow down your search and weed out some of the lower quality examples:
filetype:pdf "case study".

3.2.5 *Regulatory documents*

Regulatory documents, also referred to as normative documents, are explicit sets of rules governing the requirements for products, materials or services. Documents of this type are essentially specifications which provide clear, comprehensive and unambiguous descriptions of, for example, what a product is required to do, what characteristics a material should have or the way in which a service is to be provided. Specifications can take a more formal form in the shape of directives, laws or standards which are written by standards organizations (such as **ISO**, **DIN** or **BSI**), by trade organizations or government bodies. Standards seek to normalize and homogenize the design of products or materials or to regulate and standardize certain activities.

In both cases, regulatory documents may have a legal dimension, whether as a means of enforcement, as a justification of necessity or prevention. As such, there is a certain amount of overlap with legal translation and the documents may contain varying amounts of legal terminology and constructions as well as highly specific and detailed technical descriptions. The legal dimension is particularly apparent in the case of patents, where the aim is to protect or license an invention, i.e. the inventor's intellectual property, by giving the inventor the right to exclude others from making, using, selling or importing the invention (see DeMatteis *et al.* 2006).

Translating such documents requires meticulous attention to detail to ensure factual accuracy in the first instance, as well as compliance with specific linguistic requirements. An example of this comes in the form of what are known as **"EMEA** templates"[2]. These are quality review templates produced by the European Medicines Agency and used to ensure the quality of documents by defining the format, layout and wording of product information for medicines. Product information must be produced in accordance with these templates as it forms an integral part of the licensing and approval process and, if it is deficient in any way, the medicines may be withdrawn. The standards are very strict and they stipulate specific headings, spellings[3], phrases which have established meanings in 22 official European Union languages, as well as Icelandic and Norwegian. The fact that the templates are available in such a wide range of languages makes them quite useful for translators, as they constitute a ready-made and approved terminology resource.

Another example of a regulatory or normative text, again relating to medicine, is the *British National Formulary*. This document provides scientific definitions

---

[2] You can download the templates by going to the European Medicines Agency website [**www. ema.europa.eu**] and searching for "*product information templates*".
[3] The templates even stipulate the use of upper and lower case characters, albeit implicitly. Certain headings are written in upper case, while others are not and while the templates do not specifically tell you to copy this, your work may be sent back for correction if you not follow the templates closely enough.

and descriptions of medicines before giving practical, technical information (including prices) relating to medicines. Similarly, national and international pharmacopoeias set out precise instructions for preparing medicines and explain which compounds are currently permissible.

Practical Exercise 16: Find out more about standards
Visit the ISO website and use the *ISO Catalogue* to find out what types of products and processes are regulated by international standards. Once you have done this, try to identify at least five standards relating to any subject and find out if they have been translated into one or more of your working languages.
Next, identify the organization responsible for managing and regulating these standards in the country where you are based.

3.2.6   *Popular science*

Popular science is a generic term consisting of science writing and science journalism. The aim of popular science is to provide an interpretation of scientific material for a general audience who are outside the mainstream scientific community. Whereas popular science books are broad in their choice and treatment of topics, science journalism such as that seen in the likes of the *Popular Science* tends to focus on specific themes and recent developments.

In contrast to scientific writing such as journal papers and monographs, popular science seeks to present the observations, data and conclusions produced by scientists in an accessible way. The aim is to entertain and to educate, possibly even to provoke, but the end result is that much of the modality or cautious "hedging" that occurs in scientific texts is often absent from popular science texts because of the need to simplify or generalize scientific principles.

An interesting dimension of popular science is that it can be written either by scientists or by journalists with varying levels of scientific knowledge. The result is that certain examples of popular science may closely border what could be regarded as literary works, with all of the rhetorical devices and creative language that this entails.

In terms of identifying features, popular science texts will combine terminology, abbreviations and equations etc. from scientific texts and combine it with the linguistic features common in either literary or journalistic texts. The hybrid nature of popular science as a whole may even result in the use of unusual devices such as dialogues, story-telling, metaphors, role-plays, cartoons, extracts from other document types such as recipes, songs, poems, diaries, dramatic texts and so on, in order to ensure that texts are informative and entertaining. The flexibility required in order to convey complex information in an easy-to-understand way means that popular science texts can be particularly demanding for translators.

3.2.7   A word on how texts are structured

Understanding how and why texts are structured in a particular way can help you decide on the most appropriate translation strategy.

The way in which technical documentation is structured is not (usually) some random occurrence as a result of a writer's whims or preferences. The function of the text and the circumstances in which it will be used have as much to do with it as the idea of a logical progression of topics. To make matters even more complex, cultural preferences and norms also play a role. Some documents are written in a linked, cohesive way with individual sections which build on those previous and lead into those subsequent. Examples of this type of text would include popular science books, technical specifications, proposals, or student textbooks. Scientific texts introducing formulae, for example, might begin by stating the rule formally in words before giving the formulae in scientific notation. This is then followed by a definition of the rule and the notation to ensure comprehension and then several examples or exceptions to the rule. This logical sequence aids comprehension and fulfils what has come to be an expectation among readers of this type of text.

Other texts, however, are composed of various, more or less discrete sections which are designed to be read individually and in no particular order. Very often, it is impossible to predict the entry point from which readers will start reading and they may only read a small subset of the whole document. Examples might include reference manuals, task-based tutorials, trouble-shooting guides and online help. When translating texts like this, it is advisable to avoid anaphoric and cataphoric references (i.e. references which point backwards or forwards to content in other sections of the document) as they may be unclear or unfamiliar to the reader. It is usually possible to make the reference more specific, to simply refer to a particular chapter or, in some cases, to repeat the necessary information and delete the reference altogether.

Structure is culture-dependent
Unfortunately, once you have learned how texts are structured in your target language, for example, you then need to learn how they are structured in your source language because, even with closely related languages, they may vary considerably. In 1995, Ulijn conducted a study to establish whether culture plays a role in readers' responses to texts. His study involved 242 French and Dutch speakers whom he asked to read an English language table of contents from a user guide for a coffee maker and then to arrange the table of contents into an order that made most sense to them. While the two groups agreed on the placement of some sections, there was a significant difference in their placement of others. The results clearly showed that the cultural context in which a text is used affected readers' perceptions of whether or not the text made sense. While this type of restructuring may not always be the job of the translator, the sequencing can impact on local translation strategies. In any case, it is certainly something worth mentioning to clients.

Of course, there are times when texts can be described as hybrids – texts that display features of more than one type of text such as task-based tutorial, cookbook and reference manual. This is not as far-fetched or as uncommon as you might think. There may be cases where a document jumps back and forth between scientific and technical text, or technical and marketing text, or technical, financial, legal and promotional text. Proposals, tenders, reports, case studies and marketing material are good examples of this. Susanne Göpferich recognizes the blurred border between scientific and technical texts in her attempts to classify **LSP** texts (1995:307). For the translator this means you will need to recognize the change in function of a particular section and adapt your translation strategies accordingly.

> **Practical Exercise 17: Identifying a "logical" document structure**
> Recreate Ulijn's experiment by writing the chapter headings from a user guide on separate pieces of paper and asking different people or groups of people to arrange them in the correct order. Compare the results and discuss them. This task also works well as a class activity.

3.2.8   *Making sense of text types in translation*

Different texts are produced for different purposes and audiences, and translating them means you have to understand how they are analyzed and categorized. As translators, however, we need to look at the idea of text types in more detail. The main reason is that, as translators, we need a more in-depth understanding of the workings of a text and because we are dealing with two language/text systems, and we need to assess the compatibility of the two.

There have been various attempts to create text typologies for the purpose of classifying and profiling texts, examining specialized terminology and understanding how texts work, and there is a vast amount of literature on **text typologies**, particularly in the field of LSP. While it simply would not be feasible to look at all of these, or to discuss the issue in anything other than a relatively superficial way, it will become apparent that by grouping texts into categories and identifying types, we can hopefully arrive at strategies for translating them.

If nothing else, the very process of analyzing and categorizing texts in this way will help us to understand them better and, as Trosborg (1997:iix) points out, help us to "develop strategies that facilitate [our] work and provide awareness of various options as well as constraints". Bell (1991:206) says that the importance of creating a comprehensive and plausible text typology cannot be over-stressed because "[w]ithout the ability to recognize a text as a sample of a particular form [...] we would be unable to decide what to do with it; we could neither comprehend nor write nor, clearly, translate". This point is echoed by Schäffner (2000:214) who says that a knowledge of the cross-cultural similarities and differences regarding genres and conventions is crucial to the translator.

Schäffner (2000:211) also explains that genres or individual, specific types of texts are "embedded in sociologically-determined communicative activities", but that some are more culture-specific than others. Certain genres may be highly culture-specific genres and can vary significantly from culture to culture while others may be less culture-specific and may even be regarded as "supra-cultural" or universal (*ibid.*), meaning that they are basically the same from culture to culture. However, Schäffner also points out that, even where texts and their conventions are ostensibly universal, individual languages may require us to use different microlevel strategies when translating individual parts of a text to ensure these conventions are observed. She illustrates this by saying that giving instructions in English typically requires the use of imperative verb forms while in German it requires the use of infinitive forms.

Similarly, Nord (1995:264) examines text functions in translation and uses titles and headings as an example. She identifies six functions for titles and headings, namely *distinctive, metatextual, phatic, informative/referential, expressive* or *appellative*. Assuming that we are translating a text from one language where titles are typically expressive into a language where titles are purely informative, our strategy when translating the title may require us to eliminate any parts of the text which are not purely informative. For example when translating a journal paper, the expressive title *"When pets attack: Why does my dog hate me?"* may need to be translated as *"A clinical study into aggression and psychosis among domestic Chihuahuas."* in order to conform with target culture conventions and expectations.

While the six functions of headings and titles described by Nord (*ibid.*) can be applied to technical documentation, a more useful means of classifying texts is provided by Göpferich who highlights *normative, actualizing, didactic* and *compilatory* as categories for classifying technical text functions (1995:308). These text functions provide a more detailed and specialized framework within which we can classify texts and to help us to understand what it is certain text types are supposed to achieve.

Many of the texts which we discussed previously fall into Göpferich's *didactic-instructive* category. This means that many of the text types described earlier (which also form the basis of much of what technical communicators produce) fall into a category where the target audience is highly heterogeneous (Göpferich 1995:311) and as such can pose the greatest number of problems for us. It is for this reason that, when using the strategies described in Chapter 2, we need to understand more about the people at whom these texts are aimed.

Text Category	Communicative Function
Juridical-Normative	Like the regulatory texts described earlier, texts in this category are used to establish a legal basis or an unambiguous standard of reference. These texts always involve legal claims or some effort to impose uniformity.
Progress-orientated Actualizing	These texts are used to communicate information for the purposes of advancing science and technology by presenting new results or knowledge or a critical evaluation of existing knowledge. This category gives rise to the subcategories of *plain presentation*, which incorporates reports, dissertations, conference proceedings etc., and *sophisticated presentation*, which includes articles in learned journals.
Didactic-instructive	Didactic-instructive texts convey information for educational or entertainment purposes or for practical application. This category gives rise to various first and second order sub-categories. The first sub-category is *human/technology interaction orientated texts* which are practical texts aimed at providing step-by-step instructions to help readers perform a task. *Theoretical texts* provide a unidirectional flow of information and the reader concentrates solely on the text. Such texts can be described as *mnemonically organized* (such as text books) or *interest-arousing* (such as popular science articles, product information)
Compilation	These texts provide an accessible summary of knowledge contained in texts of the other three text categories. There are two sub-categories: *encyclopaedic* which includes encyclopaedia entries, reviews, and *dictionary*–type documents.

Example 18: Göpferich's text categories and sub-categories

Practical Exercise 18: Categorizing information types
Find three scientific or technical texts. They can be of absolutely any type, from the label on a bottle of bleach, the instructions for your mobile phone, the information sheet that came with your hair dye, an article from a popular science magazine, the package insert from a pack of aspirin or a paper from a scientific journal. Describe and categorize the main features of each text. What types of information does each text give? Be specific: is it procedural, declarative, facts and figures, descriptions, precautions etc.? Compare the results for each text. Are there any common features? What are the differences?

Suggested Reading

Göpferich, Susanne (1995) A Pragmatic Classification of LSP Texts in Science and Technology, *Target*, 7(2): 305-326.

Hoft, Nancy (1995) *International Technical Communication*, New York: Wiley

Markel, Mike (2001) *Technical Communication*, Boston: Bedford/St. Martins, 6th edition.

Rosenberg, Barry J. (2005) *Technical Writing for Engineers and Scientists*, New Jersey: Addison-Wesley.

Online Resources

- The **World Standards Services Network** is a useful site for researching technical standards and the organizations that produce them: www.wssn.net .
- The **European Medicines Agency** website provides free access to a range of useful information, including its product information templates ("EMEA templates") in 24 languages: www.ema.europa.eu. To find the templates, type "product information templates" in the site's search box.
- The **International System of Units** is available online as a website or as a brochure which you can download. It contains details, descriptions and definitions of all of the standardized units of measure, prefixes, symbols and acronyms: www.bipm.org/en/si/si_brochure.
- The **DITA World** website provides a comprehensive range of resources and reference materials which explain various aspects of the *Darwin Information Typing Architecture* which is used for authoring, producing and distributing technical information: www.ditaworld.com.

4. Case Studies

In this chapter

As a way of helping you to understand the potential challenges involved in translating specific texts as well as developing a methodology for analysing texts, this chapter presents a selection of typical scientific and technical texts that you are likely to encounter as a translator. By examining the features of each text type you will have a better idea of what to expect when you translate it. The first two examples are accompanied by detailed profiles which identify the subject, audience, text function, key features and potential problems as well as a variety of strategies for dealing with them. Using these sample profiles as a starting point, you can then complete the document profiles for the remaining texts. Appendix 4 contains sample profiles for the remaining documents, which you can use for additional information once you have created your own profiles.

4.1   Introduction

So far, we have looked at various issues relating to the production and translation of scientific and technical texts. But in order to use this knowledge in practical situations we need to look at the environment in which these issues arise. In the following pages we will examine some of the most common scientific and technical texts encountered and create a profile of each text to help us understand the issues involved with each text type and to help us approach the translation process as effectively as possible.

We will look at the generic linguistic and practical issues which may pose problems for the translator or which will require additional attention and work. Since the precise challenges facing a translator will vary depending on the nature of the text, and in particular on the language combination and direction, it is not possible to discuss issues in a high level of detail because what may pose a problem in one target language may not pose any problems whatsoever in another. Instead, the following profiles should be looked upon as a supplement to the specific issues discussed earlier.

4.2   Scientific Journal Paper

A scientific paper is a written report describing original research results whose purpose is to inform and persuade peers as to the validity of observations and conclusions as well as the effectiveness of the methods used. The format of a scientific paper has emerged over centuries of tradition, editorial practice, scientific ethics and the interplay with printing and publishing services. The result of this process is that virtually every scientific paper has a title, abstract, introduction, materials and methods, results and discussion. The typical structure of a paper, as described in Chapter 3, can be explained using the acronym *IMRAD*: *Introduction, Methods, Results, Discussion* and *Conclusions*.

An important aspect of scientific papers is that the abstract, together with the title, must be self-contained as they are also published separately from the paper in abstracting services. Together they enable the reader to identify the basic content of a document quickly and accurately, to determine its relevance to their interests, and thus to decide whether to read the document in its entirety. It is interesting to note that many abstracts are produced by the authors themselves who may be non-native speakers of the language in which the abstracts is written. Consequently, abstracts may be fraught with language errors.

> **Note**: The following text was created using *SCIgen*, an automatic computer science paper generator which uses comprehensive linguistic rules to produce texts which do not make any factual sense but which are entirely correct with regard to grammar and style.

Subject	Computer games technology, networking.
Text Category	Discussion, exposition, progress-orientated actualizing, theoretical, description.
Function	Present new research findings or review existing findings; to describe the methods used and provide an overview of previous and related work. The text is used to establish clearly and verifiably the validity and reliability of the methods and findings, and to convince peers of such.
Typical Target Audience	Scientists and academics, peer reviewers, editors; typically with the same expert scientific and educational background as author.
How the text will be used	To learn about new technologies, to examine and test methodologies used, to verify reliability of results, concepts and theories/methodologies.

Sample Text: Scientific Journal Paper

A Case for 802.11B

Gobnait Ní Mhurchu and Jörp Schudissen

Abstract

In recent years, much research has been devoted to the refinement of Scheme; unfortunately, few have synthesized the evaluation of IPv6. In our research, we prove the evaluation of architecture, which embodies the confirmed principles of cryptography. Here, we verify not only that the infamous interactive algorithm for the evaluation of Internet QoS by Jackson [1] runs in $\Theta(n^2)$ time, but that the same is true for A^* search.

1   Introduction

Many theorists would agree that, had it not been for write-ahead logging, the deployment of massive multiplayer online role-playing games might never have occurred. We leave out a more thorough discussion due to resource constraints. A typical challenge in artificial intelligence is the investigation of introspective configurations. The exploration of 802.11 mesh networks would profoundly amplify the UNIVAC computer.

In order to address this challenge, we use client-server modalities to show that the infamous event-driven algorithm for the analysis of voice-over-IP by X. Bhabha runs in $O(n^2)$ time [2]. Certainly, indeed, online algorithms and object-oriented languages have a long history of cooperating in this manner. Further, the usual methods for the emulation of robots do not apply in this area. We view electrical engineering as following a cycle of four phases: construction, construction, synthesis, and synthesis. Therefore, we see no reason not to use the Turing machine to improve probabilistic information [1].

In our research, we make three main contributions. Primarily, we argue that even though object-oriented languages and Boolean logic can agree to solve this issue, thin clients can be made client-server, semantic, and psychoacoustic. Furthermore, we use psychoacoustic configurations to disconfirm that the foremost linear-time algorithm for the synthesis of reinforcement learning by Ito et al. [3] follows a Zipf-like distribution. This is crucial to the success of our work. Furthermore, we propose new omniscient methodologies (CamGospel), which we use to disconfirm that information retrieval systems and the Turing machine can interact to accomplish this ambition [4].

The roadmap of the paper is as follows. We motivate the need for digital-to-analog converters. Along these same lines, we argue the visualization of superpages. Third, we place our work in context with the related work in this area. In the end, we conclude.

2   Related Work

In designing our solution, we drew on previous work from a number of distinct areas. A recent unpublished undergraduate dissertation proposed a similar idea for omniscient theory [4]. A novel application for the understanding of hash tables proposed by Miller et al. fails to address several key issues that CamGospel does fix. Here, we fixed all of the grand challenges inherent in the previous work. Clearly, the class of frameworks enabled by CamGospel is fundamentally different from existing methods [2].

Nehru et al. [5] suggested a scheme for visualizing the refinement of public-private key pairs, but did not fully realize the implications of the investigation of Byzantine fault tolerance at the time [3]. Further, even though Garcia et al. also explored this method, we studied it independently and simultaneously. We had our solution in mind before Roger Needham et al. published the recent seminal work on e-commerce.

1

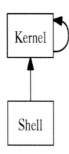

Figure 1: The framework used by our methodology [10].

The famous framework by Jones [2] does not allow wearable information as well as our approach [2, 6]. As a result, the heuristic of Wang and Robinson [7] is an extensive choice for thin clients [8]. Clearly, comparisons to this work are astute.

3 CamGospel Simulation

Next, we propose our architecture for disconfirming that CamGospel runs in $\Omega(n!)$ time. This is a key property of our application. We show CamGospel's classical deployment in Figure 1. Continuing with this rationale, consider the early model by Martinez and Thompson; our model is similar, but will actually fix this question [9]. Next, consider the early methodology by Thompson et al.; our architecture is similar, but will actually fulfill this aim. This seems to hold in most cases. Consider the early framework by Bose and Sato; our methodology is similar, but will actually fulfill this ambition. The question is, will CamGospel satisfy all of these assumptions? Unlikely.

Reality aside, we would like to emulate an architecture for how our heuristic might behave in theory. Despite the results by Watanabe et al., we can prove that courseware and e-business are entirely incompatible. Any technical analysis of RAID will clearly require that link-level acknowledgements can be made concurrent, relational, and embedded; our system is no different. This may or may not actually hold in reality. Further, the architecture for CamGospel consists of four independent components: Bayesian

methodologies, heterogeneous algorithms, Smalltalk, and compact technology. This may or may not actually hold in reality. We believe that agents and vacuum tubes can connect to answer this issue. Thusly, the methodology that our methodology uses holds for most cases [11].

Furthermore, consider the early framework by K. Martin et al.; our methodology is similar, but will actually realize this aim. Our method does not require such a theoretical observation to run correctly, but it doesn't hurt. Even though analysts largely postulate the exact opposite, our system depends on this property for correct behavior. The model for CamGospel consists of four independent components: the deployment of Byzantine fault tolerance, game-theoretic algorithms, flexible epistemologies, and pervasive information. Obviously, the design that CamGospel uses is solidly grounded in reality.

4 Implementation

Despite the fact that we have not yet optimized for complexity, this should be simple once we finish designing the virtual machine monitor. This follows from the improvement of digital-to-analog converters. The virtual machine monitor contains about 9504 lines of Fortran. Systems engineers have complete control over the hacked operating system, which of course is necessary so that e-commerce [12] and the partition table can agree to accomplish this mission [13]. Furthermore, we have not yet implemented the hand-optimized compiler, as this is the least key component of our heuristic. Our application requires root access in order to harness self-learning theory.

5 Performance Results

As we will soon see, the goals of this section are manifold. Our overall performance analysis seeks to prove three hypotheses: (1) that sampling rate is an obsolete way to measure signal-to-noise ratio; (2) that neural networks no longer impact hard disk throughput; and finally (3) that median throughput is an outmoded way to measure mean sampling rate. Note

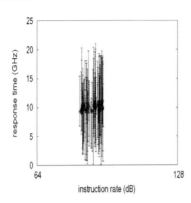
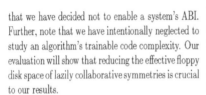
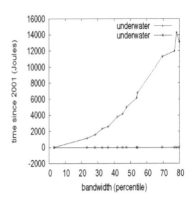

Figure 2: The expected block size of CamGospel, compared with the other methodologies.

Figure 3: The effective complexity of CamGospel, as a function of signal-to-noise ratio.

that we have decided not to enable a system's ABI. Further, note that we have intentionally neglected to study an algorithm's trainable code complexity. Our evaluation will show that reducing the effective floppy disk space of lazily collaborative symmetries is crucial to our results.

5.1 Hardware and Software Configuration

Many hardware modifications were required to measure CamGospel. We carried out a peer-to-peer deployment on our 2-node cluster to disprove the collectively autonomous behavior of DoS-ed communication. We reduced the ROM space of UC Berkeley's human test subjects. This configuration step was time-consuming but worth it in the end. Furthermore, we added a 10MB optical drive to DARPA's mobile telephones to discover our planetary-scale testbed. We removed 7 CPUs from CERN's network to consider archetypes. Furthermore, we quadrupled the time since 1999 of our desktop machines to investigate our Internet-2 testbed. Such a claim is mostly a structured purpose but is buffetted by existing work in the field. On a similar note, we added 2MB/s of Internet access to our introspective cluster. Had we emulated our XBox network, as opposed to emulating it in courseware, we would have seen muted results.

Lastly, we removed 8GB/s of Wi-Fi throughput from our mobile telephones. This configuration step was time-consuming but worth it in the end.

When Raj Reddy modified Microsoft Windows Longhorn's historical code complexity in 1970, he could not have anticipated the impact; our work here attempts to follow on. We added support for our heuristic as an exhaustive statically-linked user-space application. We added support for CamGospel as a dynamically-linked user-space application. We note that other researchers have tried and failed to enable this functionality.

5.2 Experiments and Results

We have taken great pains to describe out evaluation setup; now, the payoff, is to discuss our results. With these considerations in mind, we ran four novel experiments: (1) we ran DHTs on 40 nodes spread throughout the 10-node network, and compared them against symmetric encryption running locally; (2) we measured flash-memory throughput as a function of tape drive speed on a LISP machine; (3) we measured optical drive throughput as a function of flash-memory space on a Nintendo Gameboy; and (4) we dogfooded CamGospel on our own desktop machines, paying particular attention to effective ROM space.

We first explain the second half of our experiments as shown in Figure 4. The results come from only 9

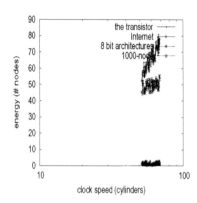

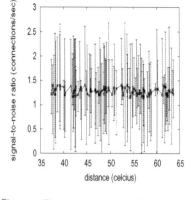

Figure 4: The mean block size of our application, as a function of latency.

Figure 5: These results were obtained by Bhabha [14]; we reproduce them here for clarity.

trial runs, and were not reproducible. Second, operator error alone cannot account for these results. Note how emulating SMPs rather than simulating them in bioware produce smoother, more reproducible results [15].

Shown in Figure 2, experiments (3) and (4) enumerated above call attention to CamGospel's distance. Note that Figure 2 shows the *median* and not *expected* provably discrete floppy disk space. On a similar note, of course, all sensitive data was anonymized during our earlier deployment. Along these same lines, error bars have been elided, since most of our data points fell outside of 52 standard deviations from observed means.

Lastly, we discuss experiments (1) and (4) enumerated above. The many discontinuities in the graphs point to amplified 10th-percentile work factor introduced with our hardware upgrades. Operator error alone cannot account for these results. The curve in Figure 5 should look familiar; it is better known as $G_{X|Y,Z}(n) = n$.

6 Conclusion

Here we introduced CamGospel, a framework for peer-to-peer algorithms. We motivated new electronic information (CamGospel), which we used to confirm that DHCP can be made constant-time, col-laborative, and unstable. We explored a relational tool for developing congestion control (CamGospel), disproving that thin clients can be made probabilistic, signed, and Bayesian. Similarly, we confirmed that scalability in our framework is not a challenge. Such a claim at first glance seems perverse but has ample historical precedence. The study of the lookaside buffer is more natural than ever, and our methodology helps information theorists do just that.

In this position paper we proposed CamGospel, new stochastic technology. In fact, the main contribution of our work is that we concentrated our efforts on confirming that the UNIVAC computer can be made symbiotic, stable, and extensible. Continuing with this rationale, we proved that usability in CamGospel is not an issue. Our framework for visualizing stochastic archetypes is dubiously good. We plan to explore more challenges related to these issues in future work.

References

[1] J. Cocke, "On the deployment of architecture," *Journal of Stable Communication*, vol. 2, pp. 58–60, Aug. 2004.

[2] R. Takahashi, C. A. R. Hoare, D. Ramani, E. Dijkstra, and B. Ramaswamy, "Prop: Compact, efficient algorithms," in *Proceedings of NDSS*, June 1990.

[3] D. Ritchie, "Contrasting the memory bus and simulated annealing," in *Proceedings of HPCA*, June 2004.

[4] E. Dijkstra, K. Lakshminarayanan, and J. Hartmanis, "Investigation of DHCP," in *Proceedings of the Conference on Ambimorphic, Relational Archetypes*, Sept. 1991.

[5] U. Nehru, "Randomized algorithms considered harmful," in *Proceedings of SIGGRAPH*, Feb. 2004.

[6] G. N. Mhurchu and I. T. Brown, "Enabling consistent hashing using modular information," in *Proceedings of SOSP*, June 1998.

[7] B. Garcia, A. Pnueli, J. Schudissen, and M. Welsh, "Deconstructing evolutionary programming," in *Proceedings of the Workshop on Autonomous, "Smart" Modalities*, Apr. 1996.

[8] M. Minsky, "A study of DHTs," in *Proceedings of FPCA*, Nov. 2005.

[9] E. Schroedinger, "Decoupling web browsers from Voice-over-IP in red-black trees," in *Proceedings of the Symposium on Stable Archetypes*, Apr. 1993.

[10] B. Lampson, "Deconstructing redundancy," in *Proceedings of OOPSLA*, Mar. 1995.

[11] M. Blum, "Deconstructing suffix trees with Slat," in *Proceedings of the Conference on Reliable, Omniscient Methodologies*, Mar. 1994.

[12] O. Bose, J. Kubiatowicz, M. Garey, F. E. Easwaran, and R. T. Morrison, "Architecting courseware and the Ethernet," in *Proceedings of the USENIX Security Conference*, May 1991.

[13] Z. U. Zhao and M. O. Rabin, "A case for web browsers," in *Proceedings of the Workshop on Certifiable, Encrypted Archetypes*, Oct. 2002.

[14] S. Cook, "A case for XML," in *Proceedings of PLDI*, Dec. 2001.

[15] K. Lakshminarayanan, J. Harichandran, T. Kumar, and R. Tarjan, "The influence of linear-time symmetries on programming languages," University of Northern South Dakota, Tech. Rep. 13, Nov. 2002.

Distinguishing Features	Scientific Journal Paper

- As is common with other types of academic writing, the text contains frequent references to other publications, especially in the literature review section.

- Some sections of the text contain declarative descriptions of procedures and phenomena.

- Given the highly specialized subject matter, the text contains a large amount of specialized terminology. This also includes the frequent use of proper nouns, eponymous terms and names of organizations, e.g. *CERN, Wi-Fi, Zipf, Turing, Bayesian.*

- A number of product names are used in the text, e.g. *Xbox, Microsoft Windows, Nintendo.*

- Several graphical elements in the form of graphs and diagrams are included. The body text of the paper contains various cross-references to the data presented in the graphs and to elements labelled in the diagram.

- A number of units of measure associated with different subject areas and physical phenomena are used; all are recognized scientific or industry-standard units.

- Various abbreviations and acronyms are mentioned in the text, e.g. *LISP, CPU, DHT.*

- Frequent use of rhetorical devices used to discuss, compare, present, contrast and convince.

- Various formulae and special characters included in the body text.

- Consistent with the conventions of academic writing, the text uses the Latinism *et al.* on a number of occasions.

- The subject material is quite complex and requires the dense presentation of information. A lot of background knowledge is assumed.

- The authors use the active voice to describe procedures and opinions, for example "In our research, we make three main contributions" and "We added support for our heuristic".

Potential Problems	Scientific Journal Paper
	▪ Abstract: The abstract must be concise and most journals specify a maximum length, typically not exceeding 250 words. They are not always cohesive texts and can be very difficult to translate from a conceptual point of view. It is usually best to translate it last once you have a proper understanding of what the text is about.
	▪ Equations and symbols are unlikely to require modification but they may present technical challenges as they may need to be inserted into the TT by the translator if the ST is not provided in electronic form.
	▪ Similarly, units of measure are unlikely to require modification as scientific work typically uses standardized international units. However, symbols used to denote units may pose technical problems if the ST is not provided in electronic form.
	▪ References in the text to graphs and diagrams must be consistent in their use of terminology
	▪ Use of active, personal language (e.g. "We added support..." "...we argue...") may not comply with norms of target language texts or the style requirements of the journal where the paper is to be published. Active constructions may need to be replaced with passive constructions, e.g. "Support was added" and "it can be argued". In such cases it is useful to ask the author where the paper will be published and/or for a copy of the publisher's guidelines for authors.
	▪ Abbreviations, acronyms, eponymous terms and organizations will require research to identify official translations or variants specific to the TL
	▪ Product names need to be researched as they may not be familiar to target audience. Correct spelling and orthography is essential.
	▪ The fact that a huge amount of background information is assumed means that the text may be relatively hard to access for the translator and this may make it difficult to render the TT in a clear and logical way
	▪ Depending on topic and nature of study, the text is likely to draw on information, facts and language from a range of disciplines
	▪ Although Latinisms often need to be replaced where the TL culture does not use them, in academic texts such as this it is a norm of the text genre and must be retained.

4.3   Technical Data Sheet (TDS)

This type of text provides detailed product information relating to a product's composition, properties and applications as well as other information relating to product safety, legal considerations and environmental issues. The precise content of such documents can vary depending on the product, the company and the legal requirements of the country where the product is produced and where it is sold. This example provides details of the product's typical applications and properties under specific conditions, general information which sets out some of the limitations of the product as well as general advice for storing, handling and using the product. In addition, the text also provides details of the product's compliance with relevant standards and regulations. This is a particularly good example of a technical data sheet as it is both comprehensive and well written.

Subject	The example presented here relates to an adhesive specially designed for the disposable medical device market (e.g. cannulae and syringes) and it provides a range of information about its properties, applications, uses and limitations.

Text Category	Informative, descriptive, instructional, regulatory/normative. Precise categories will vary according to product.

Function	To provide clear, detailed and unambiguous information on a range of aspects of the product to ensure proper use, to ensure safety and to ensure adherence to relevant legislation.

Typical Target Audience	This type of text typically has an expert audience such as engineers or designers involved in the design and construction of products. In this case, the text is likely to be aimed at people involved in the manufacture of medical devices which require specific, high-performance adhesives which are capable of providing the requisite bonding properties while complying with the various regulations and legislation governing medical devices.

How the text will be used	The text will typically be used as a reference resource to help select the correct product and to ensure that the intended application is within the product's capabilities. Additionally, the text may fulfil a marketing function whereby it convinces prospective customers or users to select this company's products over another.

Sample Text: Technical Data Sheet

Technical Data Sheet

LOCTITE® 3011™

November 2004

PRODUCT DESCRIPTION

LOCTITE® 3011™ provides the following product characteristics:

Technology	Acrylic
Chemical Type	Acrylate
Appearance (uncured)	Transparent, pale straw colored liquid^LMS
Components	One component - requires no mixing
Viscosity	Low
Cure	Ultraviolet (UV) light
Cure Benefit	Production - high speed curing
Application	Bonding

LOCTITE® 3011™ is designed for bonding and sealing clear plastic to metal substrates (e.g. disposable medical devices). Low viscosity makes it ideal for applications where wicking of the adhesive into pre-assembled parts is required or for components with close fitting tolerances. Suitable for use in the assembly of **disposable medical devices**.

ISO-10993

An ISO 10993 Test Protocol is an integral part of the Quality Program for LOCTITE® 3011™. LOCTITE® 3011™ has been qualified to Loctite's ISO 10993 Protocol as a means to assist in the selection of products for use in the medical device industry. Certificates of Compliance are available at www.loctite.com or through the Henkel Loctite Quality Department.

TYPICAL PROPERTIES OF UNCURED MATERIAL

Specific Gravity @ 25 °C   1.03
Flash Point - See MSDS
Viscosity, Brookfield - RVT, 25 °C, mPa·s (cP):
    Spindle 1, speed 20 rpm   60 to 120^LMS

TYPICAL CURING PERFORMANCE

This product is cured when exposed to UV radiation of 365nm. To obtain a full cure on surfaces exposed to air, radiation at 250nm is also required. The speed of cure will depend on the UV intensity as measured at the product surface. Typical cure condition is 20-30 seconds at 100mW/cm² using a medium pressure, quartz envelope, mercury vapor lamp.

Fixture Time

Fixture time is defined as the time to develop a shear strength of 0.09 N/mm² .
    UV Fixture Time, Glass microscope slides, seconds:
        Black light, Zeta® 7500 light source:
        6 mW/cm² @ 365 nm   ≤10^LMS

        Medium pressure mercury arc light source:
        100 mW/cm² @ 365 nm   ≤5

Surface Cure

Tack Free Time is the time in seconds required to achieve a tack free surface.
    Tack Free Time, seconds:
        Medium pressure mercury arc light source:
        100 mW/cm² @ 365 nm   5 to 10

Depth of Cure vs. Intensity

The graph below shows the increase in depth of cure with time at 100 mW/cm² as measured from the thickness of the cured pellet formed in a 15 mm diameter PTFE die.

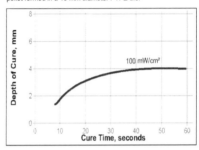

TYPICAL PROPERTIES OF CURED MATERIAL
Physical Properties

Coefficient of Thermal Expansion, ASTM D 696, K⁻¹		100×10⁻⁶
Coefficient of Thermal Conductivity, ASTM C 177, W/(m·K)		0.1
Glass Transition Temperature, ASTM E 228, °C		45
Volumetric Shrinkage, %		8
Shore Hardness, ASTM D 2240, Durometer D		68
Elongation, at break, ASTM D 882, %		160
Tensile Strength, at break, ASTM D 882	N/mm² (psi)	9 (1,300)
Tensile Modulus, ASTM D 882	N/mm² (psi)	420 (61,000)

UV Depth of Cure, mm:
    100 mW/cm² @ 365 nm for 20 seconds   ≥0.8^LMS

TYPICAL PERFORMANCE OF CURED MATERIAL
Adhesive Properties

Cured @ 100 mW/cm² @ 365 nm for 40 seconds
    Lap Shear Strength, ISO 4587:

PVC to Glass	N/mm² (psi)	1 to 5 (145 to 725)
Polycarbonate to Glass	N/mm² (psi)	1 to 5 (145 to 725)
ABS to Glass	N/mm² (psi)	1 to 5 (145 to 725)

    Tensile Strength, ISO 6922:

Steel pin (grit blasted) to Glass	N/mm² (psi)	5 to 15 (725 to 2.175)

(Henkel) **Technologies**

TDS LOCTITE® 3011™, November 2004

TYPICAL ENVIRONMENTAL RESISTANCE
Cured @ 100 mW/cm² @ 365 nm for 10 seconds plus 1 week @ 22°C
Tensile Strength, ISO 6922:
Steel pin (grit blasted) to Glass

Hot Strength
Tested at temperature

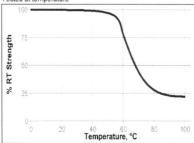

Heat Aging
Aged at temperature indicated and tested @ 22 °C

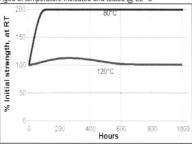

Chemical/Solvent Resistance
Aged under conditions indicated and tested @ 22 °C.

		% of initial strength		
Environment	°C	100 h	500 h	1000 h
Heat/humidity 90% RH	40	65	40	30
Gasoline	22	85	85	85
Freon TA	22	85	75	0
Industrial methylated spirits	22	80	10	0

Effects of Sterilization
In general, products similiar in composition to LOCTITE® 3011™ subjected to standard sterilization methods, such as EtO and Gamma Radiation (25 to 50 kiloGrays cumulative) show excellent bond strength retention. LOCTITE® 3011™ maintains bond strength after 1 cycle of steam autoclave. It is recommended that customers test specific parts after subjecting them to the perferred sterilization method. Consult with Loctite® for a product recommendation if your device will see more than 3 sterilization cycles.

GENERAL INFORMATION
This product is not recommended for use in pure oxygen and/or oxygen rich systems and should not be selected as a sealant for chlorine or other strong oxidizing materials.

For safe handling information on this product, consult the Material Safety Data Sheet (MSDS).

Directions for use
1. This product is light sensitive; exposure to daylight, UV light and artificial lighting should be kept to a minimum during storage and handling.
2. The product should be dispensed from applicators with black feedlines.
3. For best performance bond surfaces should be clean and free from grease.
4. Cure rate is dependent on lamp intensity, distance from light source, depth of cure needed or bondline gap and light transmittance of the substrate through which the radiation must pass.
5. Recommended intensity for cure in bondline situation is 5 mW/cm² minimum (measured at the bondline) with an exposure time of 4-5 times the fixture time at the same intensity.
6. For dry curing of exposed surfaces, higher intensity UV is required (100mW/cm²).
7. Cooling should be provided for temperature sensitive substrates such as thermoplastics.
8. Plastic grades should be checked for risk of stress cracking when exposed to liquid adhesive.
9. Excess uncured adhesive can be wiped away with organic solvent (e.g. Acetone).
10. Bonds should be allowed to cool before subjecting to any service loads.

Loctite Material Specification LMS
LMS dated February 19, 2003. Test reports for each batch are available for the indicated properties. LMS test reports include selected QC test parameters considered appropriate to specifications for customer use. Additionally, comprehensive controls are in place to assure product quality and consistency. Special customer specification requirements may be coordinated through Henkel Quality.

Storage
Store product in the unopened container in a dry location. Storage information may be indicated on the product container labeling.
Optimal Storage: 8 °C to 21 °C. Storage below 8 °C or greater than 28 °C can adversely affect product properties. Material removed from containers may be contaminated during use. Do not return product to the original container. Henkel Corporation cannot assume responsibility for product which has been contaminated or stored under conditions other than those previously indicated. If additional information is required, please contact your local Technical Service Center or Customer Service Representative.

Henkel Loctite Americas
+860.571.5100

Henkel Loctite Europe
+49.89.9268.0

Henkel Loctite Asia Pacific
+81.45.758.1810

For the most direct access to local sales and technical support visit: www.loctite.com

TDS LOCTITE® 3011™, November 2004

Conversions
(°C x 1.8) + 32 = °F
kV/mm x 25.4 = V/mil
mm / 25.4 = inches
N x 0.225 = lb
N/mm x 5.71 = lb/in
N/mm² x 145 = psi
MPa x 145 = psi
N·m x 8.851 = lb·in
N·mm x 0.142 = oz·in
mPa·s = cP

Note
The data contained herein are furnished for information only and are believed to be reliable. We cannot assume responsibility for the results obtained by others over whose methods we have no control. It is the user's responsibility to determine suitability for the user's purpose of any production methods mentioned herein and to adopt such precautions as may be advisable for the protection of property and of persons against any hazards that may be involved in the handling and use thereof. In light of the foregoing, **Henkel Corporation specifically disclaims all warranties expressed or implied, including warranties of merchantability or fitness for a particular purpose, arising from sale or use of Henkel Corporation's products. Henkel Corporation specifically disclaims any liability for consequential or incidental damages of any kind, including lost profits.** The discussion herein of various processes or compositions is not to be interpreted as representation that they are free from domination of patents owned by others or as a license under any Henkel Corporation patents that may cover such processes or compositions. We recommend that each prospective user test his proposed application before repetitive use, using this data as a guide. This product may be covered by one or more United States or foreign patents or patent applications.

Trademark usage
Except as otherwise noted, all trademarks in this document are trademarks of Henkel Corporation in the U.S. and elsewhere. ® denotes a trademark registered in the U.S. Patent and Trademark Office.

Reference 1

Henkel Loctite Americas	Henkel Loctite Europe	Henkel Loctite Asia Pacific
+860.571.5100	+49.89.9268.0	+81.45.758.1810

For the most direct access to local sales and technical support visit: www.loctite.com

Permission by Henkel Ltd.

Distinguishing Features	Technical Data Sheet

- The text contains quite a high proportion of specialized terminology which is drawn from a diverse range of disciplines and includes the names of scientific tests.

- Numerical data in the form of measurements, figures etc. along with various units of measurement. This particular example is quite helpful in that it includes a conversion table but this is by no means the norm and as such translators need to be aware of the potential problems caused by conflicting units of measurement and the issue of whether and how to convert measurements.

- Graphs are used to present numerical data and to express complex relationships and trends.

- The document contains several references to other documents, pieces of legislation and standards. Several products are also referred to within the text.

- Throughout the document a number of what appear to be set phrases are used (e.g. headings, categories and terminology) which are likely to be applied consistently across the entire range of documentation within the company.

- The text uses largely impersonal language with isolated instances of personalized speech which is used for specific purposes, e.g. to convey instructions or recommendations.

- The text uses a combination of passive and active sentences depending on the type of information being conveyed at any given point.

- Several sentences and chunks of information within the text perform a promotional or persuasive function.

- Towards the end of the text there is a significant portion of legal content which is identifiable through the use of formal language, register and constructions as well as the subject matter. This material will have quite specific meanings and will also have legal implications for the company and the reader. There is also a likelihood that in texts of this type, such legal text may be "core information" or information that is produced once and then reused in all other documents. In such cases it is useful to establish whether an existing translation exists for these sections.

- Contact details allowing the reader/customer to contact the company are also provided.

Potential Problems	Technical Data Sheet

- Terminology: various terms taken from a variety of disciplines. Care is needed to correctly identify the subject area and to find a translation appropriate to that particular area (the same word can have different meanings and translations in different areas).

- Subject knowledge: a translator would need to have a good knowledge of the basic principles and terminology relating to chemistry, physics, thermodynamics, medical devices, law. A certain amount of research will most likely be needed in order to deal with the more specialized aspects of the text.

- External references (e.g. to document titles, sections within documents, laws, documents, departments, organizations, etc.) require the translator to research whether there is an existing official translation; if such translations exist then they must be carefully copied over and used consistently. If no such translations exist, the translator needs to produce new translations which are in keeping with the style and conventions of relevant organization. The client may need to be notified if such translations are produced.

- Where the text contains product references, care should be taken to ensure that any copyright or registered trademark symbols that are used are applied appropriately and consistently.

- Graphs: Any references in the text to information provided by graphs should be checked carefully to ensure that they agree. The client should be made aware of any discrepancy between the two. There is also a need to ensure accuracy and consistency with regard to labels, axes and headings etc. The client may also want the translator to translate these graphs. If so, is the graph to be edited directly or should a glossary be produced?

- In the case of the measurements and numerical data presented in the text there are questions as to whether or not they should be converted. The original figures should always be retained even if conversions are provided because there are legal implications if figures are incorrectly converted.

- In terms of the text's register, it should be borne in mind that the direct, personal style adopted here may not be appropriate in all languages or cultures and may need to be modified.

- Some terminology appears to come from or be defined within standards, laws or regulations, e.g. Lap Shear Strength (ISO 4587). As such, a translator needs to check the authoritative documents to find any definitions and official translation, if available.

- The use of certain culturally specific terms such as *gasoline* instead of *petrol* may require intervention on the part of the translator depending on the intended audience.

- The use of Latinisms in the text, while appropriate in some target languages may not be appropriate in others; the use of Latinisms is not always appropriate even across the different varieties of English, for example. If necessary, they should be replaced with target language equivalents.

- The names of tests referred to in the text such as *Brookfield* may be known under different names in the target language and research is needed to avoid confusion. Research can also provide useful insights into the procedures described elsewhere in the text.

- In the case of abbreviations it should be remembered that some abbreviations may be industry-standard and internationally recognized while some may be unofficial or have their own national equivalents. Other abbreviations and acronyms may be company-specific and will require the translator to contact the client.

4.4 Creating your own document profiles

Using the previous examples as a starting point, create your own profiles for each of the following texts. You can use the blank boxes beside each text or you can copy the blank document profile form provided in Figure 8. If necessary, you can supplement the form with your own criteria.

Try to identify as many key features of each text and discuss the potential problems and challenges facing the translator. Your profiles should be as detailed as possible so that you can gain a thorough understanding of how to approach each text. When you have completed your profiles, you can go to Appendix 4 where sample profiles for each text are provided for reference.

Practical Exercise 19: Choose and analyse your own texts
When you have produced profiles for each of the documents presented here, you can also use this profile form to analyse the documents you collected for Practical Exercise 18: Categorizing information types.

4.4.1   Document Profile Sheet

Document Name	
Subject	
Text Category	
Function	
Typical Target Audience	
How the text will be used?	
Distinguishing Features	
Potential Problems	

Figure 8: Document Profile Sheet

4.5   Test Instructions

This text is an extract from a set of test instructions used in a manufacturing company. These instructions are essentially a type of *standard operating procedure* (SOP) which provides clear, step-by-step set explanations of how to carry out inspections on the quality of components manufactured by the company. Typically, such documents form part of a comprehensive set of instructions stored in a loose-leaf ring binder which is accessed as necessary for reference purposes.

Your document profile

Subject	

Text Category	

Function	

Typical Target Audience	

How the text will be used	

Sample Text: Test Instructions

Stacker Industries	Test Instructions 5.5.02 Shelves and Shelf Floors

Item: Portable Shelving Units

Test Regulations: ☐ in accordance with DIN ☒ Factory Standards	**Scope of random sampling:** 4 x per shift Unacceptable results must be documented on the group fault list and included in the fault analysis report.

Test Criteria:
☒ Measurement test
☒ Visual inspection
☒ Function test

Inspection Characteristics for Portable Shelving Units

Dimensional accuracy

Visual inspection of surface

Function test

Test Procedure: Portable Shelving Units
Test the Control and Function Measurements
Ensure surfaces are free from mechanical damage
Check for smooth external surfaces and burrs
Coated internal surfaces (for single-side coatings)
Check weld points:
-   Rotate bottom longitudinally through 10°
-   Tap end plates with rubber mallet

Test Material:
Caliper gauge, tape measure, rubber mallet
Visual comparison

Procedure: The test dimensions are determined from the relevant design drawing. There are two options for the test dimension drawing. The dimensions are either framed with round or square boxes or individual tolerance details can be provided. Make sure that a valid construction drawing is available.

Measures: If faulty parts are found, the production manager must be notified immediately. The production manager will then decide whether to involve the operations manager and/or the QA department depending on the severity of the problem.
Once faulty parts have been detected, the production manager will implement the appropriate corrective and preventative measures using the error analysis report and document such actions in the error analysis report.

Comments: Inspections which do not uncover any faults are not documented. Unacceptable results must be documented in the collective fault list (BE 6.1.17.) If the results are as a result of a repeated fault, an error analysis report must be completed and implemented accordingly. Implementation of the log is only deemed to be complete when it has been signed by the QM department.

Revision: 1.2   Page 1 of 1

Created	Checked	Released	Document
on: 09/11/06 by: P. Matthews	on: 11/11/06 by: Mr. Rodgers	on: 11/11/06 by: Dr. C. Redmond	HA 5.5.02 – Port SH Sys.doc

Your document profile

Distinguishing Features	Test Instructions
▪	
▪	
▪	
▪	
▪	
▪	
▪	
▪	
▪	
▪	

Potential Problems	Test Instructions
▪	
▪	
▪	
▪	
▪	
▪	
▪	
▪	
▪	
▪	

4.6   Expert Technical Report

Expert reports are a common type of text for technical translators and they are generally associated with the various engineering disciplines such as chemical, mechanical or electrical engineering as well as civil engineering and transport. These documents can vary in length and content but invariably provide details of the object of study, the circumstances surrounding the test as well as the materials and methods used. Such tests are often produced by highly qualified specialists working in an independent, consulting role.

Your document profile

Subject	

Text Category	

Function	

Typical Target Audience	

How the text will be used	

Sample Text: Expert Technical Report

T r a n s p o r t   S o l u t i o n s

Locomotive Systems Division

Document Type	Safety Assessment	Confidentiality For Internal Use Only
Title	**Assessment for TS-ETM Track Equipment**	
Subtitle		
Project Reference	TS-ETM	
Product Reference	ETCS Level 2	
Client	Allied Transport Services SA Locomotive Division Jerez de la Frontera Spain	
Expert Auditor	PJ O'Malley Transport Solutions, plc. 10 Emerald Plaza Sandyford Industrial Estate Dublin 22, Ireland +353 (0) 1-6012546	

Subject / Object of Assessment / Scope (Description of Object Being Assessed)

Assessment of Project Schedule for Installation of ETCS Level 2 Track Equipment for the TS-ETM Track Project.

Transport Solutions

Locomotive Systems Division

Contents

T r a n s p o r t   S o l u t i o n s

Locomotive Systems Division

0   Introduction

0.1   Revision History

Version	Date	Author Name	Revised Sections	Reason for Revision / Review
0.1	24/01/2009	PJ O'Malley	Document	Document created
1.0	23/04/2009	J. Lawless	Document	Document released

0.2   Aims and Objectives

This document provides an executive summary of the results of an assessment of the Transport Solutions portion of the ETCS equipment planning process on the TS-ETM project. Particular emphasis is placed on the installation of track points.

This assessment also examines the level of compliance with the relevant legal requirements. This assessment will form the basis of an evaluation of conformity with CENELEC standards [EN 50126] and [EN 50129].

This assessment is in partial fulfilment of the requirements for the decision by the National Office of Transport regarding operating approval for the TS-ETM project in accordance with Art. 6 and 8a of the [TRI].

0.3   Principles, Standards and Guidelines Referenced

Reference	Document	Document Number	Version / Date
[EN50126]	Railway Applications - The specification and demonstration of Reliability, Availability, Maintainability and Safety	CENELEC EN 50126	09/1999
[EN 50129]	Railway Applications - Safety-related electronic systems for signalling	CENELEC EN 50129	02/2003
[TRI]	Transport (Railway Infrastructure) Act 2001	SR 742.141.1	09/12/2001

Transport Solutions

Locomotive Systems Division

0.4   Documents Referenced

Reference	Document	Document Number	Version / Date
[Appl_SC_point]	Application Safety Certificate - Points	ITC 124-005	V1.1/21/11/2008
[Test_Installation_Prot ocol]	Acceptance Protocol – Balise Installation TC-NBS:	ITC 124-007	V1.0 – 23/12/2007
[Aud_point_TestProc]	Inspection Report for Technical Safety Assessment – Points Test Procedure	M0110394343	21/07/2009

0.5   Terms Used

Terms Used	Explanation
None	

0.6   Abbreviations

Abbreviation	Explanation
CENELEC	European Committee for Electrotechnical Standardization
ETCS Level 2	European Train Control System Level 2
TS-ETM	Signalling and Automation System for NBS/ABS

0.7   Validity

This assessment is valid for the project planning and initial installation of the track equipment carried out by Transport Solutions, plc. up to and including 31/12/2010.

T r a n s p o r t   S o l u t i o n s

Locomotive Systems Division

1   Scope

The assessment relates to the planning and initial installation of the track equipment carried out by Transport Solutions, plc. up to and including 31/12/2010.

2   Assessment Procedure

This safety assessment contains information from the planning and initial installation assessment of track equipment on the SA-NBS project.

The main focal points of the assessment were established as follows:

> ➢ Assessment of the level of compliance of processes as described in [*Appl_SC_point*].
> ➢ Assessment of whether initial installation of track equipment was carried out as described in [*Appl_SC_point*].

3   Observations

The project planning and initial installation of the track equipment was carried out correctly by Transport Solutions, plc. in accordance with the process described in [Appl_SC_point]. The process assessed in [*Aud_point_TestProc*] was adhered to. The [*Test_Installation_Protocol*] protocols are consistently available and verify the correct installation of track equipment on the SA-NBS project. The conditions detailed in Section 5.1 of [*Appl_SC_point*] were correctly met or communicated onwards. The conditions in Section 4.5 of [*Appl_SC_point*] must be examined by Allied Transport Services SA.

4   Overall Findings

This assessment [*Appl_SC_point*] together with the test and installation protocols [*Test_Installation_Protocol*] verifies the correct and appropriate scheduling and installation of the track equipment by Transport Solutions, plc. on the TS-ETM up to and including 31/12/2010.

The application safety regulations detailed in Section 4.5 of [*Appl_SC_point*] must be adhered to.

5   Conditions

A	The conditions detailed in Section 4.5 of the Application Safety Certificate – Point HTA 110-004 V1.1 dated 21/11/2009 must be examined by Allied Transport Services SA.

Sandyford, 23/11/09

PJ O'Malley
Senior Technical Compliance Auditor

Your document profile

Distinguishing Features	Expert Technical Report
▪	
▪	
▪	
▪	
▪	
▪	
▪	
▪	
▪	
▪	

Potential Problems	Expert Technical Report
▪	
▪	
▪	
▪	
▪	
▪	
▪	
▪	
▪	
▪	

4.7   User Guide

User guides are one of the most widely recognized and well known of all technical documents. Most people have used them at some point and, unfortunately, most of us can recount experiences with badly written instructions. The purpose of a user guide is to provide instructions to help users learn how to use a product. It does this by providing explanations, examples and advice as well as logical and structured procedural information to take users through each step of using the product. User guides invariably use simple, uncomplicated language which is supported with graphics, tables and boxes. All of this supports users' learning processes and makes the documents user friendly.

However, user guides are usually designed to be as user friendly as possible, which itself is based on human cognition and which is in theory at least universal. User guides also contain features which make them more acceptable to specific cultural groups. Coupled with the fact that user guides are rarely aimed at one particular group of people or even one single culture (e.g. native speakers of the target language), this means that translating user guides is not always a straightforward matter.

Your document profile

Subject	

Text Category	

Function	

Typical Target Audience	

How the text will be used	

Sample Text: User Guide

Chapter 3. Managing Customer Data

Global Customer Services Management (*Global CSM*) is a comprehensive suite of tools which allows you to manage client data throughout your company. *Global CSM* allows you to access, modify and track all data relating to a particular customer from initial contact, through ordering, payment, dispatch and follow-up support and service enquiries.

This chapter explains how to access and modify customer data in customer support departments and call centres. You will learn how to access existing customer incident records and update them with new information. You will also learn how to close resolved customer issues (sometimes known as "tickets"). This chapter also shows you how to create new records and how to export data for use with remote backup systems.

3.1   Why Manage Customer Data?

In large organisations dealing with large numbers of customers it is essential for the effective operation of various departments and business processes that the latest customer information is available. In customer service departments new information may become available on a daily basis. Using the data maintenance application in *Global CSM* you can modify customer Incident Records, among other things and route information to the relevant department for further processing.

Authorised Users

The sensitive nature of critical information means that certain restrictions are necessary to determine who can and cannot modify data. Both accessing and modifying personal data are subject to your company's own internal data protection regulations as well as to the *National Information Services and Data Protection Act 2003*. While all registered users within a company can access customer data, only team leaders and system administrators can modify records. The following table outlines the type of access each user has:

User	Privileges
Support Agent	Read, sort, update, redirect incident records
Team Leader	Read, sort, update, redirect incident records and delete and merge records
Group Administrator	Read, sort, update, redirect incident records and delete and merge records and create new business areas, import and export records

Table 3.1: Global CSM User Types and Privileges

Note: For more information on data access privileges, please refer to the *Global CSM Access Framework for Support Staff* or consult your IT support team.

3.2   Getting Started

- From the main Global CSM screen, log in using your username and password.

- The main application area now appears. This screen allows you to select which action you would like to carry out and in which task area. The *Action* field contains a list of possible actions and the *Task Area* drop-down menu contains a list of task areas where these actions can be performed.

- From the *Task Area* list, select *Support*. Now select *Modify* from the *Action* field.

- The *Modify Customer Records* screen now appears.

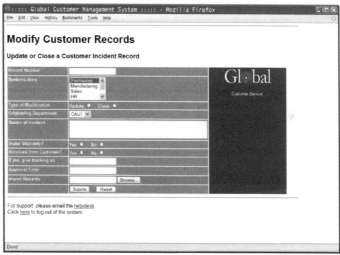

Figure 3.1: The Modify Customer Records screen

- To open the relevant customer record, enter the incident reference number in the *Record Number* field. Global CSM retrieves the record and populates the form with the existing information.

- You can now modify any of the details shown on the screen.

- If you want to redirect a record to another department, simply select the department's name from the *Business Area* list.

> **Note:** You can also distribute a record to more than one department. To do this, simply press and hold the CTRL button on your keyboard while selecting the relevant departments from the list.

- When you have finished making your changes, click *Submit*.

- You can discard any changes and reset the record to its original state at any time by clicking the *Reset* button.

Global CSM User's Guide – Version 6.02

Additional Features for Advanced Users

- **Import**: You can import record data from an external source such as a PDA, POS terminal or laptop. To do this, click on *Browse*. A pop-up window appears from which you can locate the import file on your computer or external device. When you have located the file, double-click on it to load it.

- **Close**: If a client incident has been resolved satisfactorily in accordance with the *Customer Services Charter*, you can close the active record. To do this, activate the *Close* radio button and click on *Submit*. Before closing a record, you must first provide a detailed explanation of the resolution and outcome in the *Nature of Incident* text box.

3.3   Troubleshooting

Problem	Solution
I cannot access any customer records	- Have you entered the correct username and password?
	- Do you have the necessary user privileges? If you are unsure, please contact your system administrator.
	- Is your computer properly connected to the network?
I cannot close a customer record	- You do not have adequate user privileges, OR
	- Another more senior user is editing the record at the same time as you.
I get an error message when I click on Submit	- Your browser may not be configured to accept cookies. *Firefox* users should go to the *Tools* menu and click on *Options>Privacy*. *Internet Explorer* users should go to the *Tools* menu and click on *Internet Options>Privacy*.
I cannot import .ASX files into a customer record	- ASX files are only supported by Global CSM version 6.0 and higher.
	- You must have an ASX-compliant browser pug-lin installed on your computer.

Your document profile

Distinguishing Features	User Guide
▪	
▪	
▪	
▪	
▪	
▪	
▪	
▪	
▪	
▪	

Potential Problems	User Guide
▪	
▪	
▪	
▪	
▪	
▪	
▪	
▪	
▪	
▪	

4.8   Popular Science Book

Popular science publications are intended to serve as a bridge between scientists and the general public. The term "popular science" covers a broad range of publications such as articles, books, web pages and even television programmes and they are produced by both scientists and professional writers. The aim of popular science is often regarded as being to improve the public's understanding of science and to increase public engagement with science, for example as part of policy and decision-making processes.

Popular science writers seek to take scientific findings and make them available to non-scientists through clear and accessible language. They also seek to put scientific knowledge in context and to help readers to understand the significance and implications of this knowledge. In order to achieve this, it is sometimes necessary for popular science to simplify certain concepts or to state information as fact where a scientific text would be more tentative.

Your document profile

Subject	
Text Category	
Function	
Typical Target Audience	
How the text will be used	

Sample Text: Popular Science Book

GREEN PLANET

Overall, plant photosynthesis converts carbon dioxide (CO_2) from the air into simple organic molecules such as sugars (general formula CH_2O). These are subsequently burnt by the plant in its mitochondria (see Chapter 3) to produce more ATP, and also converted into the wealth of carbohydrates, lipids, proteins and nucleic acids that make up life. We met the enzyme that cobbles hydrogen onto carbon dioxide in Chapter 5 – Rubisco, the most abundant enzyme on the planet. But Rubisco needs to be spoon-fed with its raw materials – hydrogen and carbon dioxide. Carbon dioxide comes from the air, or is dissolved in the oceans, so that is easy. Hydrogen, on the other hand, is not readily available - it reacts quickly (especially with oxygen to form water) and is so light that it can evaporate away into outer space. Hydrogen therefore needs a dedicated supply system of its own. This is, in fact, the key to photosynthesis, but for many years the lock resisted picking. Ironically, the mechanism only became clear when researchers finally understood where the oxygen waste came from.

In oxygenic photosynthesis, the hydrogen can only come from water, but the source of the oxygen is ambiguous. If we look at the overall chemical equation for photosynthesis, we see that it could come from either carbon dioxide or water:

$$CO_2 + 2H_2O \rightarrow (CH_2O) + H_2O + O_2$$

Lane, Nick (2002) Oxygen: The Molecule that Made the World, Oxford and New York: Oxford University Press, pp.134-135. **By permission of Oxford University Press.**

GREEN PLANET

At first, scientists guessed that the oxygen came from carbon dioxide – a perfectly reasonable and intuitive assumption, but quite wrong as it turned out. The fallacy was first exposed in 1931, when Cornelis van Niel showed that a strain of photosynthetic bacteria used carbon dioxide and hydrogen sulphide (H_2S) to produce carbohydrate and sulphur in the presence of light - but did not give off oxygen:

$$CO_2 + 2H_2S \rightarrow (CH_2O) + H_2O + 2S$$

The chemical similarity between H_2S and H_2O led him to propose that in plants the oxygen might come not from carbon dioxide at all, but from water, and that the central trick of photosynthesis might be the same in both cases. The validity of this hypothesis was confirmed in 1937 by Robert Hill, who found that, if provided with iron ferricyanide (which does not contain oxygen) as an alternative to carbon dioxide, plants could continue to produce oxygen even if they could not actually grow. Finally, in 1941, when a heavy isotope of oxygen (^{18}O) became available, Samuel Ruben and Martin Kamen cultivated plants with water made with heavy oxygen. They found that the oxygen given off by the plants contained only the heavy isotope derived from water, proving conclusively that the oxygen came from water, not carbon dioxide.

Lane, Nick (2002) Oxygen: The Molecule that Made the World, Oxford and New York: Oxford University Press, pp.134-135. **By permission of Oxford University Press**

GREEN PLANET

In oxygenic photosynthesis, then, hydrogen atoms (or rather, the protons (H^+) and electrons (e^-) that constitute hydrogen atoms) are extracted from the water, leaving the "husk" – the oxygen – to be jettisoned into the air. The only advantage of water is its great abundance, for it is not easy to split in this way. The energy required to extract protons and electrons from water is much higher (nearly half as much again) than that needed to split hydrogen sulphide. Controlling this additional energy requires special "high-voltage" molecular machinery, which had to evolve from the "low-voltage" photosynthetic machinery previously used to split hydrogen sulphide. To understand how and why this voltage jump was made, we need to look at the structure and function of the machinery in a little more detail.

Your document profile

Distinguishing Features	Popular Science Book
■	
■	
■	
■	
■	
■	
■	
■	
■	
■	

Potential Problems	Popular Science Book
■	
■	
■	
■	
■	
■	
■	
■	
■	
■	

4.9   Certificate of Conformity

A European Certificate of Conformity (COC) is a declaration by a manufacturer that a particular product conforms to the relevant European regulations. The purpose of this document is to ensure the free movement of goods within the European Union. This document contains information about the product and its producer's identification as well as information such as type approval number, applicable technical specifications and other data. The content of a COC is defined by EU Regulation 92/53 (Amendment IX) but may vary, depending on the product or service being certified.

Your document profile

Subject	

Text Category	

Function	

Typical Target Audience	

How the text will be used	

Sample Text: Certificate of Conformity

National Test Laboratories
Testing and Certification Consultants

National Test Laboratories Ltd.
Testing and Certification Consultants
1 Main Street, Ahascragh
Ireland

EC-CERTIFICATE OF CONFORMITY
0433 - CPD - 0293

In compliance the Directive 89/106/EEC of the Council of European Communities of 21 December 1988 on the approximation of laws, regulations and administrative provisions of the Member States relating to the construction products (Construction Products Directive - CPD), amended by the Directive 93/68/EEC of the Council of European Communities of 22 July 1993, it has been stated that the product

"AquaDry 3000"

Class IV 3000 W industrial drying machine for use on concrete, plaster and other water-based construction materials, Model No. AD3000-A13-PY6

placed on the market by

Venturi Fans and Dryers Ltd.
144 Lake Drive,
O'Hogan Business Campus,
Letterfrack, Co. Galway
Ireland

and produced in the factory

Venturi Manufacturing & Distribution Ltd.
27 Salty Lane,
Ballyneety, Co. Galway
Ireland

is submitted by the manufacturer to a factory production control and to the further testing of samples taken at the factory in accordance with a prescribed test plan and that the approved body – *National Test Laboratories* - has performed the initial type-testing for the relevant characteristics of the product, the initial inspection of the factory and of the factory production control and performs the continuous surveillance, assessment and approval of the factory production control and an audit-testing of samples taken at the factory, on the market or at the construction site.

This certificate attests that all provisions concerning the attestation of conformity and the performances described in Annex ZA of the standards

- EMC-EN61000-6-3 - *Electromagnetic compatibility (EMC). Generic standards. Emission standard for residential, commercial and light-industrial environments*
- ISO-5349-2:2001 - *Mechanical vibration – Measurement and evaluation of human exposure to hand-transmitted vibration – Part 2: Practical guidance for measurement at the workplace*

were applied and that the product fulfils all the prescribed requirements.

This certificate was first issued on 24/01/2000 and remains valid as long as the conditions laid down in the harmonised technical specification in reference or the manufacturing conditions in the factory or the FPC itself are not modified significantly, and latest on 23/01/2020.

Ahascragh, 24/01/2000

M. Clarke
Chief Technical Officer

Your document profile

Distinguishing Features	Certificate of Conformity
▪	
▪	
▪	
▪	
▪	
▪	
▪	
▪	
▪	
▪	

Potential Problems	Certificate of Conformity
▪	
▪	
▪	
▪	
▪	
▪	
▪	
▪	
▪	
▪	

4.10 Technical Case Study

The technical case study is a very common marketing text used by companies as a way of promoting their products and services and, by providing a real-world, applied context, helping potential customers understand how they can benefit from the company's expertise. These texts combine various elements of technical language with those of marketing and journalism. Their aim is to describe the product and present a very positive experience on the part of a particular client. The language used in the text, therefore, needs to reflect this without overstating or misrepresenting the reality of the product.

In terms of structure, a case study will normally start with a catchy headline and a quote or testimonial summarizing the client's experience and view of the product or service before identifying the client's business activities and needs – this is sometimes labelled as the *problem* – before describing how the company helped the client (the *solution*). Using a range of resources such as quotes from interviews, diagrams and statistics, the case study provides an explanation from the client of how the solution helped them and what they think of it and the company.

Your document profile

Subject	
Text Category	
Function	
Typical Target Audience	
How the text will be used	

Sample Text: Technical Case Study

The Power of Being There®

Case Study

WWE tag teams with AMX switches to produce action-filled programs

"From a broadcast point of view, it truly expands the capability and resource sharing beyond what a typical television production facility is doing currently... We would not be able to function with the efficiency that we have today were it not for the Avocent solution."

David "Shack" Haralambou

President

By Request Communications

● **A need for quick response**

Exciting shows with evolving storylines are what fans expect when they tune in to television shows like Monday Night RAW and WWE Smackdown! In the wrestling ring, superstar performers like John Cena, Kane and Undertaker move their muscle through emotional and physical dramas that culminate or change direction during monthly pay-per-view specials.

Behind the scenes, editing of the non-stop video action happens at the World Wrestling Entertainment's (WWE) technologically advanced production facility in Stamford, Connecticut. There, the WWE produces seven television shows, consisting of nine hours of original programming, 52 weeks per year, delivering more than 14 million viewers each week. WWE programming is syndicated in 45 of the top 50 U.S. markets and multiple versions of its U.S. programming are available in more than 100 countries in 17 languages around the world.

Just like wrestlers in the ring, the production team needs to respond rapidly to change and their small multi-port KVM switching system was pinning them down. The system had distance limitations and did not enable sharing so there were multiple computers and servers that handled the same functions. This redundancy factor and the sheer amount of equipment pointed to the need for a more state of the art approach.

In 2001, working with By Request Communications (BRC), a broadcast systems integrator, and reseller Revco, Inc., the WWE commenced a digital upgrade project and started the search for a more progressive KVM solution. Avocent quickly emerged as the leading contender. Implementing an enterprise-wide AMX® KVM switching solution from Avocent, the WWE gained the ability to share resources, eliminate duplicate hardware expenses and improve overall IT support response time.

"The WWE is a fast-paced organization and like other broadcasters, the ability to change as needed in response to production is imperative," said BRC President David "Shack" Haralambou. "When we purchased a new broadcast server, we quickly realized that putting in a standard analog KVM solution would not adequately address our needs."

Solution proves to be winner

The Avocent AMX KVM switching solution allows broadcasters to consolidate control of their machine room computers and devices into a single-user interface. This centralized interface lets operators and engineers in multiple locations access the same devices from the live studio.

"We went with the Avocent solution based on previous product history and because of the ability to run it over standard CAT 5 cable," said Haralambou. "We have a tremendous CAT 5 and CAT 6 infrastructure already built in the facility and the ability to use that infrastructure for workstations and machines produced a tremendous cost savings."

WWE purchased four 32-port AMX5000 switches and one 64-port AMX5010 switch to connect standard PCs, graphics machines, broadcast servers, music machines for MIDI, editing systems and several corporate servers. Twenty AMX5120 user stations are distributed throughout the broadcast department. Engineers effortlessly switch between Microsoft, Mac and UNIX platforms.

Haralambou also appreciates that "the user stations' video capability really helps" by supporting resolutions up to 1600 x 1200 at 75Hz with a very high quality rate of transmission – comparable to a direct computer connection experience. Another benefit is the ability to plug into a local PC at each user station, eliminating the need for a separate KVM at each desktop.

"The end result is less money on equipment and less clutter in the data center without compromising performance," said Haralambou. "Space is always an issue and having only a single monitor, keyboard and mouse is a plus."

Secure network/remote diagnostics

Another plus is the ability to be multi-user connected. Sharing of resources is the number one feature making a tremendous difference for the WWE. Haralambou appreciates the ease of ability to assign different user groups, different permissions to each user and different machines within those groups. He notes that the flexibility in setting up those types of parameters allows them to maintain a secure network.

Remote diagnostics is also enabled through the solution. With access to machines from the desktop, engineers no longer need to travel all over the building to troubleshoot, resulting in a manpower savings as well.

"The ability for engineers to access any machine on the network from their desktop shortens the time it takes to resolve user workstation issues," said Haralambou. "Now, they can just dial up from their desktop and call up the machine that's causing a problem."

The only "problem" Haralambou encountered during the implementation process was that once they began using the AMX switching solution, they found other uses for it and quickly outgrew their original purchase. When they began daisy-chaining – connecting the output of one box to the input of the next – they realized the solution was more than meeting their expectations.

Ready for growth

"The good news is the system already has a growth plan built in and you can daisy-chain, expand or swap it out very easily," he said. "It is plug and play which makes it very user friendly for instances such as an upgrade situation."

Haralambou notes that the WWE network is constantly growing and appreciates that the AMX switching system has grown with them.

"From a broadcast point of view, it truly expands the capability and resource sharing beyond what a typical television production facility is doing currently," he said. "This is a

solution that crosses multiple users, multiple locations from newsrooms to production control rooms all in one nice, little package. We would not be able to function with the efficiency that we have today were it not for the Avocent solution."

Revco, Inc. is a data center solutions reseller located in Trumbull, Conn. For more information, visit **www.revco-inc.com.**

About Avocent

Avocent® is a leading worldwide supplier IT centralized management solutions. IT administrators benefit through local and remote access and control of servers and other network data center devices.

Branded products include KVM switching, extension, intelligent platform management interface (IPMI), remote access, wireless, mobile, and video display solutions. DSView® 3 management software provides fully redundant failover authentication.

Avocent KVM solutions are in Fortune 100 companies globally. Avocent has sales, operations and R&D centers worldwide. Corporate headquarters are in Huntsville, Ala. Visit www.avocent.com for more information about Avocent products.

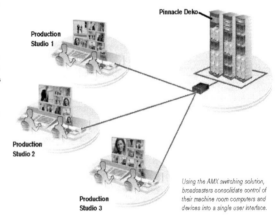

Using the AMX switching solution, broadcasters consolidate control of their machine room computers and devices into a single user interface.

The Power of Being There.

Your document profile

Distinguishing Features	Technical Case Study
▪	
▪	
▪	
▪	
▪	
▪	
▪	
▪	
▪	
▪	

Potential Problems	Technical Case Study
▪	
▪	
▪	
▪	
▪	
▪	
▪	
▪	
▪	
▪	

Basic Translation Techniques

In this chapter

This chapter discusses general translation strategies such as recategorization, modulation and adaptation and describes how they can be used when translating scientific and technical texts. Following on from the discussion of Skopos theory in Chapter 1, this chapter looks at how to formulate a translation brief and what type of information it should contain. You will also learn when not to translate sections of text and when you should contact the client. By the end of this chapter, you will be able to distinguish between the different types of translation you may be asked to produce and you will be able to develop your own translation brief to help you decide which translation strategies to use.

5.1   Introduction

Now that we have examined several typical texts and identified the typical issues and challenges they present, we are ready to start thinking about techniques and strategies for translating them. In this section, we will start out by examining some basic approaches used by translators when they translate texts. It is worth noting that these strategies are not unique to scientific and technical translation; in fact, they are used in all types of translation. What we will do here, however, is show how they are used in scientific and technical translation. Then, with the fundamentals out of the way, we will move on and look at some of the specific strategic problems you might encounter in technical documentation and explore some of the strategies you can use to deal with them.

5.2   The basics

Like most things in life, when it comes to translation there is the easy way and the not so easy way of doing things. The most straightforward way of translating is to translate literally but this will not work in all situations. Sometimes we need to take a more roundabout route as we travel from A to B to avoid traffic jams and roadworks. Just like when we are driving, the shortest route is not always the smoothest or fastest one. This is where the notions of *direct translation* and *oblique translation* as proposed by Vinay and Darbelnet (1958/1995) prove useful.

5.2.1   Direct translation

Direct translation involves relatively straightforward strategies which require less intervention by the translator and less deviation from the ST. Though relatively

Transposition

unsophisticated from a linguistic point of view, direct translation strategies such as literal translation, borrowing and calquing are useful in a range of scenarios.

5.2.1.1 LITERAL TRANSLATION

Often confused with word-for-word translation, literal translation, though related, is more sophisticated than simply replacing each ST word with a corresponding TT word. With this approach, we may start by translating individual words but, when we reach a point where the TT no longer complies with the grammatical rules of the TL, we move to translating group-by-group or clause-by-clause. Essentially, literal translation involves producing a TT which reflects the content and features of the ST as closely as possible and only deviating from this where necessary in order to produce a TT which is grammatically correct and intelligible. Literal translation will typically avoid any additions, omissions, paraphrasing or other translation techniques to produce what could be described as a faithful and simple translation.

While it is tempting, particularly in a book on technical translation, to say that translation is such a complex process that it always requires sophisticated strategies, the reality is that literal translation is not as uncommon as you would expect. Cardoso de Camargo (2001:37) shows that literal translation is actually one of the most frequently used translation strategies in technical texts. Using a corpus of 18 technical, corporate and journalistic texts, she compared the use of various translation strategies in English texts and their Portuguese translations and found that in technical texts, literal translation occurs more frequently than other strategies such as transposition, modulation, **addition** or adaptation.

Of particular interest, however, is her finding that literal translation is used to translate a smaller proportion of the total word count in technical texts in comparison with corporate and journalistic texts. This is rather surprising because we would expect journalistic texts, in particular, to feature richer and more complex language use which should not be suitable for literal translation. In fact, literal translation is used for 45.3% of the lexical items in journalistic texts as opposed to 39.6% in technical texts (*ibid.*).

But while there are situations and texts where literal translation will be our most common tool, it is not the full story and you only need to translate a few technical texts to realize this. Even the process of adjusting elements of a source text so that they conform to TL grammar can be a complex process. As we learned in Chapter 2, we know that different audiences have preferences and expectations regarding the way in which information is presented to them and this means that even though a literal translation may be grammatically, syntactically and idiomatically correct from a purely linguistic point of view, it may not be appropriate in the target text.

Nevertheless, even though literal translation may proportionally see more use in technical texts, it is by no means the most important strategy, nor does it represent the main tool in a translator's toolbox. Indeed, those instances where literal translation will not suffice are more than enough to keep us busy as we translate technical texts. In addition to literal translation, technical translation requires a range of other translation procedures.

5.2.1.2 BORROWING

Borrowing can be described as perhaps the simplest form of exchange between languages as it involves transferring an SL lexical item into the TT without any form of modification except, perhaps, for transliteration to account for different writing systems and characters. Often borrowing is used because there is no existing word or concept in the TL but it can be used deliberately in order to create a particular effect in the TT, for example to make the TT seem more foreign or "exotic". Such an approach might prove useful when translating popular science texts where the text tries to recreate a particular atmosphere or sense of the source culture. The following words are used in a variety of languages without translation, although they may be modified slightly to fit in with the grammatical rules of the receiving language.

- boot, Internet, email, pixel, ABS (Anti-Blockier System), pitot tube, diskette

5.2.1.3 CALQUE

Calquing is similar to borrowing in many ways but it involves the literal translation of the individual constituent parts of an SL word or phrase to create a new term, or neologism, in the TL. The use of calquing is something to be approached with caution, as a calque is often a rather alien-sounding thing in the TL and, with the exception of the author (or in this case, the translator) and a few others, neologisms may confound most readers and ultimately prove as uninformative as retaining the original ST term. While authors such as Mancuso (1990:197) condemn neologisms as the work of "arrogant" authors, it is sometimes necessary to introduce new words and there are various accepted calques such as those listed below. Nevertheless, introducing new words without good reason is inadvisable, particularly where there are perfectly acceptable alternatives in the TL.

- log in (German: *einloggen*),
- skyscraper (Spanish: *rascacielos*),
- command separator (Danish: *kommandoseparator*),
- disk defragmenter (Swedish: *Diskdefragmenteraren*)
- workstation (Swedish: *arbetsstationer*)

5.2.2   *Oblique translation*
More sophisticated and complex than direct translation, oblique translation is used when the grammatical, pragmatic and lexical differences between the SL and TL are too significant to allow direct translation.

While direct, especially literal, translation is quite common as a translation strategy, there are cases where a straightforward approach is not enough to allow us to produce a suitable translation. In such cases, we will need to resort to less direct approaches in order to produce our translation. This is where the notion of *oblique translation* comes into play. Coined by Vinay & Darbelnet (1958/1995),

nominalisation

it describes four translation procedures which are used where the stylistic ⌣.
linguistic features of the source text are such that a straightforward replacement
of ST elements is not possible because it would produce a TT which is unacceptable in terms of meaning, structure, idiomaticity or style.

5.2.2.1 EQUIVALENCE

Using the definition provided by Vinay & Darbelnet (1995:31), we can describe
equivalence as the process of replacing elements in the ST with corresponding
elements in the TT so as to "replicate the same situation as in the original whilst
using completely different wording" (*ibid*:342). We would use such an approach
if translating more directly would result in a translation which loses meaning
or impact, or which is missing the idiomaticity or flow of a corresponding text
originally produced in the target language.

In contrast to the more conventional notion of equivalence, which would take
several volumes to define and explain, equivalence as a translation procedure
simply involves finding the TL counterpart for a particular SL word or phrase. We
can use it, for example, to replace fixed expressions or formulaic phrases, idioms
or proverbs. More specifically, in the case of technical texts we can use this procedure as a way of translating elements such as warning signs and labels.

- Danger! → Risk of Death
- Wet Paint → Freshly Painted

5.2.2.2 TRANSPOSITION/RECATEGORIZATION

Transposition or recategorization is the process of replacing one class or type of
word in the ST with another type of word in the TT without changing the meaning. This sounds complicated but, in reality, it is quite simple and most people will
find it reasonably intuitive. This procedure is usually needed because of differences in the way information is expressed in the SL and the TL, and maintaining
the same word class would result in a translation that is awkward or unintelligible. Some transpositions are obligatory; for example, where the SL may have
a noun describing a particular process or object, while the TL can only convey
this information using a descriptive phrase. Other transpositions are optional
and may be chosen simply to improve the style or flow of the TT. Examples of
transpositions include:

- Nominalizations (noun to verb): "*The regulation* of the heating system
  is carried out by the main computer" vs. "The main computer regulates
  the heating system"
- Passive to active: "The new standard was approved by all member
  states" vs. "All member states approved the new standard".
- Passive to imperative: "The safety mechanism is engaged prior to performing maintenance work" vs. "Engage the safety mechanism before
  carrying out maintenance work".

5.2.2.3 MODULATION

Modulation refers to the process of changing the form of information by presenting it from a different point of view. It is useful where a literal translation would result in a translation which might well be grammatically correct but which is nevertheless unidiomatic. Some modulations are compulsory (or fixed), usually because of structural differences between the SL and TL, while others (known as free or optional modulations) are not. At the most basic level, modulations might involve changing a sentence from a positive to a negative, for example:

- "Never turn off the refrigeration unit" vs. "Leave the refrigeration turned on at all times".
- "Easy to use" vs. "Not difficult".
- "Protects against most viruses" vs. "Only allows a few viruses through"
- "This X-ray machine does not damage photographic films" vs. "Photographic films can be scanned by this X-ray machine without being damaged".

Other types of modulations involve replacing abstract concepts with concrete concepts:

- Reboot → Restart, Start Again
- Hardcore → Crushed Stone
- Monitor → Visual Display Unit (VDU)
- Tarmac → Asphalt

Some terms and expressions are modulated simply because of a TL preference for using a particular viewpoint to describe the concept. Take for example the *Geneva stop*, which is a type of gear mechanism used in mechanical watches and old-fashioned cinema projectors. It is also known as a *Maltese cross* because of its appearance. While both terms are equally correct and used with more or less the same frequency in English, different languages have specific preferences for which term they use.

Geneva Stop	Maltese Cross
Portuguese: roda de Genebra	<ul><li>Danish: malteserkorsmekanisme</li><li>Dutch: maltezerkruis</li><li>Spanish: mecanismo de cruz de malta</li><li>Swedish: malteserkors</li></ul>

Other modulations involve replacing a concept "part for whole" or "whole for part". In a text describing the manufacture of cars, this might involve replacing *transmission* (whole) with *gears* (part).

5.2.2.4 ADAPTATION

Adaptation can be described as a strategy of last resort in translation as it may involve a significant amount of deviation from the ST. Vinay & Darbelnet (1995:39) themselves describe it as the "extreme limit of translation". Indeed, it is a procedure to be used with caution, no matter what type of text you are translating.

Adaptation makes use of three key procedures – cultural substitution, paraphrasing and **omission** – and is used when the ST describes a situation or concept which does not exist in the TL culture or which does not have the same connotations or relevance to members of the TL audience. Such cases might include references to foods in the instructions for microwave ovens or dietary supplements, references to "mailboxes" or "zip codes" in computer software or websites, or even references to institutions such as local councils or government authorities in design and construction documentation for a manufacturing plant. We might also find ourselves forced to adapt the ST if it is poorly written, unclear or somehow resistant to translation.

Under normal circumstances, we would use cultural substitution first in order to overcome a culture-specific problem in the ST. For example, in an environmental impact report for building storage tanks in a biogas processing plant we might replace a reference to a government agency in the SL culture with a reference to the corresponding agency in the TL culture. We might even replace a reference to a particular type of soil commonly found in the source country with a reference to a comparable soil in the target country.

If such a substitution fails, we may paraphrase the ST by expressing the meaning of the ST descriptively, using words which do not necessarily correspond to those of the ST. Using the examples just given, we might instead include sentences such as "the gas collection plant must be inspected by the relevant environmental agency in your area" or "the decision to use reinforced concrete will depend on the soil composition in the area". It is perhaps the most useful of all translation procedures for technical translation as it also helps to avoid interference and unidiomatic constructions caused by sticking too closely to the ST.

If we are unsuccessful in finding a cultural substitute or paraphrasing the ST, we can, in a limited number of cases, omit information. Extreme caution is required in such instances because, as we have seen in previous chapters, technical documentation is concerned first and foremost with information so the decision to omit information should only be a last resort and you must be able to justify it completely.

Practical examples of using adaptation might include replacing a sentence in the documentation for a satellite receiver which advises users to consult a specific magazine which only exists in the SL country with a generic reference such as "more details can be found in various satellite magazines". Training materials or technical advertisements may describe typical scenarios in which a product might be used. In order to make this information as meaningful and clear to the reader as possible, the scenarios will more than likely be something to which the reader can relate, and as a result, they may be quite firmly rooted in the SL culture.

> **Transcreation – Taking adaptation to extremes**
> The term *transcreation* comes from the words *translation* and *creation* and can be defined as an extremely free form of translation (more so than regular adaptation). Transcreation probably has more in common with copywriting than it does with traditional translation and its aim is to produce texts which are fully adapted to the cultural and linguistic requirements of specific countries or regions and in which there is absolutely no trace of the original ST or culture. Transcreation is more commonly associated with advertising and marketing materials but it can be applied to other types of text where the resulting product needs to be tailor-made for the target audience and not contain any indication that it is a translation or that it was produced for anyone other than the target audience.

Scenario	Solution
The ST is an on-screen help system for a satellite receiver which advises readers to consult a named specialist magazine for details of satellite co-ordinates which only exists in the SL country.	The TT replaces the ST reference with the name of a corresponding publication in TL country (a cultural substitution). Ideally, however, generic **undertranslations** should be used to avoid problems caused by the TL being used in more than one TL country.
The source text is a technical data sheet for a chemical product advising readers to comply with the regulations set out in a specific law applicable only to the SL country when disposing of the product.	The TT replaces the reference to the SL law with one which is applicable in the TL country. Again, a generic *undertranslation* should be used to avoid problems caused by the TL being used in more than one TL country.

5.2.3   *Expansion and contraction*
Depending on the subject and your target audience's background knowledge, you may need to add explanations to your translation or remove unnecessary detail so that it meets readers' expectations.

Expansion, also known as explicitation, involves making something which is implicit in the ST explicit in the TT in order to make the TT clearer, more relevant to the TT audience, or to compensate for some perceived lack of background knowledge on the part of the TT audience. Expansion may involve adding explanatory phrases to clarify terms or statements or adding connectors to improve the flow of the text and to make it more readable. As a result of this strategy, a translation ultimately may contain a higher level of semantic redundancy or repetition, whereby the same or similar information may appear a number of times, sometimes in close proximity.

Although this may prove problematic in certain types of text, technical texts in particular are less likely to suffer as a result because they are by necessity explanatory in nature and, as mentioned in Chapter 2, present less information in a greater number of words than scientific texts, for example.

Expansion is a useful strategy for improving the cohesion and coherence of the TT when the ST has, for instance, been produced by someone other than a trained writer. In such cases, the ST may contain an excessive amount of jargon or ellipsis, which, although perfectly comprehensible to SL readers, may not be entirely intelligible to a TT audience. Expansion can also prove useful where the TT audience typically has less subject or background expertise than the ST audience and requires additional explanation. A similar scenario occurs where the ST audience can be regarded as a high context culture (see *High and Low Context Cultures* on page 39) which requires less explicit information, while the TT audience is either a low context culture or less dependent on context than the ST audience. In such cases the TT audience, although possessing a comparable level of subject knowledge, may expect and prefer certain things to be spelled out rather than left unsaid.

A very good example of this was a brand of instant mashed potato sold by the same company on both the German and Irish markets. The German packaging featured instructions for making one portion of the product and instructions for making *two* portions. The only difference between the two sets of instructions was the doubling of quantities of water and butter. The same product on sale in Ireland, however, only provided instructions for making *one* portion.

It is difficult to provide a satisfactory explanation for this apart from cultural preferences. It is something that could prove problematic for translators in either direction, as there is a risk of either patronizing one audience (by including instructions which the target audience may regard as obvious) or failing to respect the preferences of the other (by omitting instructions, which forces the target audience to resort to guesswork).

Conversely, contraction refers to the practice of making something less detailed in the TT. The motivations for this are the same as for expansion, and the aim is to adapt the TT to the perceived expectations and background knowledge of the TT audience. Taking the example of the instant potato instructions, translating the German instructions into English for the Irish market would probably involve contracting the instructions by omitting the instructions for making two portions. Translators may also choose to employ contraction as a strategy to eliminate information which can reasonably be regarded as unnecessary, irrelevant or potentially confusing for the TT audience.

5.2.3.1 RECYCLING INFORMATION

A useful way of clarifying information in a text is to expand a translation by recycling information provided elsewhere in the text. This approach bears a certain similarity to compensation, which is described later on in this chapter and which involves taking information from one part of a text and using or reusing it somewhere else in the text. This approach is also quite useful where there are problems in the way the source text is written; for example, where certain essential information is omitted from the ST and this hampers either the comprehensibility or the effectiveness of the text.

To illustrate how recycling might be necessary, let's imagine translating a maintenance guide for a large machine used in the manufacture of body panels for cars. Such documents are usually modular in design, which means that they are not intended to be read from cover to cover and the sections are not necessarily read in sequence but rather in the order in which they are needed. In one of its later sections, the document provides detailed instructions on how to replace a faulty component from inside the machine. The procedure requires an engineer to reach into the machine, underneath the large 2000 tonne hydraulic press, which is used to die-cast car panels.

However, unless the machine had been deactivated and a number of safety measures put into place, anyone following the instructions would inadvertently activate the machine and suffer severe injuries or possibly be killed. The key information needed by readers to stop this happening does appear in the document, albeit in a chapter much earlier on in the manual, crucially, in a relatively unrelated chapter. However, the information is absolutely necessary in the later section because the procedure is required as part of another task.

In this situation, the translator is faced with the choice of simply translating what is in the text, in the knowledge that someone will probably be injured as a result, or copying the information from earlier on in the text and pasting it into the other section. Admittedly, this is a rather extreme intervention, but it is wholly justified. A less controversial approach would be to raise these concerns with the client and suggest the appropriate changes.

A less extreme application of recycling is in the formulation of sentences being translated. Depending on the language combination, a translator may be faced with sentences which simply resist any attempts at idiomaticity in the target language. This can be as result of short fragmented sentences in the SL or restrictions posed by the grammar of the TL. In such cases, repeating information, particularly in the case of promotional or marketing materials, can permit translators to completely recast sentences and produce fluent and idiomatic translations. This may simply involve repeating the product name or it may involve repeating features or characteristics which have already been described previously in the text. In cases where it is not possible to combine sentences, translators can use recycling as a way of padding out sentences which would otherwise be too short and fragmented in the TL.

It is important to remember that recycling does not involve introducing new information into a text; it simply involves reusing information and wording which is already present in the ST. It should also be used sparingly so as to prevent the text becoming overly repetitive.

5.2.4 Generalizing and particularizing

Different languages, texts and audiences will require different levels of precision and specificity.

Generalizing is used to describe the practice of making information in the ST less detailed when it is transferred to the TT. This strategy can take the form of omitting information or replacing a specific word with a word which has a less specific meaning. This may be useful where the target language does not have a similarly specialized or specific word, preferring instead to use a generic catch-all term. It may also be necessary, for example, if you are translating a specialized text for a general audience where, as the translator, you might decide that a particular term in the source text will be unfamiliar to the target audience so you decide to translate it using a less specific, more generic term or hypernym in the TT.

Of course this approach can only work if the specific, detailed term (the hyponym) presented in the ST is not essential for comprehension, if it can reasonably be inferred from the context or if it can be slotted in at a suitable point somewhere else in the text; otherwise the reader will either not fully understand what is being said or will be unable to carry out some action. In such cases, the original information will have to stay in the text.

In practice, this might mean that if you are translating a text which describes how specialist paints are used to prevent rust from affecting the structure of oil rigs, you might translate the word *coating* with a word along the lines of *paint*, a less specific term, if the TT was for a general audience.

Particularization, or specification, on the other hand, is where we use a more specific term to the one contained in the ST. We may need to do this because the generic term used in the ST is simply too broad in the TL, introduces too much uncertainty or ambiguity in the TT or has connotations associated with it which are undesirable in the TT. The challenge for us as translators, however, is to ensure that we understand the subject matter of the text sufficiently well to allow us to decide which of the possible specific terms available is the correct one. For example, does *motor vehicle* mean *car, truck, van* or *motorcycle*? Often we can ascertain the correct term from the context but this will not always be the case, and thus good communication with the author or client or access to a subject matter expert is vital.

While overtranslation and undertranslation can be used intentionally as justified and effective translation strategies, it is also worth remembering that they can also be used accidentally to the detriment of the TT. One example of this relates to the translation into German of *European Council Directive 70/220/EEC* which deals with the safety requirements for vehicle fuel tanks. The English source text referred to *fuel* while the translation incorrectly referred to *petrol*, giving a more specific meaning than the one intended. This inappropriate use of particularization could have presented various safety, financial and legal problems for drivers, manufacturers and governments and the text had to be corrected as a result. For this reason, you should be careful when selecting TL terms to ensure that they have the same connotations and denotational meaning as the SL term unless there is a valid reason for doing otherwise (Byrne 2007).

5.2.5   *Compensation*

Particular features cannot always be recreated in the target text but it may be possible to add similar features elsewhere in the target text to make up for it.

Compensation is the process where we make up for the loss of certain source text features in the target text by introducing other features elsewhere in the translation which are not necessarily present in the source text. One of the best ways of illustrating this is to consider what happens when we translate a humorous text or film. There may be a scene in the film where the clever use of wordplay, for example, has a humorous effect. If it is not possible to recreate this wordplay, the joke may be lost and the film loses some of its comedic content. If, however, the opportunity presents itself later on in the film to take advantage of a potential wordplay or pun we can introduce a new joke into the film thereby restoring its "humour quota". The result is that, overall, the translated film will have the same number of jokes, although they are not necessarily in the same places as the original film.

Applying this basic idea to technical texts, we know that we are not going to be dealing with jokes or word plays but it does mean we can redistribute information and textual features throughout the text in order to balance out the information load or make the style more consistent. Hervey *et al.* (1995) describe four types of compensation:

Compensation in kind involves replacing one type of textual feature in the ST with another type of feature in the TT. This might involve replacing infinitive forms of verbs used in German to give instructions with imperative verb forms in English. Additionally, if the syntax or tone of the ST indicates a level of formality which is not reflected by the same structure in the TL, you may need to add other syntactic or stylistic devices to recreate this effect.

Compensation in place is used to make up for the loss of a particular feature or effect at a particular point in the ST by recreating it elsewhere in the TT. If, for example, a technical advertisement contains an example of wordplay which cannot be rendered accordingly in the ST, it may be possible to produce a similar play on words elsewhere in the text providing it is appropriate to the overall purpose of the text. This approach is quite similar to the strategy of recycling information described above, and involves taking information which was originally found in one part of a text and using, or reusing, it somewhere else.

Compensation by splitting may be used where the ST contains a word for which there is no corresponding TL word which conveys the same range of meanings. An example might be the English word *fastener* which is used as a collective term for all manner of objects used to attach things together such as bolts, screws, clips, clamps and pins. If we are translating into a language where a corresponding term either does not exist or is not as comprehensive we may need to spell out these meanings so as to ensure comprehensibility.

Compensation by merging allows us to condense features or information presented in the ST over a fairly long stretch of text (or in a complex compound word) and to present it in a shorter phrase or even in a single word. Using the previous example, if the source text refers to attaching a "mounting bracket to a rack unit using bolts, screws, clips, clamps or pins" we might decide to use the generic TL term *fastener* to combine all of these meanings into the expression "the mounting bracket can be attached using suitable fasteners".

It is worth noting that both compensation by splitting and compensation by merging are very similar to the ideas of generalizing and particularizing translation and the reasons for using them often overlap.

5.2.6 Restructuring
The sequence in which information is presented to readers in a text or even in individual sections, paragraphs or sentences can play an important role in the success of a translation.

Usually, information in a technical text is presented in a logical or chronological sequence. Such sequencing is particularly true in the case of instructional texts or texts which describe processes and procedures which need to be carried out. Often this will involve presenting information in the order in which it is required and the sequencing is fairly stable because it depends on real-world objects or processes. However, although perceptions of what does and does not constitute a logical or intuitive flow of information are largely culture-independent because they depend on our human cognitive processes, there are instances where cultural expectations and norms take priority and it will be necessary to rearrange the sequence of information in a text.

One example of this is the way in which people use written instructions. Some people will read the instructions in their entirety before performing any of the steps while other people may perform each step as they read it. Obviously, this is going to cause problems for readers if a particular step can only be performed after some other step has first been completed but the instructions present the steps in the wrong order.

Gerzymisch-Arbogast (1993) identified certain patterns and characteristics relating to the sequencing of information in texts and found that certain languages favoured a particular sequencing of information which could be perceived as *given* and *new* relative to the author's perceptions of the readers' background knowledge. It is worth pointing out that this is quite different from the notions of *theme* and *rheme*, which relate to given and new information within a particular sentence or discourse. She explains that in order to produce effective translations, a translator may need to alter the sequencing and even the proportion of *given* and *new* information within paragraphs or sections of text (using expansion and contraction, generalization and particularization, or even repetition). In practice, this may involve **foregrounding** certain information, omitting other information or even repeating information.

A rather extreme example of this is presented in a study by Ulijn (1995) who examined the sequencing of sections within a document. Ulijn's experiment showed that the structure of documents may need to be changed for different language audiences. He found that what might be perceived as the most logical sequence of information in a document for one audience might be counterintuitive or confusing for other language audiences. The following example illustrates how the structure of a user guide might need to be changed for two different target audiences.

Table of Contents *(Language 1)*	**Table of Contents** *(Language 2)*
1. Introduction	1. Introduction
2. Getting Started	6. Specifications
3. Advanced Features	5. Maintenance
4. Troubleshooting	2. Getting Started
5. Maintenance	3. Advanced Features
6. Specifications	4. Troubleshooting

Figure 9: Example of a table of contents modified for two different audiences

Similarly, source texts may not always be well written, with the result that information which should have been presented in a particular order, even for the SL audience, appears in some other sequence. Problems may be caused, for example, if the instructions for backing up files on a computer tell readers to delete a file before they have actually backed it up.

As a result, we may need to rearrange the information within sentences, paragraph or even chapters. However, there are limitations on what we can reasonably do as translators. So, although Ulijn's observation that the sequence of chapters within a book may need to be changed, we cannot move entire chapters or sections within a document unless we get permission to do this because it is not really a translator's job. We should at least, however, let the client know. This issue is also discussed in the section entitled *Errors in the Source Text* on page 161.

5.2.7   *Iconic Linkage*
Minimizing variation and ensuring the same information is expressed in the same way can improve the usability of translations.

In certain types of technical texts, particularly those with an instructional function, emphasis is often placed on the **usability** of the information as a way of measuring the quality of the texts. The same also applies when translating these documents. In the case of texts, usability refers to how easily and effectively readers can assimilate and act upon information that is presented to them in texts. While there are various ways of improving the usability of texts such as using diagrams, structuring chapters in particular ways, including examples and even things like using different fonts and page sizes, translators are restricted to strategies which we can implement during the writing stage of the translation process. This is because many of the strategies for improving usability go beyond the traditional role of the translator and are more commonly associated with the work of technical writers.

However, we can improve the usability of texts by implementing a strategy known as Iconic Linkage (IL) (Byrne 2006). This strategy involves reducing the number of ways in which the same information is presented in a text. It takes the idea of parallelism - using grammatically parallel structures for parts of a sentence which are similar in meaning – and expands it to include matching sentences and phrases throughout an entire text, not just those which are in close proximity. So, as the following examples show, if the same information is presented three times in the source text, but each time using a slightly different wording, instead of replicating the slight differences for each of our translations, we pick one single translation and use it for all three of the ST sentences.

- Always exit the application before disconnecting the storage device from your PC.
- The user must never remove the unit from the system without first closing the associated program running on the PC.
- To safely remove the drive, you must first close EasyUSB.

Research has shown that this strategy can significantly improve the effectiveness of texts (Byrne 2005). It does this by minimizing the amount of cognitive effort and problem solving needed in order to understand a text. Additionally, by using consistent wordings repeatedly, IL improves predictability and aids learning by taking advantage of the human tendency to form habits (Byrne 2006:172-174). In any case, it is nearly always a good idea to translate the same information in the same way because it improves clarity, aids learning and comprehension, and looks more consistent and professional. It also has a knock-on effect if the text being translated is going to be used as a **pivot** or *relay translation* because the TT becomes the ST for another translation activity. In such cases, Iconic Linkage makes the use of translation memories more effective thanks to the increased repetition the text contains.

> **Practical Exercise 20:   Identifying translation strategies in practice**
> Find one scientific and one technical text and their translations. These can be published texts and their translations, or even texts that you have translated yourself. Using the various translation procedures mentioned above, analyse each text and identify instances where each procedure is used. Explain what the translator has done and propose suggestions as to why this particular option was chosen. What are the advantages and disadvantages of the chosen procedure? If other options were available, say what they were. Does one particular strategy predominate in each text type?

5.3   What type of translation are you producing?

Perhaps the single most important factor in determining how you approach a translation is the type of translation the client actually wants. This might seem like a pointless question but it is incredibly important because it will determine what we translate, how we translate it and the amount of time we need to spend doing it. There are a number of types of translation that we may be asked to produce:

- Selective Translation
- Gist Translation
- Information Purposes
- Publication Purposes
- Instrumental vs. Documentary Translations

In the case of *selective translations*, we may be asked simply to translate certain sections of the text. For instance, a client may send us a scientific report and ask us to translate the section that deals with the results of an experiment or to translate the section that deals with the methodology. This particular type of translation job may be motivated by issues such as budget (i.e. the client cannot afford to have to whole text translated) or speed (i.e. the client cannot wait for the whole document to be translated and simply wants the most relevant information). Our job is to read through the document, identify the relevant sections and then translate them.

A *gist translation* is typically motivated by the same factors of budget and time as selective translations but rather than translating selected sections of the text, our job is to provide a rough translation which summarizes the text. The aim is simply to give the client a general idea of the content of the text. As such, we do not need to be as meticulous in terms of style, register etc.

Information purposes only translations are similar to gist translations in that we are not expected to produce polished and stylistically appropriate texts but we are, however, expected to make sure that all of the information is translated. Translations produced for information purposes are generally used internally within the company and are not intended to be seen by anyone outside the client's company. As long as the information is clear, accurate and complete, any shortcomings in style or language can be overlooked.

However, when a translation is for *publication purposes* we need to produce the best translation we possibly can in terms of content and language. This is because the text will be used for external purposes such as publication, inclusion on a website, submission to government authorities etc. This is the most time-consuming and demanding type of translation because we need to be absolutely sure not only that our texts are accurate and easy to understand but also that the language and style are flawless. When translating texts like this it is not uncommon for translators or agencies to engage a second translator or reviewer to edit or proof the translation to make sure it is of the highest quality.

In addition to the types of translation already mentioned, technical translation often involves what are known as *updates*, projects where the document to be translated is an updated version of a document which has already been translated. In an update project, we may be asked to translate a document containing 10,000 words, of which 630 are new. Along with the document itself, we may be provided with a translation memory which was produced when the original document was translated.

An alternative scenario is that we translated the original document ourselves and that we still have the translation memory we created the last time. Ethical questions arise in such instances if the client is unaware that the document is an update, if the client is unaware of the extent of repetition in the updated document or if the client is unaware that we are using a translation memory tool.

Ultimately, it is up to the translator to decide whether to inform the client that only a proportion of the text needs to be translated, or whether to say nothing and charge the client for the entire document even though not all of the words have been translated. For the sake of professional ethics and the reputation of translators, it is always best to tell the client, who will be delighted by the fact that they do not have to spend as much on the translation. Ethics aside, this is actually good business sense as the client will more than likely appreciate your honesty and become a regular customer.

Either way, in a project like this we simply translate the document as normal using the translation memory tool, allowing it to automatically insert the 100% matches from the previous translation until we reach sentences or entire sections of new, previously untranslated text. All of this is relatively straightforward but it is important to remember that the existing translations proposed by the translation memory should generally be accepted "as is" and you should resist the urge to edit or modify sentences which were previously translated in a way which you might not have chosen.

The reasoning behind this is that the existing translations have already been approved by the client and are, in theory at least, already acceptable. What's more, if the translated text was used as the basis for other translations, any changes you make will have a knock-on effect on all of those other translations which were based on the original translation. So, no matter how much you think you could produce a nicer translation, you should leave the existing translations alone and only translate the new sections, trying to replicate the style and tone of the existing translations. Nevertheless, if you do spot something which is downright wrong in the previous translation, then you should raise this with the client, preferably before you actually make any changes.

Translation memories and the art of recycling

A translation memory is a special type of database which is used to store translations produced by human translators. As you translate a text, each TL segment (usually, but not always a sentence) you translate is stored together with its corresponding SL segment to form a translation unit. This translation unit can be reused later on if you encounter the same sentence. The idea is that you should never have to translate the same sentence twice. A sentence which is identical to one which has already been translated is referred to as a "100% match". A sentence which has not already been translated is referred to as a "0% match".

Translation memories also allow you to translate sentences which are similar, but not identical, to sentences that have been previously translated. These are known as *fuzzy matches* and are described as a percentage in terms of their overall similarity to a particular sentence. They are particularly useful for texts which contain lots of internal repetition, texts which will be updated regularly or texts which are similar to other texts.

5.3.1   *Instrumental and documentary translations*

The distinction between **instrumental** and **documentary** translations was described by Nord in 1991 and it relates to the way in which translations will be used or perceived. In an instrumental translation, our translation will be used in place of the source text; it will be expected to perform as a freestanding, autonomous text in the target language. In this regard, any errors will need to be corrected if the text is to perform its intended function.

Conversely, a documentary translation is intended to describe what was said in the source text and how it was said. In professional contexts, this approach is often used where there are questions over the quality of a translation produced by somebody and you, the translator, are asked to provide a *back translation* of the text. For example, if one translator translates a text from English into Italian, a translation agency may commission a very literal and close back translation into English to assess the accuracy and quality of the original translation. This is, admittedly, a questionable practice which is extremely limited in what it can tell us about the quality and appropriateness of a translation but it is one which does take place in certain companies.

Similarly, close documentary translations may be required for judicial purposes, where, for example, the issue of liability in a court case rests on the particular wording of a document and the translation is supposed to illustrate any and all inaccuracies, errors and unclear formulations. If we think back to the faulty manual for the car manufacturing machine mentioned in the *Recycling informa-*

tion section on page 125, producing a documentary translation would mean that we would *not* correct the problem posed by the missing information.

Professional approaches to assessing translation quality

In the preceding paragraph we mentioned how some companies use back translation as a means of testing the quality of a translation. This is just one limited method and there are various alternatives which are widely used in the translation industry including the following, which are described by Louise Brunette (2000):

- ***Pragmatic Revision***: Involves a close comparison of the ST and TT in order to improve the quality of the TT. There is no contact between the reviewer and the translator and no feedback is given.
- ***Didactic Revision***: Involves a close comparison of the ST and TT in order to improve the quality of the TT **and** educate the translator. The reviewer justifies and explains proposed changes and provides feedback to the translator.
- ***Translation Quality Assessment (TQA)***: A purely diagnostic activity which is used solely to determine the quality of a TT, not to improve it. Can be carried out on a whole text or section of text.
- ***Quality Control (QC)***: QC is similar to TQA but it is only carried out on a numerically calculated number of words from one or more sections of a text.
- ***Fresh-Look Revision***: Involves examining just the TT from the point of view of the target audience to ensure that the text complies with TL norms. The TT is not compared against the ST and the translator may or may not be provided with feedback.

In ***instrumental*** translations, our job is to spot the errors and then decide what to do with them. In the case of simple linguistic errors such as spelling mistakes, typos or unclear formulations, the translator is supposed to be an expert and as such, they can and should be corrected without hesitation. Other linguistic errors such as unclear descriptions and instructions should also be rectified during the text production or drafting stage of the translation process. Other errors that should be corrected include incorrect line breaks, instances where paragraph text does not match text shown in diagrams or illustrations, or cases where the wrong unit of measurement has obviously been used (e.g., where a scientific paper describes a "250 kg" paracetamol tablet designed especially for children where "kg" should really be "mg").

Practical Exercise 21: Putting a price on your work

While we may enjoy translating and the various intellectual challenges it provides, few of us translate purely for fun. As a result, we should not ignore the financial implications of our work. Both the type of translations we produce and the subject areas we specialize in can affect how much we earn as translators. For example, a basic "information only" translation may not require the same level of editing as a text which is destined for publication. Similarly, more specialized subjects for which there is a lack of suitably qualified translators might attract more money than general technical areas. While rates in certain sectors of the translation industry are on a continuing downward spiral, qualified and skilled translators can still make a decent enough living.

To help you better understand the translation market and prepare yourself for the financial realities of working as a translator, this task involves producing a price list for your services. Using whatever resources available to you, carry out market research and produce a list of your prices for:

- *Translation*: Decide whether you are going to charge by the word, line or thousand words and whether to base your price on the source or target word count. Do you offer a different rate for general and specialized translation?
- *Editing*: Do you charge an hourly rate, or on the basis of a word count?
- *Hourly rate*: This also relates to work you might do on-site at a client's premises.

Produce a price list and keep it near your computer for future reference. You should also create invoices for each translation you produce in class.

Practical Exercise 22: Assessing the quality of translations

In this section we learned how some translation agencies may decide to test the quality of a translation by commissioning a very literal back translation. What are the drawbacks and benefits of such an approach? Draw up a list of pros and cons to help you determine whether back translations are a reliable way of gauging the quality of translations.

How does the back translation approach compare with the various translation quality assessment approaches described by Brunette (2000)?

5.3.2   *Producing a translation brief*
Your instructions and guidelines for producing a translation.

One of the cornerstones of Skopos theory is the notion of the *translation brief*, which is supposed to govern the translation process and guide the translator in the production of a suitable target text. Unfortunately, there is much debate and uncertainty as to what a translation brief should look like and what kinds of information it should contain. Hans Vermeer, who devised Skopos theory (1978), acknowledged that translators will not always get the information they need in order to produce a proper translation brief and they may end up having to use a system of educated guesses and assumptions in order to do it. There have been attempts by scholars such as Sunwoo (2007) to address this problem but the notion of the translation brief is still somewhat elusive and open to interpretation.

So what should a translator do when deciding whether to take on a translation or when establishing the best way of approaching a text? Typically, the instructions given to a translator by a client are very vague and often consist of something like "the text is about engineering and we need it translated into US English".

A useful strategy is to compile a short list of standard questions which you can ask a client at the start of a translation project. It is a good idea, however, to minimize the number of questions you ask, as you do not want to irritate a client who simply wants you to do your job and may see your interrogation of them as a lack of professionalism or ability on your part. Bear in mind also that clients simply may not understand what it is you are asking them or they may not know how to answer your questions. It is also good to remember that in the majority of cases, you are the expert, not the client, and they expect you to "just know" how to translate whatever they put in front of you.

In terms of what questions you should ask, the very minimum you should know is what language variety you are translating into (e.g. UK English or US English), what the purpose of the translation is (i.e. information purposes or publication purposes), what the deadline is, and whether there is any specific terminology you are expected to use. Professional translators' associations such as the *Institute of Translating and Interpreting* in England often provide helpful information leaflets for translators to help them ask the right questions. These can be a useful starting point for you. When you have identified this information, you can use it to create a translation brief form to help you remember to ask these questions. Figure 10 shows what a basic translation brief form might look like. Over time, as you gain more experience with specific texts, subjects, clients and your own way of working, you will develop your own questions. Eventually you may not even need to use this form or write down this information because you will instinctively ask for, or be able to identify, this information because you have done it so often. However, while you are training yourself to find answers to these questions, the translation brief form is a useful tool.

Practical Exercise 23: *Developing and using your own translation brief*

The secret to creating a translation brief and then translating a text lies in knowing what questions you need to ask so that you have enough information to make the right translation decisions. Think about the type of information you might need in order to translate a text. Compile a list of standard questions and produce a translation brief form. If you like, use the sample translation brief shown in Figure 10 as a starting point and modify it as you see fit. Which questions can you answer for yourself and which questions can only be answered by the client?

Once you have your own translation brief form, apply it to as many different texts as you can. Use the sample texts provided in the "Case Studies" chapter or to any other text you encounter.

To make things more interesting, try to think of alternate translation briefs for the same text. For example, if you needed to translate a user guide for an expert audience instead of a novice audience. Does this affect the questions you ask?

5.3.3   *When not to translate*
Dealing with authoritative texts, laws, document titles, organizations and quotes.

An interesting feature of technical documentation, which can cause confusion for translators, is the fact that in certain cases, not all of the text in a document needs to be translated. In fact, certain parts of the text either should not be translated at all or should only be translated in certain circumstances.

An example of this arises where a technical text quotes text from another publication. Again, if we translate this as a direct quote we run the risk of our translation being perceived as the actual words of the original document and this may be misleading. In such cases, we firstly need to establish whether there is already a published translation of the referenced document in the target language. If such an **authoritative translation** exists, and can be obtained, then it must be used rather than our own translation. If no such translation exists, or if we cannot obtain it, then we need to proceed carefully so that we do not misrepresent the original text.

The most useful way of doing this is to present a paraphrase translation which explains the content of the quote but which does not purport to be the official translation or the official text. The easiest way of doing this is either to omit the quote if the nature of the document permits this, or to provide the original text in the source language accompanied by our paraphrase translation contained [in square brackets] to indicate that the translation is supplementary information which is not in the original source text. Sometimes, however, the source text may reproduce a section from a publication written in a language which is neither the source nor the target language. Unless you happen to speak the other language, your best bet is to leave it alone and notify the client that this extract will need to be translated by someone else.

Translation Brief

Project Reference	Delivery Date

Source Language

Target Language & Variety

Subject(s)

Text Type

Function(s) of Target Text (incl. publication, information only, gist)

Specialised Terminology?

Intended Target Audience

Background/Occupation of Target Audience

What Will the Audience Use the Text for?

Distinguishing Features of Source Text (linguistic, terminological, subject, structure, layout etc.)

Specific Client Requirements (linguistic, conceptual, cultural, conflict of function)

Reference Sources (websites, parallel texts, dictionaries, subject guides etc.)

Figure 10: Sample translation brief form

5.3.3.1 Official translations and proper names

Quite often technical texts will refer to such things as related documents, technical standards, legislation, organizations or government bodies. Good examples of texts which do this include instructions for use, technical design specifications, data sheets or tender documents where, in addition to the actual details of the project, the document may refer to the various standards with which the work complies, to other applicable contracts or to the different organizations from which authorization may be required for particular activities.

When dealing with such organizational names, the very first course of action is to determine whether there is an existing official translation. In the case of organizations, simply visiting their website may provide either an official translation or links to other websites in your target language which refer to the organization. If no translation exists, then we can assume one of two things: either the organization has not produced a translation yet or they do not want their name to be translated, i.e. they want to be referred to by their source language name, regardless of the language context. In both cases, as long as the first reference to the organization consists of the source language name *and* your translation, you can then safely use one or the other name in the rest of the document.

5.3.3.2 Laws

If no official translation of the name of a law exists, it must be possible for an interested target audience reader to recognize what the law is about. Interested readers should be able to identify the original law and locate its original name if it is necessary, for example, to find more information relating to it. For this reason, it is important that, if you do have to provide your own translation, you do not use capital letters, as this may imply that the translated name is the official one. This can cause problems for readers if they decide to look for information on a particular law using a name which does not exist. Often the best compromise is to provide a paraphrase translation accompanied by the original name of the law in the source language.

Using Germany's *Handelsgesetzbuch* as an example, the following extracts demonstrate what to do if we can find an official translation and what to do if we cannot find one:

- "... this contract is issued in accordance with the German Commercial Code"
- "... this contract is issued in accordance with German company law (Handelsgesetzbuch)"
- "... this contract is issued in accordance with Germany's *Handelsgesetzbuch* [German company law]"

Note that in the first example, even though we have an accepted official translation, we have still added the word "German" to make it clear that we are talking about the German law, and not any other country's law which may have the same name.

A word of warning
Even if you do manage to find a common, official or existing translation for a country-specific concept or law, you should still exercise caution. In certain cases, even though such translations are available, they cannot always be regarded as authoritative because they may not be updated to reflect changes in the original language name, because certain translations are used only in certain contexts or for some other reason. As such, translations will frequently need to be accompanied by the original source language name. Remember that the ultimate aim here is that any reader, who for whatever reason is interested in this particular law, has sufficient information to be able to identify and track down the relevant law if necessary.

5.3.3.3 EUROPEAN DIRECTIVES

One of the great things about translating EU-related texts is that, assuming you are translating between official EU languages, almost all of the terminology, official names and associated documentation have already been translated into the official languages. As long as you remember to consult the relevant EU website, you should be able to find the correct authoritative translation. One potential problem relates to EU Directives. A directive is a legislative act of the European Union which requires member states to achieve a particular result, for example to criminalize certain acts, to implement technical standards or to guarantee certain legal protections, without specifying how such a result should be achieved. Directives also specify the deadline by which member states must achieve these results. They are typically named using a short reference name and a longer descriptive name, for example:

- Council Directive 85/337/EEC of 27 June 1985 on the assessment of the effects of certain public and private projects on the environment

The descriptive names can be found by searching the directory of legislation in force on the *EUR-Lex* website, so translating between EU languages should not pose a problem. However, the short reference names, while appearing relatively simple, can be problematic to the unsuspecting translator. The short references consist of three components:

- year / identifier / abbreviation, *for example: 85/337/EEC*

In English, the abbreviation will be EEC, EC or EU, depending on when the directive was issued and the legal basis upon which it was drafted. These abbreviations will differ from language to language so, for example, while 2003/35/**EC** refers to the English-language version, other versions will be represented as follows:

- 2003/35/**EG** – German version
- 2003/35/**ES** – Czech version
- 2003/35/**EY** – Finnish version
- 2003/35/**EF** – Danish version
- 2003/35/**EK** – Greek version
- 2003/35/**KE** – Maltese version
- 2003/35/**CE** – Spanish and French versions

The other abbreviations, EEC and EU, will similarly be rendered into their target language equivalents for use in these codes. To avoid confusion when translating the names of directives, you should ensure that you have selected the version with the correct short code for the target language too. Do not be tempted to leave these codes as they are.

5.4   Writing within limits

Various factors can affect your use of language, such as style guides, controlled language, preferred terminology and translation memories.

As if dealing with vast amounts of complex technical information and translating it into clear, accessible and appropriate language were not demanding enough, there are cases where constraints are placed on the ways in which you can and cannot write your target texts. There are several factors which can affect or even restrict your options when formulating a translation, and they can make technical translation more challenging and complex.

A **controlled language** (CL) is a subset of a natural language which is created using various rules to restrict the grammar and vocabulary which can be used in a text. The purpose of a CL is to reduce ambiguity and complexity in texts and it does this by limiting the ways in which information can be expressed. Some controlled languages, such as *ASD Simplified Technical English* (2005), are known as Human-Oriented Controlled Languages (HOCL) because they are used to improve readability and comprehensibility for human readers. Other controlled languages, such as *Attempto Controlled English* and *Processable English* (PENG) are known as Machine-Oriented Controlled Languages (MOCL) and they are used to make texts easier to process by computers, for example using machine translation systems (O'Brien 2003).

Sometimes, CL rules can be enforced using computerized style checkers which prevent writers (or translators) from using unauthorized grammatical constructions and vocabulary, and suggest suitable alternatives. While a source text written using a CL may actually be easier for us to understand and translate, if we are required to translate into a CL, we may find ourselves having to completely recast sentences using a limited range of grammatical and lexical options so that they conform to the rules of the CL.

Many companies and organizations seek to standardize the language used in their documents by means of style guides. A style guide is a set of standards, or guidelines, which govern the way in which documents are written and presented.

They are less strict than controlled languages and their aim is to provide a clear set of guidelines for writers to help them produce documents which are consistent and which are easy to understand; style guides are often used to help writers produce texts which are comprehensible for non-native speakers of a language. In addition to specifying such things as which grammatical constructions should be used or how sentences should be structured, style guides may specify preferred terminology as well as rules on using punctuation.

Although many companies will only have style guides governing one language, i.e. the source language, many others will produce style guides for translators. Sometimes, in-house translators themselves may be called on to produce style guides for other translators. Even where there is no style guide for the target language, the source language style guide may also provide useful information on issues such as the correct use of product names etc. The effect of such a resource for translators is that our initial choice for translating a sentence may have to be modified to take into account the style guide's rules on whether or not to use the future tense, whether or not to use direct speech or whether to use one term over another.

---

passive voice Whenever possible, don't use; use active voice. Passive voice is sometimes appropriate and necessary – when using the active voice would require highly convoluted sentence structure or excessive anthropomorphism, for example – but rewrite to avoid passive voice if you can.

In tutorials, a passive construction might be appropriate to avoid miscuing the reader – that is, when you describe an action that the user is not supposed to try yet.

> *Explanation screen*: An icon is selected by clicking it.
> *User-try screen*: You try it. Click the icon.

Figure 11: Example of a style rule from the Apple Publications Style Guide
(Apple 2003:103)

Other style rules might specify how you should address the reader, how to phrase headings or how to refer to products. The following examples are paraphrased from the *Microsoft Manual of Style for Technical Publications* (1998):

- Use second person to address the user directly.
- Do not use possessive form of product names.
- Use present tense.
- Use positive constructions where possible.
- Use consistent terminology.
- Use gerunds in headings and not infinitive verb forms.
- Avoid anthropomorphism.

5.4.1   *Terminology*

Selecting the most appropriate term can sometimes depend on more than just good research skills.

Despite its rather daunting appearance, terminology is generally the least problematic part of a technical translation *provided* you have access to the Internet and, in certain cases, to good dictionaries. However, there will be times when terminology can cause problems for you and these are often the result of factors outside the text and quite separate to what individual terms actually mean. In short, it is people who make terminology problematic.

Many large companies also have their own preferred terminology, which they insist be used in all of their corporate documents. The rules governing the use of this terminology are often incorporated into a larger style guide but they can sometimes be produced as stand-alone documents. Terminology rules might specify certain collocations so that you can *cancel* a process but not *abort* it, or *run* a program but not *execute* it. These are quite obvious examples because of the connotations associated with the "prohibited" words but other rules might be in place simply to avoid unnecessary variation in a text.

In practice, what style guides and preferred terminology mean for you as a translator is that what you might think is the most appropriate or logical way of translating a sentence or a term in the ST is not necessarily what you are expected to use. So even though some rules might even appear to be counterintuitive, odd or overly simplistic, it is part of your job as someone who provides a service to a client to accommodate wherever possible the client's wishes. It is important that you are notified of any terminological or stylistic preferences at the start of a job. It is also essential that you are given the right resources – a client cannot reasonably complain when you submit a translation which does not use their terminology if they have not given you clear instructions or the necessary resources such as style guides or glossaries.

As a general rule, however, it is always advisable to check a customer's website to get a feel for how they write their documents, even if they do not have any specific language requirements. This helps you create a text with the "look and feel" of one of the client's own documents and it will go a long way to increasing the client's satisfaction with your work.

Remember, even technical terminology can be culture-specific
You would be justified in assuming that technical terminology will be quite standard, perhaps even universal, between the different languages, but this would be a mistake (see Wilmsen & Youssef 2009, for example). Different cultures approach concepts from different angles and use different types of language to describe them. For example, what one language refers to as a "planetary gear" might be called a "sun gear" in another. If you are not absolutely certain what the target language equivalent of a term is, do your research to find an equivalent – do not be tempted to translate the individual components of a term unless there is absolutely no legitimate alternative and it is a new word.

5.4.2   *Clarity, readability and usability*
Making sure that your audience can read and understand your translations easily.

Even though it has been said several times already, it is worth restating that the primary purpose of technical texts is to communicate information clearly. In the case of translations this means that, in addition to ensuring that we produce texts which are factually accurate, we must also produce texts which the intended audience will find easy to read.

The clarity and comprehensibility of texts has traditionally been assessed by measuring their readability using methods such as the *Flesch Readability* test, the *Lensear Write Formula*, the *Fog Index* or *Fry's Readability Graph*. Many of these methods involve analysing a sample of text on the basis of factors such as the total word count, average sentence length or number of "hard" or polysyllabic words. In many versions of Microsoft Word, the spellchecker also allows you to measure the readability of texts using the *Flesch Reading Ease* test or the *Flesch-Kincaid Reading Level* test. The former measures readability on a scale from 0 to 100, with a higher score indicating a more readable text. The latter takes the 0-100 score from the Flesch Reading Ease test and maps it onto a US school grade level or a general indication of the number of years of education needed in order to understand a text. So for example, a score of 8 means that the text can be read by an average 8th grade student so the lower this number, the easier the text is to read.

As a general rule, you can make texts more readable by keeping sentences as short as possible and by using simple sentence structures and words. But while readability is a useful measure of the general accessibility of a text, it does not provide a complete picture of how comprehensible and effective a text is. In recent years, the emphasis in technical communication circles has shifted towards **usability** because a readable text is not necessarily a good text and such a text may not necessarily help readers or fulfil the text's intended function.

In the context of documents, usability can be regarded as a measure of how well a given reader can read a text, understand it and perform the required task or remember the required information effectively and efficiently, and of how satisfied or stressed the reader is afterwards. What this means is that a text must provide readers with the right type of information, in the right proportions, at the right time and in the right format. The text should be easy to understand and should either allow readers to do something, help them avoid making mistakes or help them to remember particular information. Finally, the process of reading the text should not be unduly taxing or stressful on the reader. Unfortunately, measuring usability, particularly that of texts, is a complex task and certainly not something a translator can do but there are, however, a number of strategies which can make texts more usable.

- *Use terminology consistently and avoid polysemy*: Do not confuse readers by using different terms to refer to the same thing or concept.
- *Use clear and simple language*: The reader's attention should be on *what* you are saying, not *how* you are saying it, so avoid the urge to write like Shakespeare.

- *Write instructions in chronological order*: Many users will perform actions as they read the instructions, so make sure that you put each step in the order in which it needs to be performed.
- *Use direct, active language*: Passive sentences can be unnecessarily vague and lengthy; Speak directly to the user to avoid confusion.
- *Do not provide unnecessary information*: In instructions for example, readers are only interested in performing a task, so they do not need lots of unnecessary detail; avoid overusing explicitation as a translation strategy.
- *Implement Iconic Linkage*: Wherever possible, use the same wording to convey the same information (see *Iconic Linkage on* page 130).
- *Keep the number of tenses to a minimum*: Avoid overusing some of the more complex tenses. In many cases you can survive with just the simplest of tenses.

Practical Exercise 24: Following rules
To get a feel for writing using restricted style guides and terminology, try this short task. Write a description of how to brush your teeth without using the words "mouth" or "toothbrush" and without referring to the reader directly. Instead of saying "toothpaste", you will need to say "paste-based cleaning agent". Your description should be no more than 100 words in length.

Practical Exercise 25: Testing the readability of texts
While readability cannot give us a completely reliable evaluation the quality of a text, it can give us a general insight into the effect of style on the text and the relative ease with which it can be read. There are a variety of readability tests, most of which are designed to work only with specific languages. The Flesch, Lensear and Fry methods mentioned above, for example, are intended to be used on texts written in English, but other tests are available for languages such as French (*Kandel & Moles*), Spanish (*Fernandez-Huerta*), Dutch (*Douma*), Swedish, Danish and Norwegian (*LIX*). A quick online search for "online readability calculator" will help you to find several online tools which you can experiment with.

When testing texts written in English you can use Microsoft Word to test the readability of texts and identify which sections of the texts are affecting the readability score. This function can usually be found in the *Spelling & Grammar Options* dialog but for more information on displaying document's readability statistics, use the help menu in Microsoft Word.

Once you have a figure for a text's readability, try editing the text to produce a change in the readability score. Which strategies or changes produced the most significant result?

5.4.3 Editing and proof-reading
Making final quality checks and improvements before you submit your translation.

A golden rule of any type of translation is never return a translation without first running a spellchecker and reading through the text one last time to spot and fix any errors. It is important that you read the text as well as use the spellchecker because a spellchecker will only find words which are spelled incorrectly, not words which are spelled correctly but which are the wrong words. Your spellchecker will not see a problem with the phrase "wit hall" even though you meant to write "with all".

5.4.3.1 REVIEWING THE WORK OF ANOTHER TRANSLATOR

Often, particularly on important or high-profile projects, translation agencies and customers may recruit one translator to translate a text and another to revise the translation. Usually such texts are destined for publication or some other purpose where the very highest standards are needed. From time to time, you may be asked to edit the work of a less experienced translator and provide feedback. This is what Louise Brunette (2000) calls "didactic revision". In such cases, you may also be required to fill out a report or evaluation form but more about that in a moment.

When editing another translator's work the main thing to remember is that you are being asked to look for and fix errors in the translation, not rewrite the translation so that it looks like one of your translations. The objective is to make sure that all of the information has been translated correctly and accurately, that the correct terminology has been used consistently, that the style of language is appropriate for the text type and audience and that various other factors such as spelling, orthography and punctuation are all correct. You should not replace something which is correct simply because you prefer a different phrasing or term.

Providing feedback on translations can be a challenging and time-consuming activity. Not only do you have to find errors and fix them, but you also have to provide suggestions to help the translator avoid making the same mistakes and give an overall evaluation for the client. It is important that you remain objective and simply state the facts. Remember that a real person will read your comments so they need to be useful, constructive and tactful. You should also remember that some agencies will try to include the feedback as part of your standard fee for editing even though writing the report can take longer to do than it did to edit the translation. Make sure you charge for all of the work you do, not just the editing, and agree on a rough estimate in advance.

> **Practical Exercise 26: Editing texts**
> Practice editing your translations (or those of a friend) using the *Track Changes* and *Insert Comments* functions in Microsoft Word. Make sure you turn on Track Changes before you start.

5.4.3.2 General hints for editing and reviewing translations

- *Provide two copies of the edited translation*: Start by editing the translation with Track Changes turned on. This way it is clear what changes you have made and you can add comments if necessary. This can be sent to the translator for information. When you have finished, save a copy of the edited translation without the tracking and comments. This is the file that can be sent to the client for publication.
- *Distance yourself from your translation*: Even if you are pressed for time, always step away from the translation for a while before you start editing and proofing. Have a cup of tea, walk around the block or watch some TV, anything to help you approach the translation with fresh eyes.
- *Don't be bitter*: Some translators may be annoyed that they were not asked to translate the text in the first place and will try to find as many problems in the translation as possible in the hope that the client will pick them for the next project. This is not fair and the client will probably see what you are trying to do, so don't do it.
- *Be constructive*: If you change something, add a brief comment explaining why you've changed it as it will help the original translator avoid making the same mistake again. It will also show that your changes are justified. Avoid the temptation to be sarcastic or unkind in your feedback – your job does not involve character assassination.
- *Don't be a bully*: You should not use proof-reading as an opportunity to impose your style on a text. If the translation is accurate and stylistically correct, do not propose changes just because you prefer a different wording. Changes have to be a genuine improvement, not just a matter of personal preferences.

Translator beware!
If you seem to be getting a lot of poor quality translations to edit, and it often takes as long - if not longer – to edit as it would to translate, it is possible that a translation agency is trying to save money by paying a less skilled translator a fraction of the normal industry rate to translate a text knowing that you will fix it. Instead of paying you your full translation rate, the agency saves money by paying you for a couple of hours' worth of work. If you think this is happening and you are unhappy about it, just start turning down this type of job for a while.

5.5   When in doubt

What to do when the text contains something you cannot fix, do not understand or where you need the client to make a decision.

When working as a professional translator you will invariably find yourself in situations where the text you are translating contains something which confuses you. This may be a spelling mistake, missing or illegible information, confusing phrasing or an apparent factual mistake. There may also be cases where a particular word or sentence can be translated in a number of ways depending on the context or the intended use of the translation. A lot of the time, you can use your experience, subject knowledge and research skills to resolve these issues but there will be occasions when you simply cannot and you will need to ask for help from the client.

If you are an in-house translator, you will more than likely have access to the original author and a quick phone call or email will generally produce the necessary information. If, on the other hand, you are working as a freelance translator you will probably receive a lot of your work from agencies, who act as intermediaries between you and the actual client. This means that your questions will pass through an additional stage in the communication process. As a result, any questions you have will need to be as clear as possible and they must be submitted in the correct format.

As students, we are often asked to produce annotated translations where we comment on the strategies we used in producing the translation. This will often involve using footnotes to clarify interesting or unclear features of the text and to explain what was going through our heads when we translated something. While this can be useful as a learning aid, it is very bad practice for a professional translator. In fact, using footnotes is quite often the worst thing you can do in a translation. The reason for this is that you have no guarantees that the translation will be reviewed before being sent to the client or before being published.

Always bear in mind that project managers in translation agencies do not always speak your working languages and even if they do, they will not always have the time to read through your translation, so your footnotes may go unnoticed until the translation is published and sent out to the target audience. The footnotes, in addition to demonstrating your confusion and potentially undermining your credibility as a translator, deface the text and, if they are not noticed by the agency or client, may be seen by the end reader who will be confused and possibly irritated at the poor standards of text production. In some cases, the format of the file you are translating simply will not allow you to add footnotes so the problem will not arise.

Instead, you should keep a record of your queries as you go along and, depending on the nature of your query, either send them to the client when you submit your final translation or, in the case of more serious queries, email them to the client as you are working. You should include the page number and the source sentence or word so that the client or project manager can identify the part of the text you are talking about. Make sure you phrase your questions as clearly and as concisely as possible.

If you have only one or two queries, you can simply include them in the cover email when you return your translation but remember to give specific details of what you are talking about. If you have several queries, you can use a simple word processor document or a spreadsheet to keep a record of these queries. Even if you do compile your queries into a separate document, it is a good idea to refer to them specifically in the cover email so that a busy project manager does not miss your queries. You can, if you like and if it is possible, highlight the sections of the translation to which the query relates but always mention it in the email.

> **Practical Exercise 27: Evaluating translations**
> Practice evaluating the quality of translations. Working with a friend or colleague, use the list of criteria presented in Figure 12 (or create your own list of criteria) to test each other's translations. You need to agree on what you think is an acceptable pass mark for a translation before you start work. You can also add more flexibility to the criteria by allowing errors of different severity to be weighted differently. It is also worth discussing whether there are any situations where a less than perfect translation might be acceptable and how it would be dealt with, for instance in the case of test translations.

In Chapter 6, we will build on these general strategies and look at specific challenges which arise when we translate scientific and technical texts.

Category of Error	Minor (x1)	Major (x2)	Critical (x5)	Total
Accuracy				
Unjustified omissions				
Unjustified additions				
Distortion of meaning				
Mistranslation				
Terminology				
Appropriate, e.g. usage, collocations				
Consistent				
Accurate				
Style				
Register and tone				
Fluency and coherence				
SL interference				
Appropriate for text function				

Country Standards				
Date and time				
Measurements and currency				
Local references, e.g. telephone numbers, names				
Formatting				
Tables of contents, cross-references				
Headers and footers				
Language settings				
Typography				
Formatting retained				
Client-Specific Requirements				
Adherence to style guide				
Use of preferred terminology				
Product names and company references				
Comments				

Figure 12: Sample assessment criteria for evaluating texts

Suggested Reading

Baker, Mona (1992) *In Other Words: Coursebook on Translation*, London: Routledge.

Brunette, Louise (2000) Toward a Terminology for Translation Quality Assessment, *Evaluation and Translation*, Special Issue of *The Translator*, 6(2): 169-182.

Crabbe, Stephen (2010). Controlled Languages for Technical Writing and Translation. In I. Kemble (ed.), *The Changing Face of Translation: Proceedings of the Ninth Annual Portsmouth Translation Conference*, Portsmouth: University of Portsmouth, 48-62.

Harvey, Keith (2001) Compensation. In Mona Baker & Gabriela Saldanha (eds) *Routledge Encyclopedia of Translation Studies*, London: Routledge, 47-51.

Mossop, Brian (2007) *Revising and Editing for Translators*, Manchester: St. Jerome, 2nd edition.

6. Pitfalls, Problems and How to Deal with Them

In this chapter

This chapter builds on the general approaches outlined in the previous chapter to examine specific features, challenges and problems which arise in technical documentation. These will include areas such as terminology, language constraints and register, as well as practical issues such as knowing when to contact the client, what to do with confusing or inaccurate source texts, and even how to manage your files in a translation project. By the end of this chapter, you should be able to identify the main features of technical documentation and then select an appropriate strategy in order to produce an effective translation.

6.1 Introduction

While a good awareness of some basic translation approaches and strategies can allow us to tackle texts with some kind of purpose, there will inevitably be scenarios where we need specific strategies. One of the most interesting aspects of translation is that there will always be cases like this, which cannot be neatly dealt with using a general translation strategy. There will always be a word, a sentence or even an entire text, which poses problems that depend on the text, the context, the subject, the client, the target audience or any number of other factors. In the following sections, we will look at some of the typical features, problems and potential pitfalls presented by technical documentation and examine some sample strategies which can help you to deal with them.

6.2 Abbreviations and acronyms

Alongside specialized terminology and numbers, acronyms and abbreviations are among the most attention-grabbing and potentially intimidating aspects of a technical text for translators. The primary motivation for using acronyms and abbreviations is brevity and to avoid repeated use of the same words. Abbreviations and acronyms are very useful in many cases but they can pose problems for readers and translators alike, depending on their nature and the context in which they are used. We can group abbreviations and acronyms into a number of categories:

- International Organizations, such as *NATO* (North Atlantic Treaty Organization), *EU* (European Union), *WHO* (World Health Organization)
- National Organization, *ICTU* (Irish Congress of Trade Unions), **BSI** (British Standards Institution),
- Name of Companies, such as *ICI* (Imperial Chemical Industries), *RENFE*

(Red Nacional de los Ferrocarriles Españoles), *AIB* (Allied Irish Bank)
- Technical Entities, such as *GMT* (Greenwich Mean Time), *GP* (General Practitioner), *Laser* (Light Amplification by Stimulated Emission of Radiation)
- Geographical Locations, such as *USA* (United States of America), *UAE* (United Arab Emirates),
- Latin, such as *q.e.d.* (quod erat demonstrandum), *i.e.* (id est)
- Ad-hoc or specially coined acronyms, usually only used in a particular context or document and for a finite period of time.

The way in which they are dealt with is determined by various contextual factors such as the text type and age, readership, importance, the lifespan of the acronym and how well known they are.

In the case of acronyms relating to international organizations and, in certain notable cases, national organizations, either they will remain the same regardless of the language or there will be accepted equivalents in different languages. Acronyms which form part of company names, like company names themselves, should never be translated, as they are likely to be part of the legal identity of the company. However, ad-hoc acronyms or acronyms which are used in documents solely to avoid unnecessary repetition can either be reconstituted in the target language or retained.

Some acronyms and abbreviations are not unique and they can be used in other disciplines with different meanings attached to them; some are even shared within the same general area. For example, *GP* can mean *General Practitioner*, *General Psychiatrist* or *Glycerate Phosphate*, so you need to study the context carefully. A useful way of finding more information on an acronym is to type it into a search engine along with one or two keywords from the source text to narrow down the search to what you hope will be the correct subject area.

If a specialized acronym appears in a general text, it does not always need to be transferred intact – a translation and definition will generally work quite well. However, if the acronym appears in a specialized text, transfer and possibly definition are most appropriate courses of action.

Some languages, such as Pashto, do not use acronyms and this means that acronyms cannot be translated or recreated in the target language. In such cases, the complete English acronym has to be written in its original English letters followed by a TL description of the full name, where there is sufficient space:

- RAM " یاد لوستنی-خواڅو ".

Strategies

Naturally, the first and most appropriate strategy is to check the Internet to see if there is an existing authoritative translation. If you find one, use it. If not, you can do one of the following:

- *Transfer*: If the acronym is sufficiently well known you can retain the original SL acronym in the target text
- *Reconstitute*: Translate the full name into the TL and use this as the basis for creating an acronym in the TL. This strategy is more suited to non-specialized acronyms, general texts or ad-hoc acronyms
- *Define*: If there is no way of transcribing or reconstituting the SL acronym, if it is not possible to reconstitute the acronym or where it makes more sense in the text to explain the acronym, you can replace the acronym with a definition. This is quite a useful method for rendering Latin abbreviations and acronyms into language where Latin is not used or is unknown.
- *Combine*: A combination of the transfer and definition strategies. This will usually only need to be done once in a text when the acronym is first used; afterwards, the SL acronym can be used on its own.
- *Write out SL*: A much less common approach which involves replacing an acronym with its full name in the SL. This approach would be appropriate in higher level texts where the target audience is familiar with or interested in the source culture and language.
- *Translate*: If an official or widely used translation of the full name exists and there is a corresponding acronym, they can be used instead of the SL acronym.

Practical Exercise 28: Identifying organizations
Compile a list with the names of 20 international and national organizations. Now find out what these organizations are called in different languages and whether there are any acronyms or abbreviations associated with them.

6.3   Formulae and Equations

Thankfully, in the vast majority of cases, any equations which appear in a text do not need to be modified by the translator; they are simply left untouched. It is useful to know, however, that equations can be presented in a number of different ways. This will assist us in recognizing information which is presented in a different form and help us understand the text.

One of the things that make algebra so powerful and useful for scientific and technical work is the ability to "rearrange" formulae so that another variable is the subject. At the same time, this ability can make formulae potentially more confusing for the unsuspecting translator. A practical example would be using the formula for calculating the volume of a box ($V = wdh$) to calculate the width of the box provided we know the volume, depth and height of the box. This would be done as follows:

- V = wdh
  where: V = volume, w = width, d = depth, h = height
- divide both sides by d: V / d = wh
- divide both sides by h: V / dh = w
- swap sides: w = V / dh

Although it is safe to say that a translator would never have to do this, knowing how equations can be manipulated can make texts a little easier to follow.

Equations are often included in texts as images and this means that even if we wanted to edit them, we would not be able to without using graphics editing software. Equations can also be inserted using special characters in word processors (such as those found in Microsoft Word), using ASCII codes or using tools such as Microsoft Equation Editor. For this reason, it is a good idea to learn how to insert these characters on your own computer and using your own software in the event that a sentence contains one of the symbols contained in the equation. This is also important if you are given a hardcopy of the source text instead of an electronic version.

Strategies

- Usually equations do not need to be modified in a translation and so they can be copied and pasted.
- Be careful with texts where the symbols for individual variables are used within ordinary paragraph text. It is easy to confuse symbols which look similar - for example ß and β or u and μ - so take care if you are trying to insert them yourself. A useful way around this is to copy and paste the symbol from elsewhere in the text or, if you can find one, from a parallel text on the Internet.
- If you cannot tell what a particular symbol is, try changing the font. For example, "l" and "I" look identical because of the font used but if you change the font, you can see that they are actually "l" and "I".

6.4   Quantities and units of measure

The issue of measurements and quantities can be problematic for translators. On the one hand, if your target audience only uses metric units, they may be baffled by measurements given in ounces, gallons or miles and the effectiveness of the text may be hampered somewhat. On the other hand, if precise quantities are required, converting them from one system to another can be incredibly problematic, not to mention costly or even dangerous because you do not know how precise you need to be when rounding off numbers; in some cases, such as chemistry, there can be a significant difference between 1.06 mg and 1.1 mg.

What's the point?
Remember that different languages have different conventions for formatting numbers. While this might seem rather obvious, a surprising number of translators forget this simple fact, and end up confusing their readers.

The most important thing to remember is that the symbol used to separate decimals is not the same everywhere and that decimal points may need to be replaced with commas, and vice versa. In an English text, for example, **1.495 kg** is just under *one and a half kilograms* while in a Spanish text it is *one thousand four hundred and ninety five kilograms*. While translating a document which explains how much chlorine to add to a swimming pool, remembering to replace the decimal point with a comma can mean the difference between a pool of clean water or dozens of angry swimmers complaining of minor skin burns and irritation of the eyes and nose.

The way in which numbers are grouped can also vary from language to language. Some languages group numbers using commas (10,000,000) while others use decimal points (10.000.000) and others use a space (10 000 000).

Confusing units of measure

Even in cases where we do not need to convert quantities, the units of measure used within a particular system of measurements can still give us cause for concern. In the *International System of Units* (sometimes referred to as the *SI system*), there are seven base units of measure from which all other units are derived.

Base Units			
Name	*Unit symbol*	*Quantity*	Symbol for Quantity
Metre	m	length	l
Kilogram	kg	mass	m
Second	s	time	t
Ampere	A	electric current	I
Kelvin	K	thermodynamic temperature	T
Candela	cd	luminous intensity	Iv
Mole	mol	amount of substance	n

Table 2: SI system base units

Additional units may be derived from these base units by using prefixes, which indicate either multiples of the base unit, e.g. a *kilo*metre, which is 1000 metres, or divisions of a base unit, e.g. a *milli*second, which is one thousandth of a second. The confusion can arise because of a lack of familiarity with the meanings of the different prefixes, because of similar-sounding prefixes such as *deci-* and *deca-* or, because the symbols used to indicate prefixes, e.g. ***µ*** (the Greek letter *mu* which stands for *micro-*) can be confused with other symbols, e.g. the letter ***u***.

Standard prefixes for the SI units of measure											
Multiples	Name	*deca-*	*hecto-*	*kilo-*	*mega-*	*giga-*	*tera-*	*peta-*	*exa-*	*zetta-*	*yotta-*
	Symbol	da	h	k	M	G	T	P	E	Z	Y
	Factor	10^{1}	10^{2}	10^{3}	10^{6}	10^{9}	10^{12}	10^{15}	10^{18}	10^{21}	10^{24}
Subdivisions	Name	*deci-*	*centi-*	*milli-*	*micro-*	*nano-*	*pico-*	*femto-*	*atto-*	*zepto-*	*yocto-*
	Symbol	d	c	m	µ	n	p	f	a	z	Y
	Factor	10^{-1}	10^{-2}	10^{-3}	10^{-6}	10^{-9}	10^{-12}	10^{-15}	10^{-18}	10^{-21}	10^{-24}

Table 3: Prefixes for SI units

Even units have false friends

Unfortunately, confusion can also arise from units of measure which look similar and which may even be used within the same field but which are quite different. Some examples include *pound* (lb) and *foot pound* (lbf) as well as *kilobyte* (KB or kB) and *kilobit* (kb). Interestingly, *kilo-* in computing contexts rarely means 1000, but rather 1024, a practice which has existed for so long that few people remember why. Some people use the prefix *kilobi-* instead of *kilo-* to give *kilobibyte* but this does not seem to be very a common phenomenon.

Strategies

The most common strategy for dealing with units of measure is to leave them alone, particularly if they are SI quantities. Even though in certain types of text retaining units may present some problems for readers in terms of immediate comprehensibility, it ensures accuracy and prevents the possibility of translator-induced error. This approach is especially valid if you are translating a text for a specialist audience who will, more than likely, be familiar with different units of measure or have the mathematical skills to convert the quantities if necessary. Other strategies for dealing with quantities include:

- *Convert the quantities*: You can do this if the exact quantity is irrelevant or incidental to the text, or if you are translating a text for a non-specialist audience, where quantities are simply presented for general information purposes. Converting can be highly risky and should be done after consultation with the client. To make matters even more confusing, certain languages can convert some units but not others.
- *Use a combination*: If the readers' comprehension of the text will be impaired by the lack of converted quantities, you can provide the original quantity followed by a clearly indicated approximate equivalent in brackets.
- *Check the units*: As obvious as this may seem, double-checking the units used in a text can help you find the correct symbol, learn a little more about the science and technology involved, and possibly identify any errors in the text.
- *Check the spelling*: Many units of measure are eponyms, meaning that they are named after a significant scientific figure. Examples include Kelvin, Celsius, Coulomb, Hertz and Ohm (see Appendix 2 for other examples). It is important to ensure that they are spelled and capitalized correctly according to your target language's norms, particularly as many spellcheckers will not detect spelling mistakes.
- *Use proper punctuation*: Under normal circumstances, you should put a space **between** the number and the unit. For example, write "*40 mg*" not "*40mg*". Ideally this should be a non-breaking space to stop them being separated. One peculiar exception seems to be temperatures, such as *25°C,* which only rarely seem to be written with a space. However, if a client has a preference for some other form of punctuation, you need to use that instead.
- *Watch out for similar-looking units*: Unfortunately, confusion can also arise from other, non-SI units of measure which look similar but which are quite different. For example, a sign on a UK roadside will say *8 m*, which means 100 *miles*, not 100 *metres*.

6.5   Currencies

There are a number of potential issues relating to currencies which can cause problems for translators. As was the case with quantities, the question of whether to convert amounts given in a particular currency arises with the obvious problems of accuracy and precision as well as fluctuating exchange rates. A general rule of thumb is that if the precise figure is unimportant and converting the quantity will aid the target audience's overall comprehension of the text, you can, if you wish, convert the quantities. If the precise amount *is* important, then leave it unchanged but include, if appropriate, an approximate equivalent in brackets to aid reader comprehension.

We also have the issue of how to write the currency. The Euro is a classic example of how a currency designed to introduce consistency and uniformity across a continent has resisted attempts at standardization – this is evidenced in the way it is referred to and the way in which the Euro symbol is placed in amounts:

- euro vs. euros
- €40.00 vs. 40€00 vs. 40.00€

You should also bear in mind the question of whether to name a currency specifically or simply use its symbol. Remember that not all currencies have their own unique and widely-recognized symbol. For example, several currencies use the $ symbol, which to many people is more commonly associated with the US Dollar.

Strategies

As is the case with quantities and units of measure, the most common strategy is to leave amounts in their original currency. This is particularly true in cases where the target audience is likely to have some idea of the value of the foreign currency relative to their own. However, in the case of less commonly known currencies, the following strategies can be useful:

- *Convert the currencies*: You can do this if the exact amount is irrelevant or incidental to the text, or if you are translating a text for a non-specialist audience where amounts are simply presented for general information purposes. This strategy can be highly risky and should be done after consultation with the client
- *Use a combination*: If the readers' comprehension of the text will be impaired by the lack of converted currencies, you can provide the original currency followed by a clearly indicated approximate equivalent in brackets.
- *Check the client's preferences:* The location of currency symbols will often be described in a client's style guide, if one exists. If there is none, look at the client's website to see how they deal with symbols.

6.6   Culture and Familiarity

Different languages and different target audiences may have different expectations as to how familiar or formal they want their texts to be. While technical documentation is not typically associated with "personality", there can be quite a difference, for example, in how it addresses the reader. For example, is the formal form or the informal form used? Alternatively, is a combination of both used?

You or the user?

Even though directly addressing the reader is widely regarded as the clearest and most effective way of conveying information, particularly in instructional texts, not all languages appreciate this level of informality. Conversely, texts arriving from cultures where formality is the order of the day may not find favour with a target audience which prefers direct, clear and relatively informal communication. In general, however, unless your target audience has a very strong aversion to direct address, it is almost always better to say "you" rather than "the user" as it is clearer and creates less room for misunderstandings.

Humour

When translating technical documentation, particularly texts aimed at end users, always remember that humour does not travel. Technical texts should not contain humour, jokes or anything "silly". This is one of the golden rules of technical communication which some misguided writers will, unfortunately, forget. It is highly unlikely that your target audience will appreciate humour in an instruction manual, a scientific paper or tender, so you should work on the assumption that any jokes will not make it across to your target text. If you feel uncertain about removing jokes, mention it to the client when you return the translation and explain that it is not appropriate in the target language and probably would not be funny anyway.

 Exceptions to the humour rule
There are, of course, exceptions to every rule and sometimes humour will play a valid and justifiable role in texts such as popular science articles or, less frequently, reviews in trade journals, technical journalism etc. Again, work on the assumption that the joke in the SL probably will not be funny in the TL so be prepared to adapt, modify, replace, delete or move jokes to another point in the text to make them work.

Congratulations

A rather strange feature of some instruction manuals for domestic appliances and consumer goods is the tendency to congratulate the user for purchasing the product. While this may be appropriate in some cultures, others cultures may regard such content as insincere flattery which is both irritating and patronizing. You should exercise common sense when dealing with congratulations; you know what is appropriate for your target audience.

Strategies

- Wherever possible, use direct forms of address in user-orientated texts, unless there is a very strong reason not to.
- Unless there is a compelling reason for keeping it, humour should be gently written out of texts.

- If you do need to retain humour, make sure it is appropriate for the audience, subject and text type. If you would not repeat the joke in front of your parents, it probably does not belong in a technical text. Remember too that in texts such as popular science publications, a joke may be there for a reason, i.e. to illustrate a concept or demonstrate a scenario, so your rendering of it should also fulfil this function. If you cannot fulfil this function using humour, use some other non-humorous means.
- Avoid being overly familiar. Translating into a target language which favours "you" instead of "the user" does not give you free rein to be overly familiar, to use slang or treat the reader as your friend. This is still technical documentation after all.
- Remember that different languages may approach and describe the same concepts from completely different angles so do not let the particular phrasing of a term or description overly influence your translation.

6.7   Errors in the Source Text

Hans Hönig once said "lebende Texte sind defekte Texte" (1998:162), or *living texts are faulty texts*, and this nicely prepares us for the fact that source texts can often contain errors. The errors which can occur in texts range from the simple spelling mistake to more serious and fundamental factual mistakes. The way in which these errors are dealt with depends as much on the translator as it does on the error itself.

A key consideration in deciding how to tackle these errors is the question of whether the errors need to be corrected or whether they should be preserved. This essentially boils down to whether we are producing an *instrumental* translation or a *documentary* translation. The real problems arise with regard to subject-related errors where, depending on our knowledge of the topic, we may not even recognize errors, let alone be in a position to correct them. In Germany, for example, the standard DIN 2345 published by the German Institute for Standardization provides some relief for translators because it relieves us of the responsibility for errors in the source text, saying instead that the client is responsible for resolving errors and for answering questions from translators.

If a translator spots what looks like an error in the source text, the translator should notify the client. Hopefully, similar provisions will make their way into law on a wider scale in the not too distant future. Depending on the specific text, how long it is, the subject and the deadline, you may decide to raise questions with the client as you go along.

This is particularly true with large projects or projects involving several translators where you may have to stop translating until you get an answer or if the answers will affect how you translate the rest of the text. Alternatively, you might decide to keep a list of such queries and include them in an email when you return the finished translation to the client. Whether or not you choose to send questions individually or all at once may depend on the client's preferences; they will let you know quickly enough which option they prefer.

Strategies

- **Instrumental or documentary?** Find out from the client what the intended purpose of the translation is. You may need to be persistent and possibly explain what your concerns are but in any case you need to find out whether your client needs an instrumental or a documentary translation. Generally, a translation for publication purposes will be instrumental so this helps in some cases, although the converse is not true; information purposes texts cannot be assumed to be documentary translations. If it is instrumental, fix the errors wherever you can. If it is a documentary translation, preserve the errors and translate as faithfully as you can. Bear in mind, however, that your client will most likely not understand the difference between an instrumental and a documentary translation so you should be ready to explain these terms in simple language.
- **Linguistic errors**: Simple linguistic errors such as misspelled words, incorrect punctuation and certain forms of unclear or awkward language use can be corrected quietly and without any fuss. More serious linguistic errors where the intended meaning is completely incomprehensible should be referred back to the client for clarification.
- **Factual or subject errors**: This is the trickiest category of error and detecting them depends on your own knowledge of the subject area. Minor factual errors such as a text saying, for example, that distance is measured in kilograms, can be corrected although it is usually advisable to at least notify the client that you have done this.
- **Fix definite errors**: If you spot a serious error and you are absolutely sure it is an error and you are certain that you can fix it, you should still contact the client and ask for clarification.

6.8   Sample text and computer code

When translating texts which document software – particularly texts aimed at advanced users such as programmers or system administrators – it is to be expected that they will contain frequent examples of program code to help explain concepts, features or techniques. As translators, we are not expected to be programmers but we are expected to be able to recognize code and know how to deal with it in a translation. Similarly, technical translators are often called upon to work on localization projects where they will be responsible for translating text which is displayed on-screen in a piece of software or a website. The main challenges for translators when dealing with program code are as follows:

- **Recognizing the code**: This is particularly relevant for translators working out of English because most programming languages are based on the English language. This means that commands and arguments, which are solely intended for the computer, often resemble ordinary English words, for example *verbose, print, return, getName, IF, FOR, WHILE.*

- **Working around the code**: Fragments of code may be included as part of a standard sentence and they may place restrictions on the way in which the remainder of the sentence can be translated.

Recognizing computer code can be problematic, especially if you are translating from English, because it can look a lot like ordinary English text and it is easy to mistake it for translatable text. However, there are certain clues which can help you to identify it. Words which are written exclusively in uppercase are often non-translatable pieces of code and in most cases should not be modified. Similarly, phrases consisting of several words which are written together without spaces or which are linked with underscores will probably be non-translatable. For example, fragments of text such as MENUITEM *or* Style_Caption are object identifiers used by software and should be left unchanged.

While the use of case and punctuation is usually a good indication of non-translatable text, there are cases where, even though text contains unusual punctuation, it still needs to be translated. In software localization projects, the strings of text which appear in menus, for example, regularly contain ampersand symbols (&) to indicate *hotkeys* – those underlined letters in menu items which are used to speed up access to functions by allowing users to use keyboard shortcuts.

Figure 13 shows a typical menu bar with various letters underlined. In the program code, *View* would be represented as &View while *Format* would be represented as F&ormat. It is important, therefore, that the ampersands are not deleted, that you pay attention to their placement in the word and that you do not add a space immediately after them. For more information on localizing software and in particular on how to deal with hot keys, including the need to ensure they are unique, see Esselink (2000).

Figure 13: Menu bar from a software interface with hotkeys underlined

An important feature of programming languages is their ability to use variables as a way of creating a placeholder for information in a section of code, which will be replaced with other information at a later time. Variables can usually be identified because they are preceded by the $ or % symbols. In the sentence "Your search returned $d results" the variable *$d* is replaced with a number when a search is carried out. This eliminates the need to create a sentence for every possible number of results, e.g. "Your search returned 2 results", "Your search returned 3 results", "Your search returned 4 results" and so on. Other examples of strings with variables might include:

- "Are you sure you want to delete %1?"
  which will be displayed as
  "Are you sure you want to delete PRESENTATION.DOC?", or
- "Transfer %d%% complete"
  which will be displayed as
  "Transfer 44% complete"

Hopefully, the strings, which contain variables such as these, will be written in such a way that they are simple and easy to translate but, depending on the target language, they can cause problems due to the inherent ambiguity of the information they introduce. Variables can impose a particular syntax on your translation and you have no choice but to accommodate it. For example, if a string contains two identical variables – for example, **Click %s to update %s** – you must preserve the order of the strings and rework your translation around it. This means you would not be able to produce a translation like "To update %s, click %" because it might result in "To update Refresh, click DATABASE.MDB" instead of "Click Refresh to update DATABASE.MDB".

Plurals can also impose restrictions on the way you phrase sentences, as they too can be generated using variables. Difficulties occur where languages do not have a consistent means of indicating plurals. In English the word *file* is pluralized by adding *–s* but the word *batch* is pluralized by adding *–es*. Programmers then need to find a way of letting the software know which ending to use for which word any time it is pluralized; this is both complex and unnecessarily time-consuming. Bert Esselink (1998:22) recommends deleting such variables and replacing them with translations which can represent both singular and plural forms, e.g. *batch(es)*. You should, however, exercise caution when dealing with code and variables; when in doubt, consult the client or project manager.

Files containing computer code can often feature what is known as "commented out" text. These comments are used to give other programmers additional information which is useful for understanding how the code works but which is not necessarily important for the proper functioning of software or website. Comments are preceded by one or more symbols such as /, /*, {, # or * or enclosed as follows:

```
<!-- This section is only relevant for Unix servers -->
```

Comments are not displayed in the finished program or website and as such do not need to be translated. It is, however, conceivable that you might be explicitly asked to do so in rare cases, such as sample files or training materials.

Strategies

- **Do not assume you have to translate everything**: Only some of the text that makes up computer code needs to be translated. Just because something looks like normal text, it does not necessarily mean it has to be translated.

- **Do not translate compounds**: Do not translate phrases which are linked by an underscore or which are written as one word, e.g. *CompanyName* or *File_Description*
- **Look for quotation marks**: Usually, text which is displayed between "quotation marks" needs to be translated. Be aware though that proper nouns such as font names, variable names or the names of types of elements used in an interface such as "scrollbar" may also appear in quotes but should be left untranslated
- **Preserve punctuation**: If a word has trailing ellipses, e.g. *Print...*, do not delete them. The ellipses are used to indicate menu options which, when clicked, open a dialog box in the software. Similarly, if a phrase contained in quotation marks is followed by a space, e.g. "Formatting ", do not delete the space. Often, programmers will *concatenate* or link a number of strings together and the space is necessary to separate the strings.
- **Do not change variables**: Do not delete, modify or rearrange variables in a string.
- **Beware of single-word strings**: Be very careful if you see a string such as "None" because, depending on your target language, it may have more than one translation depending on the grammatical gender of the thing "none" refers to.
- **Make sure your translation matches the software**: If a document contains examples of code which are based on the actual functioning version of the software, you need to ensure that your translations match what actually appears on screen. If an error message in the localized version of the software says "Program did not find any files", your translation of the code must reflect this; do not translate it as "No files were found".

6.9 Graphics, screenshots and menus

As we learned in Chapter 2, a key feature of technical texts is their frequent use of graphics to explain and clarify concepts and processes. A well-designed document will use a range of graphical elements to break up long stretches of text and to help readers visualize the subject being described. In technical texts, "graphics" can mean graphs, charts, diagrams, drawings, photographs, icons and screenshots. All of these elements may contain some form of annotation or labelling to indicate the name of something or to provide more information about it.

Ideally, diagrams should use numbered labels but unfortunately, some people insist on using actual words in the labels. What makes this problematic is if the diagram and labels are inserted into the document as a picture. This means that the only way of translating the labels is to import the picture into a graphics editor, edit the picture, save it and re-import it into the document – a lot of work to translate just one word and what's more, it is not strictly speaking a translator's job.

The best solution is to create a three-column table in Word or Excel with the source words and their translations as well as a reference to the relevant diagram number. You can also add a small legend beneath the image if space permits and the result will be sufficiently clear for readers (this is not advisable in texts for publication purposes without first getting the client's approval). Screenshots are typically used to illustrate software products or hardware devices which have a user interface or buttons.

Screenshots in particular can be a mixed blessing for translators. On the one hand, if they illustrate a localized version of the software, they can be an invaluable source of terminology which is specific to the particular product and company and which may not be found in dictionaries or parallel texts. On the other hand, the screenshots may be taken from software which has not been localized yet, which has been partially localized or which is in the process of be-ing localized and as such may be liable to change. Working on the assumption that the screenshot is based on a localized version of the software and is in the target language, the terms and translations used in the screenshot will be the authoritative version and it is essential that all references in text are consistent with the screenshots (if the screenshot is in your target language) or with your translations (if you can edit the graphic).

Strategies

- **Provide a glossary**: If you cannot replace the source text labels in a graph or diagram because the text is embedded in the image, create a glossary of the terms or labels and their translations. Depending on the text and its purpose, you can either include the glossary in the trans-lated text (useful for "information purposes" translations) or put them in a separate document which you will return along with your transla-tion. The second option is useful if the text is for publication purposes because the file containing the source labels and their translations can be sent to a graphic designer who will edit the image.
- **If in doubt, contact the client**: If the screenshots have not been local-ized (i.e. the screenshot is in the source language) contact the client to ask them if they want you to translate the terms in the body text. It is possible that your translations will be the first translations and will be used as the basis for localizing the software. If the client does want you to translate the text, draw up a glossary of the source terms and the target terms. It is also possible that the software has been localized but the client has simply forgotten to provide the localized screenshots or the relevant glossaries.
- **Unlocalized software**: Sometimes the client has no plans to localize the software and so the original SL terms and names will be retained, even in a translated document. This is a rare scenario and only ever occurs in the case of highly specialized products or products destined for small-er markets where the ST is widely known, so you should retain the SL terms only if the client explicitly tells you to do so.
- **Pay close attention to punctuation**: If a menu option has three ellipsis

dots after it, e.g. *Print...*, it means it will open up a dialog box. For this reason, never delete the dots.

6.10 Product names

Translating product or **brand names** takes up the time and energy of whole sections of the translation and marketing communities, and with good reason. There are countless urban legends recounting translation disasters involving the translation of Coca Cola into Chinese (reportedly translated, depending on the source, as "bite the wax tadpole" or "female horse stuffed with wax") or Ikea's *Fartfull* workbench, so the potential for embarrassment is clear. Texts may refer to products or services by brand name only and this can present challenges for the translator. Consider the following examples:

- Microsoft SharePoint
- Adobe InDesign
- Kia cee'd

The software names *SharePoint* and *InDesign* appear to be missing spaces between their constituent words while *cee'd* features an unusual use of the apostrophe and a missing initial capital letter. Despite the apparent errors, they should never be modified as they are proper names, part of the product's identity and, perhaps more importantly, central to the copyright protection of the product (copyright protection for brand names is based on a particular spelling or orthographic presentation of a word, so beware!).

In certain types of texts, references may be made to particular brands or materials. For example, a scientific paper on vascular surgery may refer to a particular brand of stent or catheter which was used during an operation, or a car instruction manual may refer to a specific brand of antifreeze to be used in the engine. These product names are usually mentioned for a particular reason so you should not change them. Simply transfer the names over to your target text without modification.

In other types of texts, if specific products are mentioned which are internationally recognized or available in the target country, all you need to do is transcribe the product name exactly as it appears in the ST. However, if the particular brand is non-existent or relatively unknown in the target language culture you may have a problem. The instinctive solution might be to replace the SL brand name with a comparable TL brand name, if one exists, but this may be just as problematic as leaving the SL brand name in the target text. This is because the two products, although similar and possibly identical in most aspects, may have different characteristics, properties or chemical compositions which, in the case of a chemistry paper, could have significant implications for the repeatability or even safety of the study.

The precise nature of the text and the needs of the target audience will naturally affect how you deal with this situation. In specialist texts where the precise

[handwritten annotation: ensure retaining ok in TL → retain, replace with equivalent]

characteristics of a product are important, one of the safest ways of dealing with brand names which do not exist in the TL is to reproduce the brand name and accompany it with a brief phrase describing its function.

In general texts, the specific brand name is not necessarily as important and you can, in principle, replace the brand name with a comparable product or, ideally, a generic description. It is essential, however, to do your research. If the source text recommends, for example, *Cleanio* for cleaning the screen of a television, you will need to find out a little more about this product before replacing it. For example, if *Cleanio* is a leading surface cleaner which does not contain bleach, you cannot replace it in the TT with *Sparklette* which **does** contain bleach because the bleach may damage the surface of the television.

Strategies

- **Retain**: Always write product names the same way regardless of whether it looks funny, ungrammatical or just plain wrong.
- **Replace**: If you do need to substitute an equivalent product name in the TL, make sure it really is comparable. Also, to avoid giving the impression of an endorsement of the product by the client, qualify the reference by saying "such as"
- **Remove**: A less problematic approach, if the specific product name is not absolutely essential, is to replace the product name with a generic description.

6.11 Contact details

The issue of contact details may seem like an unusual thing to talk about, especially in relation to technical translation, but they can present difficulties for translators, clients and readers if they are not handled with care. Many texts include contact details of some form or another and these usually include the name of a contact person, telephone and fax numbers, an email address and a website address.

In the case of contact names, if there is no title (such a Prof. or Dr.) and no indication of the gender of the person or if the name is unlikely to be recognized by a target language reader as belonging to a male or a female, using Ms. or Mr. is a useful way of helping readers avoid addressing women as *Mr.* and men as *Ms.* Admittedly, this is not an essential change but it does constitute a "value added" service for customers and it can spare readers' blushes.

Email addresses can be a source of confusion where they do not consist of a person's name. Imagine a van maintenance text, for example, contains the following email address

- van.queries@quimby.com

It is possible, depending on the target language, that speakers of the target language will not recognize that this is not the name of a person and may send emails which start *"Dear Mr Queries"* or *"Dear Van Queries"* thinking that it is a person's name. If a well-meaning but misguided translator decided to translate the email address in order to avoid this problem, emails will bounce back because that email address does not exist.

The same applies to website details contained in the text. If they are left as is, there is a risk that the reader may visit a website in the wrong language. But if the translator takes the initiative and replaces the website with the address of another language version of the site, readers may either be brought to a site with the wrong information or information in the wrong language.

In such cases, all a translator can do is leave the email or web addresses alone but notify the client of this when the translation is submitted along with some suggested translations if they decide to do the sensible thing and follow your advice. Again, while this is not an essential change it does constitute a "value added" service for customers and helps them create a more polished image.

Telephone numbers are frequently overlooked by translators but they deserve closer attention. When texts are produced in one country, they are often for-matted for readers in that country. However, when texts are translated they are destined to be read by readers outside the source country. As such, telephone numbers should be formatted to include the international dialling codes to pre-vent confusion and to save readers having to find these codes for themselves. You might also want to identify mobile telephone numbers because callers may incur substantial international call charges without realizing it.

Strategies

- **Personal names**: Add the title *Mr.* or *Ms.*, especially if it is unlikely to be clear to the target audience whether the person is male or female.
- **Email addresses**: If the email address consists of something other than a person's name, suggest a translation to the client but *do not* change the email address in the text.
- **Websites**: As with email addresses, *never* change them yourself but ad-vise the client if a specific web address points to content in a foreign language and suggest providing a suitable target language link.
- **Telephone numbers**: Convert all telephone numbers to international format with international dialling codes and prefixes. For example: the Irish telephone number 051-1234567 should become +353-(0)51-1234567.
- **Postal addresses**: Do not assume that, just because you are familiar with the source language country and its geography, the people read-ing your translation will be too. This is particularly true of smaller towns and cities so, if a document provides an address but does not iden-tify the country, consider adding the country to the address or, where appropriate, add the international country prefix to the post code, for example **LT-03500** *Vilnius* for an address in Lithuania or **B-1000** *Brussels* for an address in Belgium.

6.12   Scenarios and examples

Some texts, particularly those with an explanatory or instructional function, will provide examples or typical scenarios in which a product or procedure can be used. This is done as a way of explaining how to use something or how something works. This type of strategy is extremely useful from a technical communication and pedagogical point of view but it can throw up all sorts of challenges for translators because the examples are usually tailored to a specific audience in a specific context. For translators, the typical issues which arise in relation to examples and scenarios relate to examples which:

- are culture-specific;
- are language-specific;
- relate to a particular context, e.g. geographical, commercial, external factors;
- are constrained by technical factors, either within the text or outside the text.

The postcard shown in Figure 14 is an example which is both language-specific and constrained by technical factors.

Figure 14: Postcard with hidden message

Under normal circumstances, translating this postcard would be a straightforward task. However, if we discovered that this postcard came from a book on computer security (Plate & Holzmann 2009) where the authors are discussing steganography – the practice of hiding secret messages in otherwise ordinary-looking text – translating it might not be quite so straightforward. The purpose of the text is to demonstrate how messages can be hidden in seemingly innocuous text. In the text, the following paragraphs appear after the postcard to explain how steganography works:

To decipher the message contained in the text, we need to count the number of characters, both letters and punctuation marks, in each word up as far as the blank space immediately after it and then apply the following rule: if the number of characters is odd, we assign a value of 0 but if the number of characters is even, we assign a value of 1.

Applying this rule to the first 8 words on the postcard from David we get 01010011. This corresponds to the decimal number 83 which is also the ASCII code for the letter "**S**". The next eight words on the post card give us 01001111 which corresponds to 79 or the letter "**O**" and the last 8 words again give us 01010011 which corresponds to the letter "**S**". So despite the seemingly positive tone of the postcard, David is really sending us an SOS message asking for help. [*my translation*]

In translating this simple postcard, we must first ensure that our translation is factually correct while at the same time looking like a postcard. Depending on our language combination, it may not always be possible to produce a completely idiomatic translation so we will need to prioritize the technical aspect over the linguistic aspect. The extent to which we need to balance technical accuracy and linguistic fluency will depend on the text and subject but it is likely that the technical will need to take priority.

Strategies

- *Culture-specific examples* will need to be replaced with scenarios and examples which are familiar to the TL audience.
- *Language-specific examples* may involve significant adaptation in order for them to be comprehensible and acceptable for the target audience. It may be necessary to translate very loosely or even to create entirely new examples altogether.
- Like culture-specific examples, *context-based examples* which relate to a particular situation or context, e.g. geographical, commercial, external factors, should be replaced with corresponding TL culture examples or modified to comply with the TL environment.
- Examples which are constrained by *technical factors*, either within the text or outside the text are usually quite straightforward as the technical context will probably remain the same, unless there is an element of language-specificity as is the case in the postcard example. Normally, only minimal modification should be necessary unless different technical regulations apply.

6.13 Giving warnings and advice

Technical texts help readers to do something correctly and safely. In addition to providing clear instructions explaining the correct procedure, it is often necessary to provide warnings outlining what *not* to do or explaining the potential risks associated with a particular procedure or product. Apart from a general desire that readers do not come to any harm, there are, as we noted earlier, various legal reasons for ensuring that any warning information in a text is both clear and effective. For this reason, translating warnings and advisory information is extremely important; in some cases, it can be a matter of life or death.

Knowing the different types of notices

When providing notices to readers, a range of words can be used to indicate the relative importance of the information. To provide effective notices it is important that you think about what these words actually mean and then prioritize them in order to use them properly. The following list illustrates how a typical hierarchy of notices might be constructed.

- **Note**: This is used to remind readers of important information, to emphasize something or to highlight minor problems which may occur.
- **Warning**: This is used to warn readers of the possibility of minor injury to themselves or to others.
- **Caution**: This is used to warn readers of possible damage to equipment, data or other significant consequences of a particular procedure or course of action.
- **Danger**: This is the most serious category of warning and is used to alert readers to the possibility of serious or fatal injuries to themselves or others.

When faced with some sort of notice in a text, it may be tempting to label everything as extremely important and use *Caution* or *Danger* for all notices. While it is often difficult to correctly ascertain the level of risk or danger involved, it is just as important not to overstate risks as it is not to understate them. Understating risks means readers may not take the risks seriously enough. Overstating risks, for example using *Danger* when *Warning* is more appropriate, lessens the impact of *Danger* when it actually is appropriate.

European Hazard Symbols

In the European Union, a series of symbols has been developed for the purposes of labelling hazardous materials. Each symbol appears on an orange background and is accompanied by a text description which explains the significance of the symbol. These descriptions are translated into *most* of the official languages of the EU and should be used wherever your language combination permits.

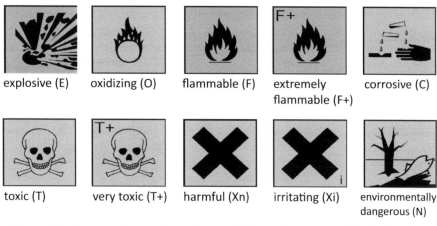

explosive (E)   oxidizing (O)   flammable (F)   extremely   corrosive (C)
                                                   flammable (F+)

toxic (T)   very toxic (T+)   harmful (Xn)   irritating (Xi)   environmentally
                                                                   dangerous (N)

Figure 15: European hazard warning symbols and accompanying indications

In the European Union, various descriptive phrases have been formulated for the different categories of hazardous materials and the risks they pose to health and safety. It is important to recognize that the precise wording of these phrases is important because it is tested, accurate, legal and recognizable. When translating descriptions relating to hazardous materials – for example packaging, data sheets, safety information, or documents relating to the approval of products – it is important that you use the same terminology and where appropriate the full wording of these descriptions.

Appendix 3 provides translations of these descriptive phrases in a variety of EU languages as well as a list of safety and risk phrases in English. A more complete list of risk phrases and safety phrases is contained in the annexes of Commission Directive 2001/59/EC of 6 August 2001, which is published in the Official Journal of the European Communities (O.J. L 225/1).

Strategies

- When translating descriptions of substances or warnings and hazards relating to their use, always use the same terminology as the official regulations and descriptions. For example, do not use *substance* if *material* is always used in similar warnings, or replace *toxic* with *poisonous* if official documents make a distinction between the two terms. The reasoning behind this is that terms used in official documents and descriptions have specific definitions and any synonyms may not have the same meaning or may render descriptions in texts invalid.
- Use warning notices consistently throughout the document; do not translate the same notice differently in the same document.
- In the case of descriptions of hazardous materials or descriptive text associated with hazard symbols, *always* try to find the official translation in your target language rather than producing your own translation. Existing translations have been tested for accuracy and any deviations, no matter how slight, may have health and safety implications.

6.14 References to other documents

In various forms of technical documentation, authors will find it necessary to refer to other documents. In the case of academic publications, references may relate to books or journal articles, while technical specifications, tenders or instruction manuals may refer to standards, contracts, regulations or supplementary documents.

In some cases, official or commonly used translations may exist, in which case the name should simply be replaced but, in the majority of cases, the translator will need to decide what to do with the reference.

Strategies

- **Paraphrase**: If the precise name of the document is not important in the context of the TL document, the name in the SL can be replaced with a descriptive phrase.
- **Retain**: If the precise name of the document is important (e.g. a book, paper etc.) and the precise meaning is either unimportant or apparent from the context, the SL name can be retained without any form of explanation.
- **Retain and paraphrase**: In cases where the SL name of the document is important but the nature of the text or the background of the target audience is such that the meaning of the SL name will not be immediately obvious, a combination of retaining the name and supplementing it with a descriptive paraphrase can be used. This means that readers will understand the name of the text but that they will also be able to identify the SL text if necessary. Depending on the point in a document where a publication name appears, the paraphrase can be incorporated into the sentence or, in the case of bullet lists, included in square brackets after the publication name.
- In the case of academic publications, it is generally not necessary to translate the names of documents, as they usually only ever appear in the bibliography at the end of the document and rarely, if ever, in the body text. It may, however, be necessary to transliterate author and publication names when translating from one writing system to another.

6.15 Partially translated source texts

A frequent feature of scientific papers for publication in journals or conference proceedings is that where the scientists speak the target language, they will often try to "help out" by translating part of the text before sending it to you. Texts may contain individual words in the target language or even phrases, sentences or entire paragraphs. This is usually done with the best of intentions and the scientists are trying to make your job easier by translating specialized terms or, because the scientists tried to translate the text themselves, realized it was either too difficult or too time-consuming and then gave up. Some clients might even try to negotiate a cheaper rate for doing this but you should politely refuse to entertain such requests.

Depending on the language abilities of the scientist, this can be either a blessing or a curse. Where scientists speak the language well, they have reduced the amount of subject and terminology research you will have to do. If their use of language is poor, you will not only have to understand the source language text but also decipher whatever it is the scientist was *trying* to say, fix it and make sure your translation fits around it. In the worst-case scenario, you might need to contact the client and ask them what it is they mean.

Strategies

- If you run into problems understanding what the scientist's attempt at a translation means, *be tactful* when you ask them to clarify what a particular sentence means. Some people can react negatively to what they perceive as a criticism of their language skills.
- If a scientist uses a different term for a concept to what you would use, err on the side of caution and work on the assumption that the scientist knows more about this subject than you do and they are probably correct in their choice of terminology. If you do change the terms they will spot what you have done so be prepared to justify your actions (tactfully!).

6.16 Latinisms and scientific nomenclatures

Scientific texts and technical texts dealing with certain topics such as medicine are frequently littered with terms and phrases which are either in Latin or have Latin origins. For an inexperienced translator or layperson, the use of Latin can be daunting. Yet, despite their intimidating appearance, Latinisms are actually quite a useful feature of texts and can make the job of translating texts on complex subjects substantially easier, or at least, less problematic. The use of Latin in scientific and technical texts – especially in relation to medicine and the natural sciences such as zoology and botany – stems from the traditional role of Latin as a common language or *lingua franca* among scientists. Ironically, Latin was seen as the language of knowledge and was used as a way of communicating with colleagues, thereby removing the need for translation.

Consequently, many significant scientific works were published in Latin with the result that many key concepts were only known by their Latin name. Technical terms that were assimilated into national languages often retained their overall Latin appearance with only minor modifications to allow the terms to function within a particular grammar or orthography. In European languages in particular, many specialized terms bear a striking resemblance from one language to another precisely because of this common ancestry in Latin.

Latin in scientific language is introduced using what is known as *scientific nomenclature*, a system of assigning unique names to various species of animals and plants. This system is needed in order to provide scientists with stable, simple and internationally acceptable ways of naming objects in the natural world. The best known of these methods is based on a complex system of Latin terms proposed by Swedish scientist Carolus Linnaeus in the tenth edition of his book *Systema Naturae* in 1758. *Linnaen classification*, as the system is known, is a standard feature of scientific and technical discourse. It is described as a binomial nomen-clatural system and it assigns a unique two-part name in which the first word indicates the genus and the second the species, e.g., *Corydoras paleatus*, which is commonly known as the rather tasty-sounding "peppered Cory catfish".

Latin is also used in medical contexts as a way of naming the anatomy of animals, including humans. This gives rise to standard anatomical terms of loca-tion, which consist of a noun usually in Latin or based closely on Latin to indicate the part of the anatomy, and frequently words which are known as *directional terms*:

Directional term	Explanation
superior	top, towards the head (Can be used relatively)
inferior	bottom, towards the feet (Can be used relatively)
anterior	to the front of the body
posterior	to the back of the body
dorsal	front (Less common when referring to body as a whole, more applicable to particular organ or structure)
ventral	back (Less common when referring to body as a whole, more applicable to particular organ or structure)
lateral	away from the middle, to the side
medial	Middle
proximal	away from an extremity (In relative terms, a closer part)
distal	towards an extremity (In relative terms, a more distant part)
intermediate	away from either end (Only used in relative terms)
ipsilateral	same side
contralateral	opposite side
superficial	shallow, not deep (Only used in relative terms)
deep	not shallow (Only used in relative terms)

Figure 16: Directional terms for human anatomy

CAROLI LINNÆI

I. QUADRUPEDIA.	II. AVES.	III. AMPHIBIA.
Corpus hirsutum. Pedes quatuor. Femina vivipara, lactifera.	Corpus plumosum. Alæ duæ. Pedes duo. Rostrum osseum. Femina ovipara.	Corpus nudum, vel squamosum. Dentes molares nulli : reliqui semper. Pinnæ nullæ.

(Detailed taxonomic table listing orders, genera, generic characters, and species across the three classes Quadrupedia, Aves, and Amphibia — including genera such as Homo, Simia, Bradypus, Ursus, Leo, Tigris, Felis, Mustela, Didelphis, Lutra, Odobenus, Phoca, Hyæna, Canis, Meles, Talpa, Erinaceus, Vespertilio, Hystrix, Sciurus, Castor, Mus, Lepus, Sorex, Equus, Hippopotamus, Elephas, Sus, Camelus, Cervus, Capra, Ovis, Bos; Psittacus, Strix, Falco, Paradisea, Coracias, Corvus, Cuculus, Picus, Certhia, Sitta, Upupa, Ilpida, Grus, Ciconia, Ardea, Platelea, Pelecanus, Cygnus, Anas, Mergus, Graculus, Colymbus, Larus, Hæmatopus, Charadrius, Vanellus, Tringa, Numenius, Fulica, Struthio, Casuarius, Otis, Pavo, Meleagris, Gallina, Tetrao, Columba, Turdus, Sturnus, Alauda, Motacilla, Luscinia, Parus, Hirundo, Loxia, Ampelia, Fringilla; Testudo, Rana, Lacerta, Anguis.)

PARADOXA

HYDRA corpore anguino, pedibus duobus, collis septem, & totidem capitibus, alarum expers, asservatur Hamburgi, similitudinem referens Hydræ Apocalypticæ § 3. Jo. ANNE CAP. XII. & XIII. descriptæ...

RANA-PISCIS 1. RANA IN PISCEM METAMORPHOSIS valde paradoxa est, quum Natura mutationem Generis unius in aliud diversæ Classis non admittat...

MONOCEROS Veterum, corpore equino, pedibus ferinis cornu recto, longo, spiraliter intorto...

PELECANUS rostro volens infigens femori suo...

SATYRUS oculorum hirsutus, barbatus, humanum referens corpus...

BOROMETZ 1. AGNUS SCYTHICUS plantis accensetur...

FILICIN Americanis compositus...

PHOENIX, Avis species, cujus unicum in mundo individuum...

BERNICLA 1. ANSER SCOTICUS & CONCHA ANATIFERA...

DRACO corpore anguino, duobus pedibus, duabus alis Vespertilionis instar...

AUTOMA MORTIS Horologii minimi sonitum edens in pariebus...

Figure 17: Part 1 of Table of the Animal Kingdom (Regnum Animale) from Carolus Linnaeus's first edition of Systema Naturae (1735).

REGNUM ANIMALE.

IV PISCES.	V. INSECTA.	VI. VERMES.
Corpus apodum, pinnis veris inftructum, nudum, vel fquamofum.	*Corpus crufta cutis loco tectum. Caput antennis inftructum.*	*Corporis Mufculi ab una parte bafi cuidam folidæ affixi.*

Figure 18: Part 2 of Table of the Animal Kingdom (Regnum Animale) from Carolus Linnaeus's first edition of Systema Naturae (1735).

For scientists, the advantages of using scientific nomenclature are that every species is uniquely named and these names are understood by experts in all countries and languages. In addition, they ensure consistency through standard spelling and punctuation and, because they can only be revised by expert committees, they are stable and tend not to gain connotations as conventional language does. These benefits are also of use to the translator who, depending on the text being translated, can either leave the Latin terms as they are or, if a target language translation is necessary, can use the standard international terms to identify their commonly used equivalents in the target language.

Of course, Latin terms are not without their problems. For scientists and laypersons alike, they can be difficult to remember and they are liable to being misspelled. If this is the case in a text to be translated, searching for background information and target language equivalents becomes more difficult, though not impossible.

Common is not always common!
Part of what makes Latin terms so useful is that they always have the same meaning whereas not all common names are "common" in the target language. So if, for example, you want to replace *Batrachian larva* with a plain English term, bear in mind that this would be *tadpole* in England but *polliwog* in the USA. If you are going to replace Latinisms, do so with care and remember who the target audience is likely to be.

Strategies

- **Retain**: In the vast majority of cases the most appropriate strategy is to retain the Latin name as this ensures the concept being referred to is identified accurately. Latin terms are invariably printed in *italics* to indicate that it is a different language.
- **Explain**: Latin names alone may not always be appropriate in the target text, especially in cases where the target audience does not have the same background as the original audience (e.g. translating a medical article for a general audience or translating the technical description of a surgical procedure for use in a patient information sheet). In such cases, use the Latin name to identify the common target language name and include this either in parentheses or as an explanatory phrase before or after the Latin term.
- **Replace**: Specialist scientific and technical audiences will almost universally be familiar with Latin terminology, although some may have certain preferences for or against their use. Similarly, virtually all European audiences will recognize Latin as a scientific *lingua franca* and this means that when translating between any of the European languages, Latin terms will not pose too much of a problem. However, where the target audience or language have had no exposure to Latin, the inclusion of such terms may be confusing and rather pointless. In such cases,

Latin terms may be replaced with their common names in the target language.

- **Finding translations**: If you need to find out what a Latin term means in your target language, type it into a search engine along with one or two related words in your target language (you can also search for phrases by enclosing them in quotes). This should return a list of pages in your target language which contain the Latin term; one of them is bound to contain a translation for you. If you type in a Latin term and it produces no results, it may be because it has been misspelled. In such cases, search engines such as Google may propose alternative spellings or you can try entering a shorter fragment of the term and performing a fuzzy search. This can also be done in Google using a ~ in front of the search term.

Practical Exercise 29: Linguistic detective work
Find out what the following Latin terms refer to and find out what the common name is for each one in both your source and target languages:

- *Chamomilla recutita*
- *Dactylorhiza incarnata*
- *Primula veris*
- *Troglodytes aedon*
- *Fasciola hepatica*
- *Phytophtera infestans*
- *Hypericum perforatum*
- *Halichoerus grypus*
- *Hippodamia tredecimpunctata*
- *Glaucomys volans*

6.17 Instructions that do not make sense

Translating instructions is a core part of a technical translator's job, yet all too frequently, readers have to contend with translated instructions which do not make sense or which make the job of the reader much more difficult than it needs to be. We're all familiar with instructions like the ones shown in Figure 19 (which is both poorly written and incorrectly numbered) which leave us scratching our heads in confusion.

PUZZLE BALL

HOW TO ASSEMBLE
2. Hold A1 hand. Put A2 and A3 on both side of A1.
2. Slide B1 and B2 on both side of A2 & A3.
3. Slide C1 for the side of B1 though the side of B2

Figure 19: Confusing instructions for a child's toy (Michael O'Mara Books 2004:87)

One of the most important aspects of translating instructions is to make sure that you use words which you know the reader will understand. For this reason, you must be consistent in your use of terminology and only use terms (for example relating to parts of a product) which have already been used or which are clearly identifiable. If you know what the product is, what it looks like or how it works, do not be afraid to make your translation clearer by rephrasing instructions or by adding a little more description. A quick search on the Internet for photos of the product can often help you to visualize the product and write clearer instructions.

Instructions which are out of sequence

Most people do not enjoy reading instructions and will only do so as a last resort. Of these people, a great number will perform each step described in instructions as they read them before moving on to the next step. For this reason, instructions should be presented, wherever possible, in chronological order. In other words, they should describe steps in the order in which they will be carried out to account for readers who will work with the instructions in one hand and a screwdriver in the other.

The following sentences are taken from the instructions for a disposable hypodermic syringe:

- Throw used syringe into a sharps box
- Do not replace the cap on the needle

By the time the reader finds out that the cap should not be replaced before disposing of the syringe, they will probably have already thrown the syringe into the box full of dirty needles. At this point, it is much too late to do anything unless readers want to risk injury and possibly contracting a disease by reaching into the sharps box to take the cap off!

Strategies

- **Do your research**: Try to find out what the product looks like and, if necessary, modify the instructions to make them clearer
- **Rebuild the instructions**: If instructions are not presented in a logical or chronological sequence rearrange the order of individual steps in a set of instructions.
- **Give the reader some space**: If the SL instructions are densely packed with information and you think it is likely to be confusing, split complex sentences into smaller, more manageable units. This lets you focus the reader's attention on the important information and divert attention away from less important information.
- **Give the reader a hint**: If the instructions are a little vague or do not make something perfectly clear, provide the additional clarification necessary to make the reader's job easier.

- **Contact the client**: If the instructions do not make any sense or if you cannot figure out what it is you are describing, contact the client and ask them to walk you through the process if they have time.

> **Practical Exercise 30: Putting your writing skills to work**
>
> A useful way of learning how to translate instructions is to try writing some yourself. For most of us, however, the idea of writing instructions often seems pretty simple until we actually try to do it for ourselves. This task not only helps you develop your writing skills but also gives you an insight into how and why written instructions can go wrong.
>
> To do this task, you will need a small toy car and a copy of the parking diagram provided in Figure 20. Your task is to write instructions explaining how to park the car in the space indicated between the two other cars. You must only use written instructions and you cannot use diagrams to help you. Make sure your instructions are as clear as possible but make sure that they are appropriate for the most likely target audience, i.e. do not give so much information that the instructions are patronizing or so little information that the readers are confused.
>
> After spending approximately 20 minutes writing your instructions, find a volunteer to help you test them. Your volunteer should read and follow your instructions precisely in order to perform the task. The volunteer must not use any common sense, initiative or problem-solving skills at all. Instead, they must do *exactly* what your instructions say. Your role is simply to observe the volunteer while using your instructions and make a note of any problems encountered. You should not answer any questions unless it is clear that your volunteer cannot proceed any further on the basis of your instructions. If this happens, you can provide advice but you must make a note of this as it represents a significant problem with your instructions.
>
> This task helps you work on your writing skills and it also lets you test your instructions to identify potential weaknesses in the way you explain information. Alternative scenarios for your instructions can include any step-by-step procedure such as connecting a plug to a piece of electric cable (obviously not a live piece of cable), inserting a picture into a picture frame, adding a new contact to a mobile phone address book or changing a light bulb.

6.18 Tables of contents and indices

Lengthy technical documents will contain tables of contents as a way of helping readers identify and locate the main sections in a document. Some documents may also feature an index of key terms at the end which helps readers locate specific information. Although it might seem logical to translate a table of contents – often referred to as a TOC – because it appears early on in a text, there are important linguistic and technical reasons for not translating it.

From a technical point of view, many professionally-produced documents are created using word processors or text editing applications which automatically generate tables of contents. Word processors typically do this by scanning the document and compiling a list of the various chapter, section and paragraph headings. In the case of documents created in Microsoft Word, for example, the text you see in one of these automatic tables of contents is not actually there; it is like a hologram or a projection of text which is located elsewhere in the document. This means that in order to translate the table of contents, you must translate the actual heading text which is being "projected" into the table of contents. You can try to translate the table of contents, but as soon as you print or update the document, your translation will be lost.

There are more compelling reasons for not translating tables of contents first and these relate to the accuracy of your translations. The section headings, which make up a typical table of contents, are used to describe the content of a particular section or chapter. If you choose to translate the headings without having first read the sections they describe, you are translating without the full context and you risk mistranslating some or all of the headings. It is always best to wait until you have read and translated the rest of the text before tackling tables of contents so that you have a better idea of what the text is about.

A similar situation applies to indexes (or indices if you prefer) at the end of a document which, like TOCs are also generated automatically. Some people suggest translating them first because it helps you identify and translate your main terminology before you start working on the body of the translation. This, they claim, can save you a lot of time when you translate the rest of the text. While this would appear to make sense – after all creating your own specific terminology list for a text in one go sounds like a great way of saving time – the same problem of translating terms out of context also applies so you may end up using the wrong term in your translation. You may realize this halfway through a translation and have to go back and replace each instance of the wrong term. For this reason, be very careful if you do decide to translate the index and use it as a glossary because you may end up wasting time using the wrong terms and having to fix your translation.

6.19 Formatting and layout

The idea of translating within strict space constraints is something which we usually associate with the subtitling of films, but it also affects several aspects of technical translation. Certain types of documents such as information leaflets or instructions may be restricted to a single side or sheet of paper whether for cost reasons, or to allow multiple language versions to be printed on the same piece of paper. Similarly, when localizing software, the design of the interface may impose limits on the maximum number of characters permitted in a text string which will appear in a dialog box, for example. The same situation may also arise when translating the text labels in a diagram or graph.

While tackling the challenging task of making sure you convey all of the necessary information in the space available you will need to bear in mind the fact that, depending on your language combination – and just as importantly, your language direction – your translation may undergo a natural process of expansion or contraction. In some cases, the difference in word count between your ST and TT can be quite significant so you may have to rethink your translation strategies if it looks like you are going to run out of space.

Strategies

- *Use short, simple words and sentences*: Formulate your translation so that it is as concise as possible while still remaining clear and easy to understand.
- *Use abbreviations where necessary*: Try to find abbreviations and acronyms, ideally ones already used by the company or in the general subject area; if not, make sure that any abbreviations are clear and easy to decipher. Do not overuse abbreviations – the text must be clear and easy to understand.
- *Avoid sticking too closely to the source text*: If using a different grammatical or syntactic structure in the TL will allow you to produce a shorter translation, do not be afraid to deviate from the ST.
- *Where appropriate, use imperative verb forms*: Sentences which use imperative forms of verbs are invariably shorter than sentences which use passive constructions. They are also easier to understand.
- *Be flexible and creative*: Be prepared to try several possible wordings and use modulation, transposition and adaptation strategies

6.20 Managing and naming files

As a technical translator, the majority of texts you deal with will be sent to you in electronic format. In technical translation projects, you will often be presented with multiple files to translate. There are various things that can go wrong when managing multiple files such as accidentally overwriting the original source files, not being able to find the file you're supposed to translate, not being able to tell which files are for translation and which are for reference purposes and so on.

To help you manage the files and to help prevent problems when you return your translation, you should create a folder for each project in which you will store all of the files for that project. Always retain a copy of your source files in a separate folder, preferably on a separate drive, computer or online file storage facility (this could be as simple as a web-based email account or as fancy as your own file server). This way, if your computer crashes or the file you are working on is corrupted, you will always have the original file and you will not have to ask the client to send you the files again (this is embarrassing and does not create a very professional image).

Storing your files

- Create a master folder for the project
- Create one folder for your source files and one for your target or translated files
- If necessary, create separate folders for reference materials or translation memories
- Set up your computer to create daily back-ups of your files which should be stored on a separate hard drive or another computer.

Translating your files

- **Overwrite the source text with your translation**: Generally, if you are sent a file in electronic format, you are expected to overwrite the source text with your translation. (This does not apply if you are sent a PDF file because these files cannot be edited like normal documents). This means you should use the source text as a template so that your translation is formatted in exactly the same way as the source text. Do not make the mistake of typing up your translation in a blank Word document, for example, without the formatting.
- **Never work on the only copy of your source file**: When you open a file to translate it, the first thing you should do is save it under a different name to your target file folder. This way you are not working on the only copy of your source text.
- **Give your translated files clearly identifiable and unique names**: You should retain the original file name as this makes it easy to identify related files but append the **ISO language code** for your target language to indicate that it is a translation. For example, when translating the file *specification-doc-2010.doc* into Chinese, save the file as *specification-doc-2010_ZH.doc*. These codes are easy to find on the Internet but here are some examples: *_DE* for German, *_ES* for Spanish, *_GA* for Irish, *_AR* for Arabic and *_EN* for English.

6.21 Using the Internet

Translating a text on a topic with which you are unfamiliar or if the text refers to a concept which is new to you can be a stressful business for any translator. If you are lucky, you will have a bookcase full of assorted encyclopaedias, which you can use to get up to speed on a particular area. More often than not, however, the concepts will be quite new or quite specialized so it is unlikely that you will have the right books. Thankfully, the Internet provides a gateway to all of the information you need but the problem is how to find it and, when you have, how to decide which information is the most reliable.

Using search engines can open up a wealth of useful information and save you a lot of time when researching a translation. It can also prove to be a frustrating waste of time if you cannot get the most out of your search engine.

Strategies

- **Find parallel texts**: Parallel texts are one of the most useful resources available to a translator as they help to explain the subject material and they are often a rich source of terminology. Certain technical documents will typically be published in a particular format. For example, manuals, reports and specifications will usually be published in PDF format, marketing material will appear either in HTML or PDF format while training materials and corporate information may appear in PowerPoint format. Use the advanced search function in search engines such as Google to restrict your search to these formats to help reduce the number of results and find more suitable documents.
- **Use synonym searches**: In Google, type a tilde ~ in front of a search term to find similar terms
- **Exclude useless information**: If your search for information about the *buffers* used to stop trains crashing in train stations keeps suggesting links to pages about computers, you can exclude them from your search. In search engines such as Google you can type a minus symbol – in front of whatever term appears in the pages you do not want, e.g. *buffer -**computer*** to exclude pages about computers. Other search engines may allow you to do the same thing using the *NOT* operator.
- **Finding terminology**: If you want to find a TL equivalent for an SL term, try searching for the term along with a word in the TL which is related to the subject or your best guess at what the SL term means. This will produce a list of sites which contain both the SL and the TL and will increase your likelihood of finding a translation or a glossary.
- **Using translators' forums**: Various websites contain translator forums where translators can ask for advice and help from other translators. This can be a useful strategy if you are having trouble with a particular word or phrase because, in theory at least, it allows you to draw on the expertise of other translators, some of whom will have many years of translation experience. Although most sites allow users to rate or comment on the answers provided, you should exercise extreme caution when relying on answers from others. This is because there are no real mechanisms for ensuring the quality of answers provided and you, the person – who does not know the answer – have to select what *you think* is the correct answer. Also, the people answering the question, well-meaning as they may be, might not know the entire context of your translation and may give you an answer which is correct in one situation but not another.

Once you have found what looks like useful information, you will need to assess it to decide whether it is actually reliable. There are some general rules of thumb which can guide you through this process, although ultimately, practice and a little commonsense are your best tools:

- Websites belonging to international organisations, government bodies or state organizations are usually a very reliable source of subject information. Find out what the typical suffix for government websites is in your target country and use it as a way of limiting your search.
- Company websites may not be as objective as you might like but they will often have specialized terminology. If you are lucky, the website will have been localized so you might have multiple versions of the site in different languages. If this is the case, you have a ready-made bilingual terminology resource.
- Be careful with sites that supposedly offer impartial reviews of products or technologies as they may present information with a particular slant or agenda so you may not get the most accurate description.
- Personal websites hosted by free website services are usually the least reliable resource on the Internet. The reason for this is that anyone can start up a website and there are no quality controls so you may be reading completely inaccurate or biased information.
- While a lot of people use Wikipedia, its use is not entirely unproblematic and you should never rely solely on the information you find there. The philosophy behind the online encyclopaedia is that because it is a collaborative endeavour, its users as a group will ensure that all information is accurate. The result is supposedly a form of peer review on a massive scale. However, the volume of information contained in Wikipedia combined with the ease with which anyone can change information makes quality control difficult. One problem affecting the reliability of articles is the incidence of deliberate acts of vandalism where incorrect information is added to articles. Even where moderators are active and alert, there may be a period of several hours during which the incorrect information can be unwittingly used by visitors to the site. For this reason, if you do decide to use Wikipedia you should use it as a first port of call only – always try to identify other sources to corroborate any information you find on Wikipedia before you use it.

Suggested Reading

Baker, Mona (1992) *In Other Words: Coursebook on Translation*. London: Routledge.

Bird, Mary (2008) *Medical Terminology and Clinical Procedures Revised*, Dartford: National Services for Health Improvement, 3rd edition.

Chesterman, Andrew (2005) 'Problems with Strategies', In Krisztina Károly & Ágota Fóris (eds) *New Trends in Translation Studies: In Honour of Kinga Klaudy*, Budapest: Akadémiai Kiadó, 17-28.

Kearns, John (2009) Strategies, in Mona Baker & Gabriela Saldanha (eds) *Routledge Encyclopaedia of Translation Studies*, Abingdon: Routledge, 282-285, 2nd edition.

Lörscher, Wolfgang (1991) *Translation Performance, Translation Process and Translation Strategies: A Psycholinguistic Investigation*, Tübingen: Gunter Narr.

Muñoz Martin, Ricardo (2000) 'Translation Strategies: Somewhere Over the Rainbow', In Allison Beeby, Doris Ensinger & Marisa Presas (eds) *Investigating Translation: Selected Papers from the 4th International Congress on Translation*, Barcelona, 1998, Amsterdam & Philadelphia: John Benjamins, 129-38.

Strunk, William & E.B. White (1999) *The Elements of Style*, Massachusetts: Longman.
University of Chicago (2003) *The Chicago Manual of Style*, London/Chicago: The
    University of Chicago Press.

Online Resources

- The **EUR-Lex** website is a useful searchable database of information relating to laws of the European Union. http://eur-lex.europa.eu.

- **EServer TC Library** is a useful way of accessing various resources relating to technical communication. This particular link takes you to a selection of technical writing style guide resources which are useful and informative. http://tc.eserver.org/dir/Reference/Style-Guides/Technical-Writing.

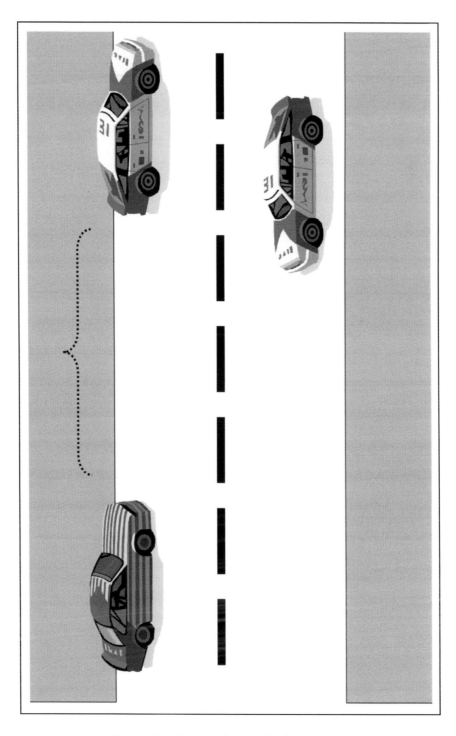

Figure 20: Diagram for Practical Exercise 25

Bibliography

Apple (2003) *Apple Publications Style Guide – May 2003*, California: Apple Computer, Inc.

ASD Simplified Technical English (2005) AeroSpace and Defense Industries Association of Europe Specification ASD-STE100(tm).

Austermühl, Frank (2001) *Electronic Tools for Translators*, Manchester: St Jerome.

Baer, Brian J. and Geoffrey S. Koby (2003) *Beyond the Ivory Tower: Rethinking Translation Pedagogy*, Amsterdam/Philadelphia: John Benjamins.

Baker, Mona (1992) *In Other Words: Coursebook on Translation*, London: Routledge.

Bates, Daniel and Fred Plog (1990) *Cultural Anthropology*, New York: McGraw-Hill, 3rd edition.

Bell, Roger T. (1991) *Translation and Translating*, London and New York: Longman.

Bird, Mary (2008) *Medical Terminology and Clinical Procedures Revised*, Dartford: National Services for Health Improvement, 3rd edition.

Boucau, Fernand (2005) *The European Translation Industry: Facing The Future*, Brussels: European Union of Associations of Translation Companies.

Bowker, Lynne (2002) *Computer-Aided Translation Technology,* Ottawa: University of Ottawa Press.

Bowker, Lynne, Michael Cronin, Dorothy Kenny and Jennifer Pearson [eds] (1996) *Unity in Diversity? Current Trends in Translation Studies*, Manchester: St Jerome.

Brunette, Louise (2000) Toward a Terminology for Translation Quality Assessment. *Evaluation and Translation*, Special Issue of *The Translator*, 6(2): 169-182.

Bryson, Bill (2003) *A Short History of Nearly Everything*, London: Black Swan.

Byrne, Jody (2003) Freelance Translation: Teaching Students to Create Their Own Jobs. Daniel Gouadec and Daniel Toudic (eds) *Traduction, Terminologie, Rédaction*. Paris: La Maison du Dictionnaire, 161-174.

------ (2005) Evaluating The Effect of Iconic Linkage on the Usability of Software User Guides. *The Journal of Technical Writing & Communication*. 35(2): 155-178.

------ (2006) *Technical Translation: Usability Strategies for Translating Technical Documentation*. Dordrecht: Springer.

------ (2007) Caveat Translator: Understanding the Legal Consequences of Errors in Professional Translation. *Journal of Specialised Translation*, 2007 (7): 2-24.

Cardon, Peter W. (2008) A Critique of Hall's Contexting Model: A Meta-Analysis of Literature on Intercultural Business and Technical Communication. *Journal of Business and technical Communication*, 22(4): 399-428.

Cardoso de Camargo, Diva (2001) Estudos Tradutológicos em Córpus de Textos Técnicos, Corporativos e Jornalísticos. *Tradução & Comunícação*, (10): 33-49.

Catford, John (1965) *A Linguistic Theory of Translation: An Essay in Applied Linguistics*, London: Oxford University Press.

Chandran, K. S. Ravi (2005) Duality of fatigue failures of materials caused by Poisson defect statistics of competing failure modes. *Nature Materials*, 4, April 2005: 303-308.

Chesterman, Andrew (2000) Translation Typology, in A. Veisbergs and I. Zauberga (eds), *The Second Riga Symposium on Pragmatic Aspects of Translation,* Riga: University of Latvia, 49-62.

Commission Directive 2001/59/EC. Official Journal of the European Communities (O.J. L 225/1) [Online] Available from: *http: //eur-lex.europa.eu/LexUriServ/LexUriServ. do?uri=OJ: L: 2001: 225: 0001: 0333: EN: PDF*

Council of the European Union (1998) *Council Resolution of 17 December 1998 on operating instructions for technical consumer goods*. Official Journal of the European Communities (98/C 411/01).

Crabbe, Stephen (2010). Controlled Languages for Technical Writing and Translation, in I. Kemble (ed.), *The Changing Face of Translation: Proceedings of the Ninth Annual Portsmouth Translation Conference*, Portsmouth: University of Portsmouth, 48-62.

Delisle, Jean and Judith Woodsworth [eds] (1995) *Translators Through History*, Amsterdam: John Benjamins.

DeMatteis, Bob, Andy Gibbs and Michael Neustel (2006) *The Patent Writer: How to Write Successful Patent Applications*, New York: Square One Publishers.

DePalma, Donald and Renato Beninatto (2006) *Ranking of Top 20 Translation Companies for 2005*. Common Sense Advisory, Inc. [online] Available from: http: //www.commonsenseadvisory.com/Research/All_Users/060301_QT_top_20/ tabid/1429/Default.aspx

Deslisle, Jean and Pierre Cloutier (1995) The Invention of Alphabets, in Delisle, Jean and Judith Woodsworth (eds) *Translators Through History*, Amsterdam: John Benjamins, 7-21.

DIN (1998) DIN 2345: 1998. *Übersetzungsaufträge* [Translation Contracts], Berlin: Beuth Verlag.

Esselink, Bert (1998) *A Practical Guide to Software Localization*, Amsterdam: Benjamins.

------ (2000) *A Practical Guide to Localization*, Amsterdam/Philadelphia: John Benjamins.

Finlay, I.F. (1971) The Staff Translator, in J.B. Sykes (ed.) *Technical Translator's Manual*, London: Aslib, 30-41.

Gerzymisch-Arbogast, Heidrun (1993) Contrastive Scientific and Technical Register as a Translation Problem, in S.E. Wright and L.D Wright (eds) (1993) *Scientific and Technical Translation*, Amsterdam: Benjamins, 21-52.

Göpferich, Susanne (1995) A Pragmatic Classification of LSP Texts in Science and Technology, *Target*, 7(2): 305-326.

------ (2009) Comprehensibility assessment using the Karlsruhe Comprehensibility Concept. *Journal of Specialised Translation*, 11, 31-51.

Grant, Edward (1992) *Planets, Stars, and Orbs: The Medieval Cosmos, 1200-1687*, Cambridge: Cambridge University Press.

Gutt, Ernst-August (1991) *Translation and Relevance: Cognition and Context*, Oxford: Basil Blackwell.

Hall, Edward T. (1976) *Beyond Culture*, New York: Anchor Books.

Harvey, Keith (2001) Compensation, in Mona Baker and Gabriela Saldanha (eds) *Routledge Encyclopedia of Translation Studies*, London: Routledge, 47-51.

Herman, Mark (1993) Technical Translation Style: Clarity, Concision, Correctness, in S.E. Wright and L.D Wright (eds) *Scientific and Technical Translation*, Amsterdam: Benjamins, 11-20.

Hervey, Sandor, Ian Higgins and Louise Haywood (1995) *Thinking Spanish Translation*. London: Routledge.

Heyn, Matthias (1996) Translation Memories: Insights and Prospects, In L. Bowker *et al.* (eds) *Unity in Diversity? Current Trends in Translation Studies*, Manchester: St Jerome, 123-136.

Hofstede, Geert (1991) *Cultures and Organizations: Software of the Mind*. New York: McGraw-Hill.

Hoft, Nancy (1995) *International Technical Communication*, New York: Wiley.

Hönig, Hans G. (1998) "Wissen Übersetzer eigentlich, was sie tun?" *Lebende Sprachen* 1, 10-14.

Horton, William (1994) *Designing and Writing Online Documentation*, New York: John Wiley & Sons.

House, Juliane (1977) *A Model for Translation Quality Assessment*, Tubingen: Gunter Narr Verlag.

Institute of Translating and Interpreting (2008) *The thirty-nine steps: Questions you need to ask yourself when undertaking a translation*. [online] Available from: http: //www.iti.org.uk/pdfs/newPDF/10FH_39Steps_(02-08).pdf [Accessed: 01/10/2009].

Kasner, Edward and James R. Newman (1940) *Mathematics and the Imagination*, New York: Simon & Schuster.

Katan, D. (1999) *Translating Cultures: An Introduction for Translators, Interpreters, and Mediators*, Manchester, St. Jerome Publishing.

Kenny, Dorothy (1998) Equivalence. Mona Baker (ed.) *Routledge Encyclopaedia of Translation Studies*, London and New York: Routledge, 77-80.

Kingscott, Geoffrey (2002) Technical Translation and Related Disciplines, in *Perspectives: Studies in Translatology*, 10(4): 247-255.

Koller, Werner (1979) The Concept of Equivalence and the Object of Translation Studies, *Target*, 7(2): 191-222.

Komissarov, Vilen (1977) Zur Theorie der linguistischen Übersetzungsanalyse, In: Otto Kade (ed.) *Vermittelte Kommunikation, Sprachmittlung, Translation*, Leipzig: VEB Verlag, 44-51.

Lane, Nick (2004) *Oxygen: The Molecule That Made the World*, Oxford: Oxford University Press.

Linnaeus, Carolus (1758) *Systema naturae per regna tria naturae: secundum classes, ordines, genera, species, cum characteribus, differentiis, synonymis, locis*, Leipzig: Impensis Georg Emanuel Beer, 1788-1793, 10th edition.

Locke, David (1992) *Science as Writing*, New Haven, USA & London, England: Yale University Press.

Maclean, Leonard, Alex Richman, Stig Larsson and Vincent Richman (2005) The Dynamics of Aircraft Degradation and Mechanical Failure, *Journal of Transportation and Statistics*, 8(1): 1-11

Mancuso, J.C. (1990) *Mastering Technical Writing*, Menlo Park, USA: Addison-Wesley Publishing Company.

Markel, Mike (2001) *Technical Communication*, Boston: Bedford/St. Martins, 6th edition.

Michael O'Mara Books (2004) *The World's Stupidest Instructions*, London: Michael O'Mara Books Ltd.

Microsoft (1998) *Microsoft Manual of Style for Technical Publications*, Washington, US: Microsoft Press, 2nd edition.

Montgomery, Scott L. (2002) *Science in Translation*, Chicago, London: The University of Chicago Press.

Mossop, Brian (2007) *Revising and Editing for Translators*, Manchester: St. Jerome, 2nd edition.

Murray, Patrick R., Michael A. Pfaller, Ken S. Rosenthal (2005) *Medical Microbiology*, Philadelphia: Mosby, 5th edition.

Myers, Greg (2000) Powerpoints: Technology, Lectures, and Changing Genres, in Anna Trosborg (ed.) *Analysing Professional Genres*, Amsterdam: Benjamins, 177-192.

Newmark, Peter (1977) Communicative and Semantic Translation. *Babel*, 23(4): 163-180.

------ (1988) *A Textbook of Translation*, London: Prentice Hall.

Nida, Eugene anaTaber, Charles (1969) *The Theory and Practice of Translation*, Leiden: E.J. Brill.

Nida, Eugene (1964) *Toward a science of translating*, Leiden: E.J. Brill.

Nord, Christiane (1991) Scopos, Loyalty and Translational Conventions, *Target* 3(1): 91-109.

------ (1995) Text-Functions in Translation: Titles and Headings as a Case in Point, *Target* 7(2): 261–284.

O'Brien, Sharon (2003) Controlling Controlled English: An Analysis of Several Controlled Language Rule Sets, In *Proceedings of EAMT-CLAW-03*, Dublin City University, Dublin, Ireland, 15-17 May 2003, 105-114.

O.J. L 225/1: *Commission Directive 2001/59/EC of 6 August 2001*, Official Journal of the European Communities.

O'Hagan, Minako (1996) *The Coming Industry of Teletranslation*, Clevedon, Philadelphia: Multilingual Matters.

O'Reilly, Tim (2005) *What is Web 2.0: Design Patterns and Business Models for the Next Generation of Software*. [online] Available from: http: //www.oreillynet.com/pub/a/oreilly/tim/news/2005/09/30/what-is-web-20.html [Accessed: 1st August 2007].

Pinchuck, Isadore (1977) *Scientific and Technical Translation*, London: André Deutsch Ltd.

Plate, Jürgen and Jörg Holzmann (2009) *Sicherheit in Netzen*, Munich: Netzmafia/Fachhochschule München.

Price, Jonathan (1984) *How to Write a Computer Manual*, Menlo Park, CA: The Benjamin/Cummings Publishing Company.

Pym, Anthony (1995) European Translation Studies, une science qui dérange, and Why Equivalence Needn't Be a Dirty Word, *TTR* 8(1): 153-176.

------ (2010) Translation Theory Today and Tomorrow – Responses to Equivalence, in Lew N. Zybatow (ed.) *Translationswissenschaft – Stand und Perspektiven*, Frankfurt am Main: Peter Lang, 1-14.

Radkea, P.W., A. Kaisera, C. Frost and U. Sigwarta (2003) Outcome After Treatment of Coronary In-Stent Restenosis, *European Heart Journal* 24(3): 266-273.

Reiß, Katharina (1971) *Möglichkeiten und grenzen der Übersetzungskritik. Katagorien und Kriterien für eine sachgerechte beurteilung von Übersetzungen*, Munich: Hueber.

Ricketts, Wendell (2010) *The Revolution of the Translators – It's My Business, and I'm Minding It*. [online] Available from: http://vitavagabonda.blogspot.com/2010/02/

revolution-of-translators-its-my.html [Accessed: 22nd September 2010].

Rosenberg, Barry J. (2005) *Technical Writing for Engineers and Scientists*, New Jersey: Addison-Wesley.

Sager, Juan (1993) *Language Engineering and Translation*, Amsterdam: John Benjamins.

Schäffner, Christine [ed.] (1999) *Translation and Norms*, Clevedon: Multilingual Matters.

------ (2000) The Role of Genre for Translation, in Trosborg, Anna (ed.) *Analysing Professional Genres*, Amsterdam: Benjamins, 209-224.

Schatzman, E.L. and F. Praderie (1993) *The Stars*, trans. A.R. King, Berlin: Springer.

Schriver, Karen (1996) *Dynamics in Document Design*, New York: Wiley.

Schubert, Klaus (2009) Positioning Translation in Technical Communication Studies. *Journal of Specialised Translation*, 11, 17-30.

Selfridge, R. J. and Sokolik, S. L. (1975). A Comprehensive View of Organizational Development. *Business Topics*, 47.

Stahl, W.H. (1962) *Roman Science: Origins, Development, and Influence on the Later Middle Ages*, Madison: University of Wisconsin Press.

Steiner, George (1975) *After Babel*, Oxford, England: Oxford University Press.

Strunk, William and E.B. White (1999) *The Elements of Style*, Massachusetts: Longman.

Sunwoo, Min (2007) Operationalizing the Translation Purpose (Skopos). Heidrun Gerzymisch-Arbogast and Gerhard Budin (eds) *Proceedings of the Marie Curie Euroconferences MuTra: LSP Translation Scenarios.* [online] Available from: http: // www.euroconferences.info/proceedings/2007_Proceedings/2007_Sunwoo_Min. pdf [Accessed: 1st October 2009].

Sykes, J.B. [ed.] (1971) *Technical Translator's Manual*, London: Aslib.

Tebeaux, Elizabeth (1997) *The Emergence of a Tradition: Technical Writing in the English Renaissance 1475-1640*, New York: Baywood Publishing Company.

Toury, Gideon (1995) *Descriptive Translation Studies and Beyond*, Amsterdam: John Benjamins.

Trompenaars, Fons (1993) *Riding the Waves of Culture: Understanding Cultural Diversity in Business*, London: Nicholas Brealey.

Trosborg, Anna [ed.] (1997) *Text Typology and Translation*, Amsterdam: Benjamins.

------ [ed.] (2000) *Analysing Professional Genres*, Amsterdam: Benjamins.

Ulijn, Jan (1995) Is Cultural Rewriting of American Technical Documents Needed for the European Market: Some Experimental Evidence from French and Dutch Technical Documents, *International Dimensions of Technical Communication*, Arlington, VA: Society for Technical Communication.

University of Chicago (2003) *The Chicago Manual of Style*, London/Chicago: The University of Chicago Press.

Van Laan, Krista and Catherine Julian (2001) *The Complete Idiot's Guide to Technical Writing*, Indianapolis: Alpha Books.

Vermeer, Hans J. (1978) Ein Rahmen für eine allgemeine Translationstheorie, *Lebende Sprachen*, 3: 99-102.

------ (1982) Translation als Informationsangebot. *Lebende Sprachen*, 27(2): 97-101.

------ (1987a) What Does it Mean to translate? *Indian Journal of Applied Linguistics,* 13(2): 25-33.

------ (1987b) Literarische Übersetzung als Versuch interkultureller Kommunikation. Alois Wierlacher (ed.) *Perspektiven und Verfahren interkultureller Germanistik*, Munich: Iudicum, 541-549.

Victor, David A. (1992) *International Business Communication*, New York: Harper Collins.

Vinay, Jean-Paul and Jean Darbelnet (1958) *Stylistique Comparee du Francais et de l'Anglais*, Paris: Didier.

------ (1995) *Comparative stylistics of French and English: A Methodology for Translation*, trans. and ed. by Juan C. Sager and M.J. Hamel, Amsterdam/Philadelphia: John Benjamins.

Wagner, Emma, Svend Bech and Jesús M. Martínez (2002) *Translating for the European Institutions*, Manchester: St. Jerome.

Wilmsen, David and Riham Osama Youssef (2009) Regional standards and local routes in adoption techniques for specialised terminologies in the dialects of written Arabic, *Journal of Specialised Translation*. 11: 191-210.

Wright, S.E. and L.D Wright (eds) (1993) *Scientific and Technical Translation*, Amsterdam: Benjamins.

Wright, Sue Ellen (2006) The Creation and Application of Language Industry Standards. In: Keiran J. Dunne (ed.) *Perspectives on Localization*, American Translators Association Scholarly Monograph, Series XIII, Amsterdam/Philadelphia: John Benjamins.

Appendix 1.   Glossary of Terms

This appendix provides definitions of some of the key terms as they are used in this book. The terms presented here range from technical acronyms, translation-specific terms relating to concepts and strategies as well as concepts which occur in the wider technical communication community, the translation profession and business in general.

addition (of information)	Related to the translation procedure of *explicitation*, addition relates to adding extra information to a text during the translation process. This may be motivated by factors such as the clarity and comprehensibility of the target text, legal requirements, and political, cultural or social influences.
authoritative translation	An existing published translation of a name, title or document which must be used rather than producing a new translation. In the case of laws, institutions, departments, organizations, publications or other text, they are often official translations and are produced by the relevant organization itself.
Brand name	The name by which a product or service is known. They are usually registered trademarks which are protected by copyright and form part of the legal and commercial identity of a brand.
BSI	*British Standards Institution*. The national standards body for the UK, it develops and publishes standards.
CAT	Computer-assisted (or aided) translation. The use of computerized tools such as translation memory software and terminology management databases to *assist* the work of the translator. This should not be confused with Machine Translation whose purpose is to *perform* the work of a translator.
commercial text	Any text relating to business in general. Commercial texts may frequently incorporate subject areas such as technology, law or other specialized areas, making them difficult to distinguish from texts typically associated with specific genres or subject areas.
commercial translation	Any translation which is carried out for payment. This is not the same as the translation of *commercial texts*.

contaminare (contamination)	An old translation practice which involves translating extracts from several different texts and combining the results to produce a new text. This was typically carried out by ancient Greek and Roman writer/translators. Also known as *compilation*.
covert translation	Defined by Juliane House (1977) as a translation which is functionally equivalent to the source text and where it is not obvious that the target text is a translation; it could easily have been written in the target language. Contrast with *overt translation*.
DIN	*Deutsches Institut für Normung.* Based in Berlin, the German Institute for Standardization develops norms and standards.
distinguishing features	The main structural, technical, linguistic and content-related factors which characterize a particular text and which allow it to be classified as belonging to a particular text type and which help translators decide on the most appropriate translation strategy.
documentary translation	First described by Nord (1991:73) it refers to a translation which describes some communicative action between the author and the reader of the original source text. A documentary translation describes and documents what was said and how it was said. This type of translation is not intended to serve as an independent target language text and readers will be aware that it is a translation. Contrast with *instrumental translation*.
DTP	Desktop Publishing
EMEA	*European Medicines Agency.* A European organization responsible for evaluating, regulating and controlling medicines and pharmaceuticals in the European Union.
foregrounding	When translating, foregrounding means adding additional emphasis to information in a text so that it is more obvious and explicit, possibly at the expense of other information
freelancer	A freelance translator; a self-employed independent translator who works with direct clients and/or translation agencies.
FTP	File Transfer Protocol; a way of transferring (usually large) files directly between computers on the Internet or some other network.

function	As distinct from the purpose of a text described in Skopos theory, the function of a text can be described as the *effect* a text has on its audience or the way the text "interacts" with the audience.
functionalism	An approach to translation which, in addition to various levels of equivalence on linguistic, semantic and textual levels, traditionally regards the function of the source text and the translator's ability to maintain it in the target text as being important.
HTML	*Hypertext Mark-up Language*, used to format and structure information on websites.
instrumental translation	First described by Nord (1991:73) it refers to a translation which is intended to serve as a new communicative tool which gives the impression of having been written in the target language and which readers will not detect is a translation. The text is intended to function as a free-standing, autonomous text in the target language and must be adapted to the needs of the target audience. Contrast with *documentary translation*.
inventio (invention)	An old translation practice which involved rewriting or rewording texts during translation and often involved the large-scale addition of new information.
ISO	*International Organization for Standards*; a non-governmental organization which is the world's largest developer and publisher of international standards.
locale	In computing, a locale is a set of parameters used to define the user's language, country and any special variant preferences that need to be reflected in a piece of software. In general translation terms, it can be defined as all of the linguistic, cultural, geographic, technical and political factors that identify a particular target audience.
loyalty	Typically means favouring one aspect of the translation process over others, usually used in the context of the original author or the target audience but this can also mean favouring the form over content and vice versa. Usually, the issue of loyalty is associated with the original author and is, therefore, linked with source based translation approaches.
LSP	*Language for Special Purposes.*
manuals	see *user guides*.

MT	Machine Translation
omission (of information)	A translation strategy whereby information contained in the source text is deliberately omitted from the target text, usually because it would be deemed unnecessary for the target audience or because it would affect the clarity of the translation. This strategy is usually necessary because of different levels of cultural specificity or background knowledge on the part of the target audience.
original language texts	Texts which are originally written in a particular language, i.e. texts which have not been translated.
overt translation	Defined by Juliane House (1977) as a translation where the function of the source text is not maintained, i.e. it is not functionally equivalent. In this type of translation, the target language audience is overtly not being addressed and it is obvious that the text is a translation, usually because the source text is inextricably linked to a specific period of time, culture or language. Contrast with *covert translation*.
PDF	*Portable Document Format*; a file format developed by Adobe Inc. to aid in the distribution of documentation across various operating systems.
pivot translation	In cases where no translators are available for a particular language combination a text may be translated into an intermediate language before being translated again into the desired target language. For example, if no German into Japanese translator is available, the German text may be translated into English and then into Japanese. Pivot translations are also sometimes referred to as *relay* or *indirect* translations.
purpose	The purpose of a text or translation is the ultimate, intended use to which a text will be put. For example, the purpose of a translated patent application may be to allow the client to file a patent application or to allow engineers to understand the technology behind the object being described. This should not be confused with the function of a text.
scientific text	A text which presents scientific information, typically for an expert audience and which utilizes a wide range of linguistic and rhetorical devices to explain, discuss, illustrate, entertain and persuade.

Skopos	A key term in *Skopos Theory* developed by Hans Vermeer, the Skopos of a text is the intended purpose to which a translation will be put; it describes what the translation will be used for. Ideally, the Skopos is determined jointly by the translator and the client on the basis of a *translation brief* but in reality, translators usually have to determine this for themselves.
SL	see *source language*.
source language	The language *from* which a text is translated.
source text	A text which provides the starting point or basis for a translation process. The SL text which is to be translated.
ST	see *source text*.
target language	The language *into* which a source text is translated.
TL	see *target language*.
TT	see *target text*.
target text	The target language text which is produced on the basis of a source text. The end-result of the translation process.
task-orientated	Information which is designed and written around a specific task or process so as to provide all of the necessary information in one logical, self-contained unit.
technical communication	The process of communicating technical information, as well as a generic term for a range of allied professions aimed at communicating scientific and technical information, including writers, translators, editors, illustrators.
technical documentation	As used in this book, technical documentation refers to any text which contains scientific or technical information
technical text	A text designed to present technical or applied information of a scientific origin for a specific practical purpose in as clear and efficient a manner as possible.
technical writer	A professional communicator who is responsible for designing, researching, creating and testing technical texts which are destined to be used by specific audiences for specific purposes.
TL	Target language.

translation brief	A key concept in *Skopos Theory*, the translation brief is a largely hypothetical or mental construct which sets out the specifications for producing a translation in accordance with a particular *Skopos*.
translation memory	A bilingual database used by translators to store sentences and their translations so that they can be reused at a later stage if appropriate.
translator community	Websites or online forums such as Proz.com, Translators Café and Aquarius.net where companies, agencies and translators post and bid for translation projects, where translators can share expertise or discuss issues relevant to the profession.
TT	see *target text*.
undertranslation	A generic translation which lacks the specificity and detail of the ST but which nonetheless conveys enough information for the TT to be comprehensible to readers.
usability	When applied to texts usability measures the extent to which readers can read a text, understand its content and perform whatever task is required by the text quickly and accurately and the extent to which they find the experience difficult or easy.
XML	Extensible Mark-up Language. A technology used to structure documents and label their specific components to make distributing and editing information more efficient and flexible.

Appendix 2. Scientific Notation & Units of Measure

In this section

This appendix provides an overview of the key units of measure used in various scientific and technical texts and explains what they mean, how they are written and how they are used. It also explains the various abbreviations and prefixes used in conjunction with units of measure.

lbs	Pounds. An Imperial unit of weight corresponding to 0.45359237 kg.
±	Plus or minus
°	Degree
Ø	In mathematics used to indicate an empty set but is also used to indicate diameter
π	Pi
α	The Greek letter alpha, similar to the symbol for "is proportional to" ∝
β	The Greek letter beta, not to be confused with the German letter ß
Δ	The Greek letter delta, which is used in calculus to indicate the rate of change in something
Ω	Greek letter omega, also used to indicate "Ohm", a measurement of electrical resistance
∞	Infinity
≈	"Is approximate to"
≠	"Is not equal to"
l	Litre
t	Tonne or 1000 kg. Different from the Imperial *ton* which can be either *long,* as used in the UK and which is equivalent to 1020 kg, or *short,* as used in the USA and which is equivalent to 907.1847 kg.
KB	Kilobyte
Kb	Kilobit
iff	In texts relating to logic and mathematics, *iff* is not a misspelling but rather a less commonly used symbol for the logical connective "if and only if". More commonly used symbols are ↔ or ⇔.
≤	"Less than or equal to"

| ≥ | "Greater than or equal to" |
| √ | "Square root of" |

SI Prefixes

10^n	Prefix	Symbol	Short scale	Long scale	Decimal
10^{24}	yotta	Y	Septillion	Quadrillion	*1000000000000000000000000*
10^{21}	zetta	Z	Sextillion	Trilliard	*1000000000000000000000*
10^{18}	exa	E	Quintillion	Trillion	*1000000000000000000*
10^{15}	peta	P	Quadrillion	Billiard	*1000000000000000*
10^{12}	tera	T	Trillion	Billion	*1000000000000*
10^{9}	giga	G	Billion	Milliard	*1000000000*
10^{6}	mega	M	Million		*1 000 000*
10^{3}	kilo	k	Thousand		*1000*
10^{2}	hecto	h	Hundred		*100*
10^{1}	deca	da	Ten		*10*
10^{0}	*(none)*	*(none)*	One		*1*
10^{-1}	deci	d	Tenth		*0.1*
10^{-2}	centi	c	Hundredth		*0.01*
10^{-3}	milli	m	Thousandth		*0.001*
10^{-6}	micro	μ	Millionth		*0.000001*
10^{-9}	nano	n	Billionth	Milliardth	*0.000000001*
10^{-12}	pico	p	Trillionth	Billionth	*0.000000000001*
10^{-15}	femto	f	Quadrillionth	Billiardth	*0.000000000000001*
10^{-18}	atto	a	Quintillionth	Trillionth	*0.000000000000000001*
10^{-21}	zepto	z	Sextillionth	Trilliardth	*0.000000000000000000001*
10^{-24}	yocto	y	Septillionth	Quadrillionth	*0.000000000000000000000001*

• Long scale and short scale as used here refer to the alternate systems used in countries such as the UK and the USA. This is particularly apparent with regard to the different definitions of the
term billion.

Eponymous Units of Measure

Ampere (A)	The basic unit of electric current intensity.
Becquerel (Bq)	Named after Antoine Henri Becquerel, is a measure of the radioactive strength of a source.
Coulomb (C)	The coulomb is the unit of electric charge, and it is the charged particles which flow when electricity is said to flow.
Farad (F)	The standard unit of electrical capacity.
Gray (Gy)	Unit of measurement for exposure to radiation.
Hertz (Hz)	Hertz is a unit of frequency (of change in state or cycle in a sound wave, alternating current, or other cyclical waveform) of one cycle per second.
Henry (H)	The unit of electric induction.
Joule (J)	A unit of work which is equivalent to the energy expended in one second by an electric current of one ampere in a resistance of one ohm.
Kelvin (K)	The Kelvin scale of temperature is an absolute scale; that is the lowest possible temperature has the value 0 K. It is worth noting that unlike other temperature measurements, you would not say 100 degrees Kelvin, just 100 Kelvins.
Newton (N)	The absolute unit of force It is defined as that force necessary to provide a mass of one kilogram with an acceleration of one meter per second *per second.*
Ohm (Ω)	The standard unit used to measure electrical resistance.
Pascal (Pa)	Pascal is the standard unit of pressure in the SI metric system and is defined as the pressure exerted by a force of one Newton (N) on an area of one square metre.
Siemens (S)	Bearing the same name as the large German industrial conglomerate, Siemens is the official SI unit measuring the electric conductance of a material.
Sievert (Sv)	A unit used to measure human exposure to radiation. It is an SI-derived unit expressing the amount of radiation needed to apply 1 joule of energy to each kilogram of human tissue.
Tesla (T)	Named after Nikola Tesla, it is the SI unit for magnetic flux density.
Volt (V)	A Volt is the basic unit of electrical potential. It is defined as the amount of electro-motive force is needed to produce a current of one ampere in a conductor whose resistance is one ohm.
Watt (W)	A unit of power, one watt is the amount of work done by applying one joule of energy per second.

Non-SI Units

Ångström (Å)	The Ångström (represented by the symbol Å) is a unit of length equal to 1×10^{-10} of a metre.
Celsius (°C)	The Celsius scale is used for measuring temperature. Measurements in the Celsius scale are indicated by the suffix °C. The scale is designed such that the freezing point of water is 0°C, and the boiling point of water is 100°C at a pressure of one atmosphere.
Curie (Ci)	A unit of radiation; the radiation produced by a gram of radium in one second.
Fahrenheit (°F)	Temperature scale devised by Gabriel Fahrenheit in the 1700's. Using this scale, at sea level the boiling point of water is 212 degrees Fahrenheit and the freezing point of water is 32 degrees Fahrenheit.
Gauss (G)	Unit of density of a magnetic field, equal to a field of one line of force per square centimetre.
Roentgen (R)	Refers to a unit of exposure, based on an amount of ionization (charge) produced by the absorption of gamma radiation energy in air under standard conditions. Scientific Definition: A unit of radiation exposure equal to the quantity of ionizing radiation that will produce one electrostatic unit of electricity in one cubic centimetre of dry air at 0°C and standard atmospheric pressure.

Scalar units

Neper (Np)	A dimensionless logarithmic unit used to describe ratios of measurements, such as amplitude, current or voltage.

Appendix 3. Hazard, Risk and Safety Phrases

In this section

This appendix provides a list of risk and safety phrases which are used internationally to advise readers on potentially dangerous substances. The main internationally-recognized symbols used to label hazardous materials are also illustrated along with their associated descriptions in a range of languages. For reasons of space, it is only possible to provide the Safety and Risk phrases in English but official translations in a range of European languages are available for each phrase in the *Official Journal of the European Communities*, details of which are presented at the end of this appendix. These set phrases should always be used when translating safety information.

Hazard symbols and their associated descriptions in several languages

The following symbols (which consist of a black symbol on an orange background) and their associated indications of danger are published in Commission Directive 2001/59/EC of 6 August 2001 (Annex II), Official Journal of the European Communities L 225/1

Code: E
ES: Explosivo
DA: Eksplosiv
DE: Explosionsgefährlich
EL: Εκρηκτικό
EN: Explosive
FR: Explosif
IT: Esplosivo
NL: Ontplofbaar
PT: Explosivo
FI: Räjähtävä
SV: Explosivt

Code: O
ES: Comburente
DA: Brandnærende
DE: Brandfördernd
EL: Οξειδωτικό
EN: Oxidizing
FR: Comburant
IT: Comburente
NL: Oxiderend
PT: Comburente
FI: Hapettava
SV: Oxiderande

Code: F
ES: Fácilmente inflamable
DA: Meget brandfarlig
DE: Leichtentzündlich
EL: Πολύ εύφλεκτο
EN: Highly flammable
FR: Facilement inflammable
IT: Facilmente infiammabile
NL: Licht ontvlambaar
PT: Facilmente inflamável
FI: Helposti syttyvä
SV: Mycket brandfarligt

Code: F+
ES: Extremadamente inflamable
DA: Yderst brandfarlig
DE: Hochentzündlich
EL: Εξαιρετικά εύφλεκτο
EN: Extremely flammable
FR: Extrêmement inflammable
IT: Estremamente infiammabile
NL: Zeer licht ontvlambaar
PT: Extremamente inflamável
FI: Erittäin helposti syttyvä
SV: Extremt brandfarligt

Code: C
ES: Corrosivo
DA: Ætsende
DE: Ätzend
EL: Διαβρωτικό
EN: Corrosive
FR: Corrosif
IT: Corrosivo
NL: Bijtend
PT: Corrosivo
FI: Syövyttävä
SV: Frätande

Code: T
ES: Tóxico
DA: Giftig
DE: Giftig
EL: Τοξικό
EN: Toxic
FR: Toxique
IT: Tossico
NL: Vergiftig
PT: Tóxico
FI: Myrkyllinen
SV: Giftig

Code: T+
ES: Muy tóxico
DA: Meget giftig
DE: Sehr giftig
EL: Πολύ τοξικό
EN: Very toxic
FR: Très toxique
IT: Molto tossico
NL: Zeer vergiftig
PT: Muito tóxico
FI: Erittäin
myrkyllinen
SV: Mycket giftig

Code: Xn
ES: Nocivo
DA:
Sundhedsskadelig
DE:
Gesundheitsschädlich
EL: Επιβλαβές
EN: Harmful
FR: Nocif
IT: Nocivo
NL: Schadelijk
PT: Nocivo
FI: Haitallinen
SV: Hälsoskadlig

Code: Xi
ES: Irritante
DA:
Lokalirriterende
DE: Reizend
EL: Ερεθιστικό
EN: Irritant
FR: Irritant
IT: Irritante
NL: Irriterend
PT: Irritante
FI: Ärsyttävä
SV: Irriterande

[image-42]
Code: N
ES: Peligroso para
el medio ambiente
DA: Miljøfarlig
DE:
Umweltgefährlich
EL: Επικίνδυνο για
το περιβάλλον
EN: Dangerous for
the environment
FR: Dan-
gereux pour
l'environnement
IT: Pericoloso per
l'ambiente
NL:
Milieugevaarlijk
PT: Perigoso para
o ambiente
FI: Ympäristölle
vaarallinen
SV: Miljöfarlig

Safety Phrases

These phrases are used to describe safety procedures to be used in relation to dangerous materials. They are used internationally, not just in Europe, and work is being carried out to harmonize them internationally. Authoritative translations of these phrases in several European languages can be found in the *Official Journal of the European Communities* (O.J. L 225/1).

- S1: Keep locked up
- S2: Keep out of the reach of children
- S3: Keep in a cool place
- S4: Keep away from living quarters
- S5: Keep contents under ... (appropriate liquid to be specified by the manufacturer)
- S6: Keep under ... (inert gas to be specified by the manufacturer)
- S7: Keep container tightly closed
- S8: Keep container dry
- S9: Keep container in a well-ventilated place
- S12: Do not keep the container sealed
- S13: Keep away from food, drink and animal feedingstuffs
- S14: Keep away from ... (incompatible materials to be indicated by the manufacturer)

- S15: Keep away from heat
- S16: Keep away from sources of ignition - No smoking
- S17: Keep away from combustible material
- S18: Handle and open container with care
- S20: When using do not eat or drink
- S21: When using do not smoke
- S22: Do not breathe dust
- S23: Do not breathe gas/fumes/vapour/spray (appropriate wording to be specified by the manufacturer)
- S24: Avoid contact with skin
- S25: Avoid contact with eyes
- S26: In case of contact with eyes, rinse immediately with plenty of water and seek medical advice
- S27: Take off immediately all contaminated clothing
- S28: After contact with skin, wash immediately with plenty of ... (*to be specified by the manufacturer*)
- S29: Do not empty into drains
- S30: Never add water to this product
- S33: Take precautionary measures against static discharges
- S35: This material and its container must be disposed of in a safe way
- S36: Wear suitable protective clothing
- S37: Wear suitable gloves
- S38: In case of insufficient ventilation wear suitable respiratory equipment
- S39: Wear eye/face protection
- S40: To clean the floor and all objects contaminated by this material use ... (*to be specified by the manufacturer*)
- S41: In case of fire and/or explosion do not breathe fumes
- S42: During fumigation/spraying wear suitable respiratory equipment (*appropriate wording to be specified by the manufacturer*)
- S43: In case of fire use ... (indicate in the space the precise type of fire-fighting equipment. If water increases the risk add – **Never use water**)
- S45: In case of accident or if you feel unwell seek medical advice immediately (show the label where possible)
- S46: If swallowed, seek medical advice immediately and show this container or label
- S47: Keep at temperature not exceeding ... °C (*to be specified by the manufacturer*)
- S48: Keep wet with ... (appropriate material to be specified by the manufacturer)
- S49: Keep only in the original container
- S50: Do not mix with ... (to be specified by the manufacturer)
- S51: Use only in well-ventilated areas
- S52: Not recommended for interior use on large surface areas
- S53: Avoid exposure – obtain special instructions before use
- S56: Dispose of this material and its container at hazardous or special waste collection point
- S57: Use appropriate containment to avoid environmental contamination
- S59: Refer to manufacturer/supplier for information on recovery/recycling

- S60: This material and its container must be disposed of as hazardous waste
- S61: Avoid release to the environment. Refer to special instructions/ safety data sheet
- S62: If swallowed, do not induce vomiting: seek medical advice imme- diately and show this container or label
- S63: In case of accident by inhalation: remove casualty to fresh air and keep at rest
- S64: If swallowed, rinse mouth with water (only if the person is conscious)

Combinations of Safety Phrases

Some of the safety phrases listed above can be combined in specific instances. The following is a list of the approved combinations and authoritative transla- tions of these phrase combinations can be found in several European languages in the *Official Journal of the European Communities* (O.J. L 225/1).

- S1/2: Keep locked up and out of the reach of children.
- S3/7: Keep container tightly closed in a cool place.
- S3/9/14: Keep in a cool, well-ventilated place away from ... (incompat- ible materials to be indicated by the manufacturer).
- S3/9/14/49: Keep only in the original container in a cool, well-ventilated place away from ... (incompatible materials to be indicated by the manufacturer).
- S3/9/49: Keep only in the original container in a cool, well-ventilated place.
- S3/14: Keep in a cool place away from ... (incompatible materials to be indicated by the manufacturer).
- S7/8: Keep container tightly closed and dry.
- S7/9: Keep container tightly closed and in a well-ventilated place.
- S7/47: Keep container tightly closed and at a temperature not exceed- ing ... °C (to be specified by the manufacturer).
- S20/21: When using do not eat, drink or smoke.
- S24/25: Avoid contact with skin and eyes.
- S27/28: After contact with skin, take off immediately all contaminated clothing, and wash immediately with plenty of ...(to be specified by the manufacturer).
- S29/35: Do not empty into drains; dispose of this material and its con- tainer in a safe way.
- S29/56: Do not empty into drains, dispose of this material and its con- tainer at hazardous or special waste collection point.
- S36/37: Wear suitable protective clothing and gloves.
- S36/37/39: Wear suitable protective clothing, gloves and eye/face protection.
- S36/39: Wear suitable protective clothing and eye/face protection.
- S37/39: Wear suitable gloves and eye/face protection.
- S47/49: Keep only in the original container at a temperature not ex- ceeding ... °C (to be specified by the manufacturer).

Risk Phrases

These phrases are used to describe risks posed by dangerous materials. They are used internationally, not just in Europe and work is being carried out to harmonize them internationally. Authoritative translations of these phrases in several European languages can be found in the Official Journal of the European Communities (O.J. L 225/1).

- R1: Explosive when dry
- R2: Risk of explosion by shock, friction, fire or other sources of ignition
- R3: Extreme risk of explosion by shock, friction, fire or other sources of ignition
- R4: Forms very sensitive explosive metallic compounds
- R5: Heating may cause an explosion
- R6: Explosive with or without contact with air
- R7: May cause fire
- R8: Contact with combustible material may cause fire
- R9: Explosive when mixed with combustible material
- R10: Flammable
- R11: Highly flammable
- R12: Extremely flammable
- R14: Reacts violently with water
- R15: Contact with water liberates extremely flammable gases
- R16: Explosive when mixed with oxidizing substances
- R17: Spontaneously flammable in air
- R18: In use, may form flammable/explosive vapour-air mixture
- R19: May form explosive peroxides
- R20: Harmful by inhalation
- R21: Harmful in contact with skin
- R22: Harmful if swallowed
- R23: Toxic by inhalation
- R24: Toxic in contact with skin
- R25: Toxic if swallowed
- R26: Very toxic by inhalation
- R27: Very toxic in contact with skin
- R28: Very toxic if swallowed
- R29: Contact with water liberates toxic gas
- R30: Can become highly flammable in use
- R31: Contact with acids liberates toxic gas
- R32: Contact with acids liberates very toxic gas
- R33: Danger of cumulative effects
- R34: Causes burns
- R35: Causes severe burns
- R36: Irritating to eyes
- R37: Irritating to respiratory system
- R38: Irritating to skin
- R39: Danger of very serious irreversible effects

- R40: Limited evidence of a carcinogenic effect
- R41: Risk of serious damage to eyes
- R42: May cause sensitization by inhalation
- R43: May cause sensitization by skin contact
- R44: Risk of explosion if heated under confinement
- R45: May cause cancer
- R46: May cause heritable genetic damage
- R48: Danger of serious damage to health by prolonged exposure
- R49: May cause cancer by inhalation
- R50: Very toxic to aquatic organisms
- R51: Toxic to aquatic organisms
- R52: Harmful to aquatic organisms
- R53: May cause long-term adverse effects in the aquatic environment
- R54: Toxic to flora
- R55: Toxic to fauna
- R56: Toxic to soil organisms
- R57: Toxic to bees
- R58: May cause long-term adverse effects in the environment
- R59: Dangerous for the ozone layer
- R60: May impair fertility
- R61: May cause harm to the unborn child
- R62: Possible risk of impaired fertility
- R63: Possible risk of harm to the unborn child
- R64: May cause harm to breast-fed babies
- R65: Harmful: may cause lung damage if swallowed
- R66: Repeated exposure may cause skin dryness or cracking
- R67: Vapours may cause drowsiness and dizziness
- R68: Possible risk of irreversible effects

The official translations of all of these phrases are contained in the *Official Journal of the European Communities* (O.J. L 225/1) which can be accessed at the following address:

http://eur-lex.europa.eu/LexUriServ/LexUriServ.do?uri=OJ:
L:2001:225:0001:0333:EN:PDF

Appendix 4.   Sample Document Profiles

In this section

This appendix provides sample document profiles for case studies 3-6 which were presented in Chapter 4. You might find it useful to consult these profiles after you have created your own profiles for each of the texts.

Profile: Test Instructions (see page 91)

Subject

- Instructions indicating the correct approved procedure for conducting quality control tests on products. In this case, the instructions relate to the testing of manufactured components in a warehouse shelving system. The tests described in the document are used to help identify defective components and to ensure conformity with pre-approved standards. The instructions also ensure that all relevant persons and departments are notified of any manufacturing problems.

Text Category

- Procedural, descriptive, normative, reference

Function

- The primary function of the text is to instruct, although because it is an authoritative document, it also has a regulatory function in that it specifies not just the procedure for conducting the test but also the required course of action if defects are discovered. The text provides clear and repeatable instructions to allow the same tests to be performed consistently, even by different people.

Typical Target Audience

- Typically produced for engineers in a supervisory role or managers. The typical audience will have in-depth knowledge of the company's products as well as a background in engineering and test procedures. The document may also be used by people from a legal background or by potential investors/business partners although these would be very much secondary to the main audience.

How the text will be used

- As a reference resource. It is unlikely that the text will be used as a step-by-step document accompanying the performance of the test but rather as the basis for a supervisor providing instructions to others.

Distinguishing Features

- The text provides clear procedural information which is presented in chronological order.

- In addition to procedural information, the text provides declarative information which is clear, unambiguous and definitive.

- The text uses short and highly specific sentences to present information.

- There appear to be various set phrases and fixed terms throughout the text. Some of these are likely to be company-specific while others will be universally known or defined in relevant regulations or laws. Examples include "free from mechanical damage", "inspection characteristics" and "visual Inspection of surface".

- The text refers to other documents, e.g. *"the collective fault list (BE 6.1.17)"*.

- The text also refers to departments which, in this case, are identified by means of acronyms, e.g. *QA* and *QM*, and to organizations, e.g. *DIN*.

- The first section of the document consists of a checklist.

- One specific unit of measure, i.e. degrees "10°", is mentioned in the document.

Potential Problems

- The short sentences in the text may be quite condensed in places and may not provide enough context for clear translation.

- External references (e.g. to document titles, sections within documents or to the names of departments or work groups) require the translator to carry out research to establish if there are existing translations; if such translations exist then they must be carefully copied over and used consistently. If no such translations exist, the translator needs to produce new translations which are in keeping with the style and conventions of the relevant organization. The client may need to be notified if such translations are produced.

- References to legislation, standards and documents may not be applicable in the target language culture, in which case appropriate translation strategies will be needed (see Chapter 4).

- Some abbreviations may be universally used and recognized while others may be standard but have their own national equivalents. Other abbreviations and acronyms may be company-specific and will require the translator to contact the client.

- Job titles should be given in accordance with customer preferences. Similarly, this type of text may include academic titles such as Dr, Prof. or regional variants such as *Dipl.Ing.* (in Germany) etc. which may need to be preserved in the target language as different cultures place different emphasis on titles.

- Product terminology: is it specific to the company or is it generic, industry-standard? Does the client have a preferred terminology which precludes the use of certain terms?

- Set phrases such as headings, categories etc. may have been translated already elsewhere and need to be consistent across all documents.

Sample Profile: Expert Technical Report (see page 94)

Subject

- Details of a scientific and technical evaluation of an electrical system on a railway network to ensure the project is designed and implemented in accordance with standards and agreements.

Text Category

- Authoritative, juridical-normative, descriptive

Function

- To provide an expert opinion on the characteristics of a system. The document also needs to establish a technical, theoretical and regulatory basis as evidence for the test's validity and that of its implications.

Typical Target Audience

- Senior management and engineers, consultants, government/local authority officials and regulatory bodies.

How the text will be used

- As the basis for approving construction, commissioning, licensing or using a system. Can also form the basis for activities relating to financing, regulatory approvals, decisions to proceed with projects etc. May sometimes be useful in the event of legal disputes.

Distinguishing Features

- References to project numbers, client and expert auditor. Generally this involves set terminology and it is essential that the client names and project names be correct for legal and technical reasons.

- The document contains a table of contents which usually indicates a reasonably substantial document and can also alert the translator to the fact that the electronic version of the document may contain complex technical features relating to formatting and layout.

- Revision history outlining the provenance of the document and the parties involved is provided at the start of the document.

- The document sets out the aims, scope and nature of the tests carried out as well relevant documents, standards and legislation. This is important for establishing the reliability and accuracy of the test and to allow reader to consult supplementary information if necessary.

- Various abbreviations and terms are used which may or may not be explained.

- The document provides clear, concise and unambiguous descriptions of the test procedure, data observed and an interpretation of the findings.

- Some texts of this type may present large amounts of numerical data in tables as evidence of the claimed test results.

- Variants of this document type may be more extensive with lengthier and more detailed discussions, numerical data, graphical representations etc.

- This type of document typically provides details of any conditions attached to the test findings, limitations or provisos relating to the report/approval, including their validity.

Potential Problems

- For legal and technical reasons it is essential that references to project names and numbers, clients and auditors be correct.

- Some documents contain clauses prohibiting translation or a clause requiring the addition of a phrase by the translator stating that text is a translation and as such is not the definitive version.

- If abbreviations and acronyms are not explained, the translator will either have to explain them while keeping the original letters or to produce new abbreviations based on the translation of the full meaning (often problematic).

- Numbers and measurements, particularly numerical data presented in tables, require particular care, especially if they have to be typed up by the translator. The possibility of typing mistakes is significant and any errors will be missed by a spellchecker.

Sample Profile: User Guide (see page 101)

Subject

- User guide for a customer relationship management tool explaining how to use certain functions and providing answers to help specific problems.

Text Category

- Instructional, procedural, human-technology interaction-orientated.

Function

- To explain the purpose of the software, give clear instructions for using various functions and help users troubleshoot problems.

Typical Target Audience

- Novice users with experience of the company's business activities. Users will be unfamiliar with the product being described but will have at least basic computer skills. Users may be apprehensive about using the new software.

How the text will be used

- As a training resource; readers will read individual chapters and refer to them as they use the software. Some sections of the document will also be read by experienced users as a quick reference source.

Distinguishing Features

- Introductory paragraph setting out the aims and objectives of the chapter as well as its context. This serves to prepare users for subsequent sections and to clearly identify the goals of the chapter.

- User guides contain a combination of descriptive, declarative and procedural information to fulfil various functions in support of the learning process.

- Clear headings which identify content of subsections. Most headings use the gerund form of verbs.

- The paragraphs in the document are generally quite short.

- Simple and clear language is used throughout the document but especially in procedural sections.

- Text adopts a relatively personal tone by directly referring to the reader, e.g. *you*, and through the use of imperatives. These features reduce the perceived distance between the reader and author.

- Tables are used to provide clear comparisons of user roles.

- The document layout includes headers and footers which contain translatable text.

- References to product names such as *Global CSM*.

- Use of company's own abbreviations.

- Frequent references to product concepts such as *tickets* and interface items, e.g. menus, buttons etc.

- The text contains a screenshot illustrating the software interface. Where the screenshots are in the target language, all references to these items in the text must be consistent.

- References to other documents such as internal company documents and legislation.

- Procedural information is generally short and logical, in chronological order and contains one idea per sentence.

- Important information is highlighted in boxes.

- Internal cross-references to chapters and headings elsewhere in the document.

- References to external technology such as ASX and other software.

Potential Problems

- Care must be taken to ensure that the clear headings which identify content of subsections are maintained and that they demonstrate structural parallelism to aid readers when using the table of contents.

- References to product names and official abbreviations require research to establish whether specific orthography is required (e.g. "FrameMaker" and never "Frame maker" or "Frame Maker") or whether different names are used indifferent markets. Abbreviations may not always be universally recognized. In the case of company-internal abbreviations, the abbreviations may not always be translated and as a result are unclear to the target audience.

- Laws can pose problems and the translator may need to use generic paraphrases if no equivalent laws exist in the target culture. Alternatively, one of the strategies discussed in Chapter 5 may need to be used.

- Screenshot illustrating the software interface. In this case the screenshot shows the source language version. The frequent references to the interface text throughout the text mean that care is needed to ensure that the paragraph text matches the actual software which the target audience will ultimately use. Although a relatively uncommon occurrence, a screenshot which shows the source language version of the software will need to be replaced after translation. Sending a friendly reminder to the client is not a bad thing.

- Internal cross-references to chapters and headings elsewhere in the document require consistency and may cause technical problems (for example through the deletion of bookmarks and reference codes).

- With several references to external technology such as *ASX* and other software, the translator may need to research the product names (and whether they are subject to copyright restrictions) and the actual menu names and items.

- The headers and footers provide additional information about the document and can easily be overlooked during translation. In this case, only the header needs to be translated although the text may have been created by means of a cross-reference to the relevant paragraph in which case it will be automatically replaced as soon as the relevant section heading is translated. Additionally, such text can be ignored by spellcheckers if the language settings are not changed specifically for the headers and footers. Text inserted automatically by word processors will often be formatted using the source language conventions (e.g. "Page 1 of 7" or dates) and may have to be reinserted by the translator using the appropriate function in the target language version of Word.

Sample Profile: Popular Science Book (see page 106)

Subject
- Properties of oxygen and its reactions with other chemicals as well as their implications for plant nutrition.

Text Category
- Essay, explanatory, discussion, didactic-instructive

Function

- Educate, explain and entertain. Arouse interest in subject.

Typical Target Audience

- Keenly interested in various aspects of science, many readers could be described as "hobbyists" or "self-improvers". Typical audience will have a relatively high level of education (though not necessarily with qualifications in science). It is likely that readers would have some form of scientific education, perhaps at secondary school level (apparent in this text through their assumed familiarity with basic scientific concepts).

How the text will be used

- Entertainment, information, self-actualization, unlikely to be read more than once.

Distinguishing Features

- The text uses a combination of ordinary, semi-specialized and specialized language, particularly terminology.

- The text uses scientific formulae and equations accompanied with textual explanations and discussions.

- The structure of the text is narrative, to a certain extent, to make the information more engaging for the reader who is reading for pleasure, not solely for education.

- The text uses various rhetorical devices such as figurative and metaphorical language to explain concepts and issues. This brings concepts closer to reader and makes the subject more accessible (examples in this particular book include the use of expressions such as "spoon-fed" or "jettisoning" to explain complex concepts).

- The text contains various personalizing features such as "we need to" which are used to decrease the distance between author and reader as well as to make the subject matter more relevant.

Potential Problems

- Achieving the correct tone combined with clarity and factual accuracy may require recasting, rephrasing and adaptation. Depending on the assumed level of background knowledge of the target audience, you may need to use explicitation to ensure clarity and explain unknown concepts.

- The intensity of the personal, direct tone of text, achieved using features like "we need to", may not be compatible with textual norms and audience expectations in target language.

- Vivid language use and imagery will need to be assessed on a case-by-case basis to establish its suitability and meaningfulness for the target audience.

- Formulae may need to be reproduced but will not need to be changed or modified.

- References to other authors and works need to be researched. There may be different conventions for spelling the names of scientists in different languages. Publications will need to be researched to identify existing translations and, where they do not, to find additional information to allow a paraphrase translation. Looking up references will also help in the identification of terminological resources.

- Only some of the specialized terms in the text are explained, while others (e.g. fundamental scientific terms such as photosynthesis), are not. This implies that the SL audience has a particular level of background knowledge and education. Care needs to be given to ensure that the level of explanation is appropriate to the assumed level of background knowledge.

Sample Profile: Certificate of Conformity (see page 111)

Subject

- This document is used to confirm that a specific make of drying machine used in the construction industry has been tested and found to comply with certain legal requirements.

Text Category

- Regulatory, juridical-normative.

Function

- To certify and demonstrate compliance with specific laws, regulations and directives.

Typical Target Audience

- Compliance inspectors, health and safety personnel, purchasers and importers, in rare cases end users.

How the text will be used

- The text will be used as a reference document and is likely to be read just once in order to verify the suitability and legal compliance of the product.

Distinguishing Features

- In addition to technical terminology relating to the product and its area of application, the text also contains legal terminology such as *"administrative provisions"* and *"harmonized technical specification"*.

- The text contains specific, set phrases and preferred wording, which are often based on a template. Examples include *"on the approximation of laws..."*, *"is submitted by the manufacturer to a factory production control"* and many phrases and sentences in the first and second body paragraphs.

- The text contains various references to directives and laws such as *Directive 89/106/EEC* and *EMC-EN61000-6-3* in order to illustrate the legal and regulatory basis upon which the product has been tested and approved.

- Certificates of Conformity contain precise technical descriptions of the product being certified (for example *"Class IV 3000 W industrial drying machine..."*) to aid in identifying the product and the correct certificate.

- The text contains trademarks and product names, e.g. *"AquaDry 3000"*.

Potential Problems

- References to directives and laws: you will need to see if there are official translations of names and descriptions. This can pose problems if translating into a non-EU language as you may need to produce your own translations if no comparable official equivalents exist.

- Names and addresses of both the manufacturer and the testing authority (and in certain certificates, a distributor) may need to be clarified and modified to minimize confusion and speed communication.

- The various instances of legal and technical terminology will require research to identify parallel texts or comparable templates in the target language.

- Specific, set phrases and preferred wording: it may be possible to copy and past certain sections from approved EU templates.

- The precise content may vary depending on nature of product and applicable regulations.

- Technical descriptions of the product must be clear and accurate so that there is no confusion as to the actual product being certified.

- When handling trademarks and product names, care must be taken to use identical spelling and orthography, otherwise the product may not be correctly identified and consequently, not certified.

- Certificates of conformity are also produced outside the EU, for example in the USA, and may be formatted differently or contain different information and terminology.

- Depending on the specific layout of the document, it is possible that a translator may need to maintain a one-to-one page correspondence between ST and TT. This is to ensure printing costs are kept to a minimum and to achieve consistent presentation across different language versions. If this is the case, translations may need to be edited so that they are more concise.

Sample Profile: Technical Case Study (see page 114)

Subject

- The text provides a detailed description of how the company's centralized IT management products were used to help the client manage its broadcasting and computing activities.

Text Category

- Promotional, persuasive, descriptive

Function

- To persuade potential customers of Avocent's expertise by presenting a practical example of how the products can be used, along with testimonials from the client outlining their motivation for using Avocent and their satisfaction with the product and company.

Typical Target Audience

- Senior level IT experts, engineers and systems administrators.

How the text will be used

- As an initial introduction to the company and its products; possibly also as part of sales and marketing presentation; as part of initial research into potential solutions and as a way of identifying contact details for company.

Distinguishing Features	
• Various cultural references and terms (e.g. American wrestling terms, organizations and personalities).	
• Frequent use of journalistic style such as direct quotes to add a personal, "real" dimension to text and topic so that reader can relate.	
• Alternates between journalistic, personal accounts and impersonal technical narrative from outside the text.	
• Depending on the client, this type of text will frequently contain a certain level of language (phrases and jargon) and interdisciplinary terminology which is related to the client's business but which is not necessarily related to the technology of the company. Texts may also involve various culture-specific references.	
• The text is divided into several subsections, each of which is introduced by a short, snappy heading.	
• A key feature of this type of text is the emphasis on identifying both companies and the products involved (e.g. *AMX5000* and *AMX® KVM*). This is done to personalize the text and make it easier for readers to identify, remember and relate to the company and its products. Case studies also identify specific people and their job titles within the client's company, again to personalize the text and also to add credibility to the text.	
• References to other product and brand names such as UNIX, Mac, etc.	
• Generic technical terms and acronyms (e.g. IP, MIDI).	
• Specialized (product-specific) terms and acronyms such as KVM.	
• Measurements and units of measure (e.g. "1600 x 1200" and "75 Hz").	
• Jargon such as "daisy-chaining" and "pay-per-view".	
• Descriptive and figurative language (e.g. "pinning them down", "daisy-chaining" "a nice little package").	
• The overall tone of the text is very positive – it talks about benefits, satisfaction and expectations being met or surpassed rather than problems, difficulties and compromises.	
• The text provides contact details, including addresses, websites and telephone numbers. It also contains geographic references such as *Ala.* or *AL* which represent the US state of Alabama but which would not be immediately obvious to non-US readers.	

- Corporate profile or biography providing a succinct overview of the company. Sometimes can include reference to the company being listed on stock exchange by providing its stock exchange *symbol* (e.g. *"...Avocent (NASDAQ: AVCT)..."*).

- The text contains a diagram with labels to illustrate how the product was used in the client's business.

Potential Problems

- Many of the cultural references in this text must be retained as they relate directly to the client's core business (e.g. *WWE Smackdown*, *Monday Night Raw*, *Undertaker* and *John Cena*). They will more than likely require explanation to make them comprehensible to the target audience even if the full significance of the reference is lost.

- Quotes used in the text need to be retained as they are used primarily as a stylistic device aimed at personalizing the text and making it relevant to the reader (as opposed to presenting a verbatim account of what someone said). Clients will have agreed to their statements being used for publicity purposes so a certain amount of minor deviation will be accepted as long as you do not misrepresent what the client has said.

- The corporate profile or biography at the end of the text may be what is known as "core information", which is written once and reused from text to text to ensure consistency and also, in certain cases, for legal or compliance reasons. If this is the case, there may be an existing translation and this should be reused. Check the company's website or contact the client.

- In translating the *problem* section it is important not to present the client as being incompetent or unprofessional so care is needed when phrasing descriptions, for example when choosing adjectives, etc.

- The alternation between journalistic and technical writing styles must be preserved to ensure the overall "documentary" and informative tone of the text. You will need to modify your translation strategies depending on the specific paragraph to ensure that you do not homogenize the text.

- Language, terms and jargon relating to the client's business area will require additional research so that you can fully understand the meaning and connotations and to ensure that you do not assign a particular term to the wrong subject area.

- Company and product names must be retained; check company websites to find out if there are any accepted TL equivalents of job titles mentioned in the text.

- Generic technical terminology and acronyms such as MIDI may be industry standard and not require translation but should be checked in any case to make sure.

- Measurements can generally be left unchanged because of the specialized background of the audience.

- Jargon such as "daisy-chaining" needs to be researched as it can pose comprehension problems; if no TL equivalents are available, you will need to explain what it is.

- Contact details and geographic references (such as *AL* and *Ala.*) need to be localized.

- If it is not possible to edit the diagram to translate the labels, produce a side-by-side list of ST phrases and their translations. Ensure that any references in the body text to diagram labels are translated consistently.

- Great care must be taken to ensure the tone and language of the translation is positive and lively and emphasizes the client's satisfaction and the benefits of the product. This will require, among other things, careful consideration of the connotations of various words and phrases. Be careful not to overstate the positive experience as this may be both inaccurate and potentially problematic from a legal standpoint.

Index